IRELAND

a sacred journey

ATLANTIC OCEAN

Malin Head

Tory Island

RATHLIN ISLAND

Coire Breccáin

Straits of Moyle

Grianan Ailligh · Broighter

Lough Foyle

DONEGAL

Londonderry

LONDONDERRY

ANTRIM

Toome

Lough Derg

Derg

Foyle

ULSTER

Butterlump

Donegal Bay

Ess Ruaid

Inis Samer

Ballyshannon

Plains of Tribute

Ben Bulben · Boho

Pettigoe

Kiltierney

TYRONE

Lough Neagh · Belfast

Erne

Lough Erne

Knockmany tomb

Slieve Beagh

Emain Macha (Navan Fort)

LEITRIM

FERMANAGH

(Site of Bith's tomb)

ARMAGH

DOWN

Shannon Pot

Marble Arch Caves

SLIGO

Doohat

MONAGHAN

Slieve Gullion Tomb

Moytirra

Keshcorran

CAVAN

LOUTH

ACHILL ISLAND

MAYO

ROSCOMMON

LONGFORD

Sleave Beagh

Dunany Point

Clew Bay

Croagh Patrick

Crúachain (Rathcroghan)

Brí Léith (Ardagh Hill)

Loughcrew

Knowth

Dowth

Tailte

New Grange

IRISH SEA

MAM EAN

CONNACHT

Lough Derravaragh

Sliab na Caillígh

Fremu

Lough Owel

Tlachtga

Fourknocks

WESTMEATH

MEATH

Hill of Tara

GALWAY

Athlone

MIDE

Boyne

LAMBAY ISLAND

Galway

Clonmacnoise

Uisnech

Lough Ennell

Liffey

Dublin

Hill of Howth (Benn Étair)

Clarinbridge

Ballinasloe

Shannon Bridge

Croghan Hill (Brí Éle)

Dublin Bay

Galway Bay

EISCIR RIADA

Shannon

OFFALY

Almu (Hill of Allen)

Drimnagh

ARAN ISLANDS

SLIEVE AUGHTY MTS.

Banagher

Kildare

The Curragh

Bray Head

BRÂZIL

Liscannor (St. Brigit's Well)

Ard Éireann

Lough Dergderc

LEINSTER

Glendalough

Lough Graney

LAOIS

WICKLOW

CLARE

Slieve Bernagh

ARRA MOUNTAIN (Tountinna)

Barrow

WICKLOW MTS.

MOTHER MOUNTAIN (Mauher Slieve)

CARLOW

Shannon

Limerick

Slieve Phelim (Fódla's Seat)

TIPPERARY

KILKENNY

Shannon Mouth

LIMERICK

Lough Gur

Cnoc Grene

Cashel

WEXFORD

Ardamine (Ladra's Landing)

Connla's Well

Cnoc Fírinne

Cnoc Áine

Slievenaman

Nore

Cloghan

Harps of Cliu

MUNSTER

Rath Luirc

Suir

Slieve Mish (Ériu's Seat)

Cullen (Latiaran's Heart)

WATERFORD

KERRY

Carrig Cleena

Paps of Anu

Waterford Harbour (Cesair's Landing)

Cork

Cork

BHEARÉ PENINSULA

CORK

Hag of Bheare's Home

0 — 60km

IRELAND

N

IRELAND

a sacred journey

Michael Dames

TED SMART

© Element Books Limited 2000
Text © Michael Dames 1992

First published as *Mythic Ireland* in Great Britain
by THAMES & HUDSON 1992

Published in Great Britain in 2000 by
ELEMENT BOOKS LIMITED
Shaftesbury, Dorset, SP7 8BP

Published in the USA in 2000 by
ELEMENT BOOKS INC
160 North Washington Street, Boston,
MA 02114

Published in Australia in 2000 by
ELEMENT BOOKS
and distributed by Penguin Australia Ltd
487 Maroondah Highway, Ringwood,
Victoria 3134

This edition produced for
The Book People Ltd.
Hall Wood Avenue, Haydock,
St Helens WA11 9UL

Designed and created with
The Bridgewater Book Company Limited

ELEMENT BOOKS LIMITED
Editorial Director Sue Hook
Project Editors Kate John,
Annie Hamshaw-Thomas
Group Production Director Clare Armstrong
Production Controller Fiona Harrison

THE BRIDGEWATER BOOK COMPANY
Art Director Terry Jeavons
Designers Caroline Marklew, Alistair Plumb
Editorial Director Fiona Biggs
Managing Editor Anne Townley
Project Editor Caroline Earle
Picture Research Vanessa Fletcher
Computer Artwork Trevor da Costa, Derek Lee
Maps Kevin Jones Associates
Photographer Zul Mukhida assisted by
Catherine Gellaty

Printed and bound in Great Britain by
Butler & Tanner Ltd, Frome and London

British Library Cataloguing in Publication
data available

Library of Congress Cataloging in Publication
data available

Hardback ISBN 1–86204–446–5

Page 1: Gold disk, Tedavnet, Co. Monaghan, c. 2000 B.C.E.
Page 3: Achill Island, Co. Mayo, Connacht.
Page 4: Stone of Divisions, Co. Westmeath, Leinster.

CONTENTS

"The oldest of the old follows behind us in our thinking, and yet it comes to meet us."
MARTIN HEIDEGGER

SETTING OUT

Ireland and myth

I t is often said that the Age of Myth is over, and that the gods of humanity's childhood have been supplanted, first by the real Christian god, and then by the reality of scientific reason. The assumption is made that only in traditional places like Ireland, does the shadow of myth still fall across the country and all its customs.

In this book it will be argued that Irish mythology is far from dead. Instead, it springs to enjoyable and valuable life through the interplay of language with place-names, medieval manuscripts, contemporary folklore, and modern Irish literature. Together these words are found to complement Ireland's landscapes, and her ancient monuments, art, and objects of common use, to tell stories of deities that have been presumed lost. They return to illuminate contemporary life in Ireland and help to define the future prospects for the world in general.

Since the first communities settled in Ireland nine thousand years ago, the country has received and developed at least four major canons of myth. They are first, 7000–2000 B.C.E., the myths of the Mesolithic hunter-gathers and of the New Stone Age (Neolithic) farmers. The latter, according to P. C. Woodman, were "present throughout most of the island by about 3200 B.C.E., with evidence of their arrival from 3700 B.C.E. onwards." The myth of this era, termed "Old European" by the prehistorian Marija Gimbutas, revolved around a female goddess of birth, death, and regeneration, matched by a matrilineal human order.

LEFT *Ruined Franciscan friary, Quin, Co. Clare. Built 1402. On journeys through Ireland, one sees and hears evidence of attempts to reach sacred Otherworlds.*

BELOW *Passed down the generations, Irish myths serve as sources of ancestral wisdom, emotional attachment, further inspiration, and creative renewal.*

✠ FACT OR FICTION ✠

Ireland, scholars affirm, has preserved the richest store of mythological traditions of any country north of the Alps. This legacy sometimes caused bewilderment to those trained exclusively in the Christian tradition. For example, a medieval Irish monk wrote, in a colophon to his copy of the Táin Bó Cualgne myth:

I do not accept as matter of belief certain things in this history, or rather fiction; for some things are diabolical superstitions, some are poetical inventions, some have the semblance of truth, some have not; and some are meant to be the entertainment of fools.

Second were the myths of Indo-European warriors that emphasized a male sky god, reflected in a patriarchal human society. (Present in the Irish Bronze Age, c. 2000–800 B.C.E., this mythic wave is most clearly represented by the Celtic-speaking invaders of the Iron Age, beginning c. 800 B.C.E.)

Third, from 500 C.E., Christian mythology introduced concepts of Original Sin and a dualistic division between body and soul, world and spirit, previously unknown in Ireland. The subdivision of the Christian myth between Catholic and Calvinist followed the seventeenth-century settlement of Ulster by an Anglo-Scottish population.

Fourth, 1700–2000, came Scientific Rationalism, introduced by English and Anglo-Irish urban populations. At first glance this is not a mythology, since it rejects all supernatural accounts of reality, preferring to describe the cosmos through an ostensibly objective language of numerical abstraction (mathematics) – an entirely subjective choice.

The recent appreciation by Karl Popper and others that "scientific discovery is akin to explanatory storytelling, to myth-making, and to the poetic imagination" places science in the broad mythic field where, in any case, it was born and nurtured. There, the idea of objectivity appears as one among many storytelling techniques. The nineteenth-century conviction that the modern world had entered a post-mythic state now appears to be a delusion. Instead (especially in Ireland), we inhabit a commonwealth of interacting mythic states that includes modern science among its number.

In present-day Ireland, there are four seemingly incompatible mythologies that interact. Each in turn has claimed an exclusive grasp of the truth, before merging with its rivals to create new hybrids that are gradually accepted as authentic. As a result, evidence of the very oldest mythic layer can still be recognized at the contemporary surface of Irish life, offering hospitality to later inputs.

Marija Gimbutas, when visiting Ireland in 1989, commented:

Old European monuments stand here in all their majesty. In its legends and rituals, this country has preserved many elements which in other parts of

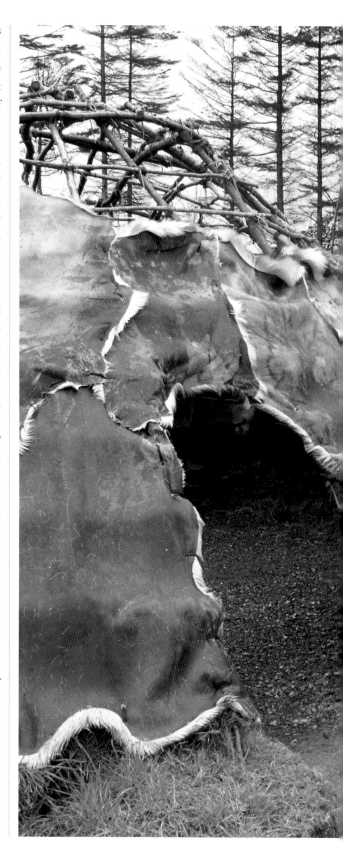

LEFT *Reconstructed
Mesolithic huts in
Ulster History Park,
c. 7000 B.C.E. In
ancient Ireland, the
divinities lived inside
Nature, just as a cow or
bull is integral to its
hide; and people dwelled
within the sacred
dramas, both light and
dark. Ireland is a
country of sacred
imaginings, tied
loosely together.*

*Europe vanished long ago. Much that stems from pre-
Indo-European times . . . is still very much alive in
Ireland. I would say that the ancient spirit of Ireland
is closer to the Old European [fourth millennium
B.C.E.], despite the rather early appearance of Indo-
European peoples here.*

In Ireland, the oldest is not necessarily the faintest, or
most distant, so instead of attempting a chronological
account of Irish mythic sequences, this book accepts
that the layers are now thoroughly intermingled, and
they are described accordingly.

IRELAND AND OTHERWORLD

The coexistence of the archaic within the modern
makes Ireland a complex place, and its power to fasci-
nate stems partly from its endemic ambiguities. These
are now reflected by the multifaceted reality presented
to the entire world by modern physics, where ghostly
interlacings are inferred at the subatomic level. In its
old habits, Irish life may be said to epitomize this
emergent sensibility. Thus a markedly conservative
culture coincides with the latest view of nature, and
archaic practices are supported at a fundamental level
by today's theory. Traditional Irish attitudes may
literally be said to offer prescience or foreknowledge
of recent science at its most kaleidoscopic.

There are numerous senses in which Ireland is a
multiple world. On the political level, the current division between the Irish Republic and Ulster (declared
to be part of the United Kingdom in 1921), means that
on both sides of the border people are aware that there
is another version of island reality, a fact emphasized
further by divisions within Ulster. These outward
disparities stem from different ways of imagining,
embodied in two languages, Gaelic and English. Even
when, as now, Gaelic is little spoken, its supernatural
assumptions infiltrate and affect the use of English
in the Republic, contrasting with Ulster's Anglo-
Scottish employment of the same words. In Ulster,
pre-Christian mythic layers tend to be suppressed,
whereas in Eire even the primary Neolithic stratum
continues to impinge on the collective imagination.

ABOVE *An Irish post office, signed in Gaelic and English. Through song, poetry, storytelling, and in written form, Irish mythology has been posted back and forth between languages.*

This amazing continuity of myth can be explained in part by the fact that Ireland is still a mainly rural country, where agriculture has been regarded as a sacred art for at least five thousand years. Recent mechanization has yet to dismantle this attitude completely. Nor has it totally eradicated those traces of the original Neolithic deities who lived on as *aes síde* – the fairies, or people of the mounds. These lesser spirits of the land remained fearfully vivid through the first half of the twentieth century. They enabled people to stay in touch with their ancestral gods, who had taken refuge in the *síd*. Such magic halls were located inside mountain or monument, or in an "Otherworld" beneath a lake, or "somewhere" in the western ocean.

"Otherworld" has long since waned, but another version is waxing strong. To most Irish people today, their land is a place across the sea, rarely if ever visited. Forty millions of Irish descent live in North America, and millions more in Britain and Australia. For them Ireland is a point of ancestral reference – an

island hidden in cloud, whose profile looms the larger the less it is seen. With the Irish population scattered across the world, Ireland's position is elusive, both in space, and (as this book tries to show) in time. Ireland lies here *and* there, now *and* then. The Other is often heard knocking on both sides of her door.

WORD OF MYTH

Those who prepare for a mythological journey in Ireland by looking for a definition of myth in almost any English dictionary will receive a discouraging shock. Myth, it appears, has a very bad name.

The 1989 Oxford Dictionary defines it as "a purely fictitious narrative usually involving supernatural persons, actions or events, and embodying some popular idea concerning natural or historical phenomena; in generalized use, an untrue or popular tale, a rumour." Longman's says: "Myth is a false story or idea, something or someone invented, not real." Collins' Cobuild adds: "An untrue idea or explanation; the word is often used to show disapproval." "A widespread but false idea," contributes Penguin, while Scribner-Bantam emphasizes the degrading consequences: "A false belief held by a people to justify social institutions, such as slavery."

Fortunately, some obsolete Scottish usages of the word take us nearer the role played by myth in contemporary Ireland. They include, "To show, to mark, to notice, to measure," and "the marrow of a bone." With that we come to the archaic pith of the word.

MYTH, RITE, AND SYMBOL

Myth can be regarded as one of three interrelated aspects of religious expression. Its word and story is reenacted on the human plane by means of ritual (sacred acts). Myth reactivated by human rites also requires a sacred place and tangible sacred objects. These physical symbols can be discovered in landscape features and are emphasized by enclosure, temple architecture, and sacred art.

The word symbol comes from the Greek "to throw together, to unite," and the symbols employed by myth, whatever their size, represent the visible convergence of the cosmic pattern within the living body of the godhead. The "walks" that are undertaken in this book are a movement toward integration of myth with ritual and symbol.

The attempt to join myth, symbol, and ritual into one is helped in Ireland by the *Dindshenchas*. These are collections of sacred stories (Irish, *senchasa*), written down in verse and prose from 1160 C.E. onward using archaic oral sources, explaining the origin of note-worthy Irish place-names, or *dind*. *Dind* is cognate with Old Norse *tindr* – a "spike, tooth, mountain peak." Both traditions compare mountain peaks to the

teeth of the gods, and the Irish stories typically conclude with absolute union between god and place, when the deity dies and is buried at the spot carrying his or her name.

The *Dindshenchas* stories were arranged to make a clockwise, or rather a sunwise, circuit of Ireland, starting in the northeast. They are mythical rather than historical tales, and they bring sacred topo-graphic memories under the scrutiny of solar and lunar "eyes." These scripts offer a valuable means of access to a neglected pagan landscape, lying close to Christian or prosaic surfaces.

Step by hesitant step one follows the tracks. Some are still kept open by living pilgrims; most have long since been abandoned.

BELOW *Early medieval stone sculptures, White Island, Co. Fermanagh, combining Christian and Pagan influences. Through their open mouths they speak the holy words. Icon and utterance merge, when supported by human ritual.*

THE FIVE CÓICED (PROVINCES)

A five-fold structure is fundamental to Irish myth. It follows that the Old Irish word for province is *cóiced*, literally "a fifth." Parts one to four of this book describe journeys into the provinces of Ulster, Munster, Leinster, and Connacht. Each of these regions can be shown to have developed its own emphasis, while drawing from the common store of national experience. This is demonstrated by focusing attention on selected sites within each province. These provincial findings are then brought together in the fifth province, Mide, from where a web of relationships is seen to run to and from every part of the island, making a mythological web spun by the deities.

The first "walk," in Ulster, encounters the relationship between Irish Catholicism and the pre-Christian myths that found shelter within the body of the early Church and have remained therein ever since. This theme is explored at St. Patrick's Purgatory on Lough Derg, Co. Donegal, still the scene of annual pilgrimage. This starting place is chosen because Christianity represents the most recent and widespread overt claim to godhead and is the gauze through which other deities are largely seen.

The Munster "walk" focuses on Cnoc Áine and Lough Gur, where Neolithic and Iron Age myths are seen to combine in twentieth-century folk belief.

RIGHT The division of Ireland into four quarters around a central point was basic to Irish myth-making long before the Celts arrived, c. 2,500 years ago. It is reflected in Gaelic sayings such as "into the five points" and "the five parts of the world," meaning in all directions.

Ulster

Mide

Connacht

Leinster

Munster

Here the central figure (befitting the southern province of Ireland's high noon) is the sun goddess Áine. Her cult is traced through the rich assemblage of monuments erected around the lough, where the archeological evidence is interpreted with the help of oral traditions of equal antiquity. Listening to Mr. Tom MacNamara, a Lough Gur inhabitant, running through his repertoire of stories (which he learned word-for-word from his neighbor, Tom Carroll, who died in 1988 aged 93), one is reminded that these are not illustrations of ideas, but a liturgical evocation of deities who live in monument and landscape.

From the inhabitants of Lough Gur one learns that myth, even in its decline, is best known from the inside. To wear the stories makes for an understanding denied to objectivity and opens the way toward dozens of holy wells and Marian shrines, Finn's seats, and sea coves remembered for supernatural landings.

LEFT *The great Yew at Crom Castle, Co. Fermanagh. Certain trees of immense antiquity were revered as living symbols of the tribe and its ancestors, whose roots were traced to underworld gods. When such a tree fell, the future of the community was considered to be at risk.*

gods. They in turn modeled their behavior on the elemental play of natural forces. The Slighe Mhór, or great east–west road across Ireland, formed the axis of these rivalries. Where it crossed the Shannon, Connacht's eastern boundary (and a major mystical and physical axis), the qualities of western-ness is developed in the legends of Goll, King Eochaid, and the hags of Keshcorran. Endings and deaths mingle with a new-found desire at the Ess Ruaid Falls in North Connacht, where a Samain or end-of-year love feast was central to a myth of national importance. In Connacht the themes of love and war, life and death, are merged, in a manner that made the province the proverbial seat of wisdom.

The vertiginous grandeur of Mide, the fifth province, is approached in Part Five. Mide gathers together sites from the surrounding provinces, to make a rotation taking a year to complete, and annually repeated. Mide presides over a dynamic pattern, where the entire island is affected by four "provinces" of Time. These traditionally began at the festivals of *Samain,* or Halloween (November Ist), the start of the New Year; *Imbolc* or *Oimelg*, also called St Brigit's Day or Candlemas (February Ist); *Beltaine* (May Day), the start of summer; and *Lughnasa* or Lammas (August 1st), the start of harvest and fall.

Mythic Ireland is centered on the story of a divine space–time cycle in which provinces of time continuously interact with provinces of space, thanks to a mythic narrative that draws them together as the visible life of the gods.

Finally, the mythic narrative is carried across the domestic threshold in sacred attitudes to the house, based around the fire goddess (Saint) Brigit. Through her, the dwelling and its ceremonies are seen to flare on the hearthstone of infinity, bringing the furthest lights of divinities within the scope of the family. This possibility, it is suggested, has by no means gone, any more than has our only source of domestic light and heat, the sun. By its light, the inhabitants of a modern bungalow may yet consciously transform their dwelling into the occasional fulcrum of the universe, provided the mythic words (whether of liturgical or spontaneous utterance) are sounded.

The third "walk," in Leinster, concentrates on Dublin as a mythic construct. Prehistoric, neoclassical, and modern attitudes are seen to merge in the internationally renowned achievements of Leinster's poets, novelists, and playwrights. Her word artists have revealed the mythic nature of urbanism *per se* by lifting the mundane metropolis into a series of new universes, as Cyril Connolly remarked in 1929. Joyce, Yeats, O'Casey, and Beckett have revitalized a tradition whereby "poets" act as priest-midwives to Leinster. They hint at the reintegration of urban with rural Ireland in pursuing their visions beyond the constraints of historical time and simple geometric location. In Ireland's capital, thanks to them, we see the archaic turn up on the doorstep of the Here and Now.

Connacht, the western province, is rich in myths of war, honed by the Iron Age enthusiasms of a warrior society, who followed the exploits of their

ULSTER

St. Patrick's Purgatory

Mythological walks are bound to follow the tracks of the ancient gods and the revelatory journeys of the first carriers of a new god's name. In the northern province of Ulster this leads us straight to the location of St. Patrick's Purgatory, where, by the manipulation of both hope and terror, the dominant Irish deity of the present day achieved and sustained his supremacy, with the help of the patron saint.

OPPOSITE *Lough Derg (Red Lake), Co. Donegal, Ulster, is sacred in both pagan and Christian belief. It has drawn pilgrims since the twelfth century.*

To Catholics, Lough Derg is by far the most sacred lake in Ireland. It lies broad and gray, 8 miles (5 kilometers) wide, among unpopulated, heathery hills, in Co. Donegal. The placid surface is dotted with woody islands, and when the wind drops the whole scene sustains an intense silence, as if the universe is holding its breath in preparation for a fresh start.

Today, the believers have come and gone, leaving their cars and minibuses behind, parked in rows along the lakeside.

Beyond the cars are a clutch of single-story buildings, in the style of a country railroad station of the last century, known as the Ferry House. Inside there is a stout deal table, some benches arranged around the walls, and a black empty grate at one end. The drivers and passengers have all departed for the other world of Station Island. Like a battleship it lies moored in mist, a mile offshore. Capped by the octagonal cone of its basilica roof, the first officer can peer through clerestory windows in all directions over the tops of dormitories whose gray walls fall sheer as a hull into the water on all sides.

This stone ship is designed for the transportation of human souls to Purgatory. Although from a distance no passengers are visible, the vessel is crowded with the devout, reliving the agony of the early Middle Ages in complete mythic identification. This is no place for tourists, which is why none come. Lough Derg is a place for pilgrims only. A pamphlet on the waiting room table explains why:

> Lough Derg has been Ireland's national shrine of pilgrimage since the time of St. Patrick (fifth century). Pilgrims arrive daily and do not need to make any booking arrangements for their three-day stay. About twenty thousand make the pilgrimage every year.

BELOW *Pilgrims at Ferry House, on the south shore of Lough Derg, prepare to embark for Station Island, July 1990.*

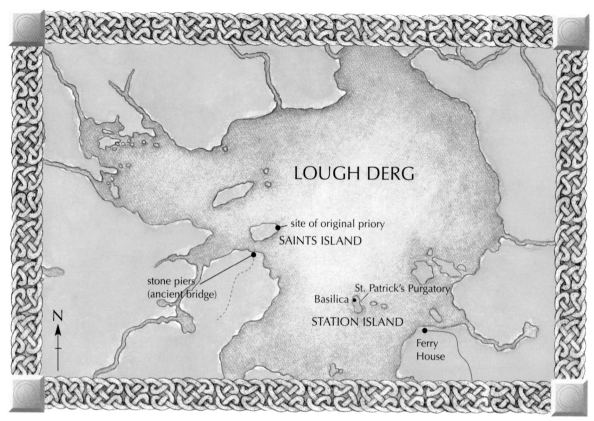

LOUGH DERG

site of original priory
SAINTS ISLAND

stone piers
(ancient bridge)

St. Patrick's Purgatory
Basilica

STATION ISLAND

Ferry
House

N

WHAT TO BRING

Because many of the Exercises take place in the open air pilgrims should bring warm and waterproof clothing. They may not bring to the island cameras, radios, musical instruments, or articles to sell, distribute, or for games.

Pilgrims may arrive on any day of the season until August 13 and they must have fasted from all food and drink (except plain water) from the preceding midnight. . . .When registering at the lake-shore pilgrims pay in advance for their accommodation, leaflet of instructions, boat fare, etc. There is no other charge. [In 1989 the rates were £12 Irish currency, or £11 Sterling, which is approximately $20.]

WHEN TO COME

Boats are available from 11:00 a.m. to noon and from 12:45 to 3:00 p.m. The crossing to the island takes about five minutes.

Pilgrims must be at least fourteen years of age, and free from disability. The nature of the penances excludes anyone under doctor's care and the very old.

THE EXERCISES

Having arrived on the island the pilgrim goes to the hospice, removes all footware and begins the Stations. A twenty-four hour vigil, a night of continuous prayer, is the chief Exercise of the pilgrimage. To do this successfully pilgrims need to be well rested before arriving. On the second night they go to bed on the island and leave Lough Derg for home on the following morning at 10:00 a.m.

Pilgrims are expected to attend all the Exercises of the pilgrimages as approved by the Bishop of Clogher in 1988. Three Stations are to be completed before 9:20 p.m. All the prayers of these Stations are to be said silently.

Begin the Station with a visit to the Blessed Sacrament in **St. Patrick's Basilica**.

Then go to **St. Patrick's Cross**, near the Basilica: kneel and say one Our Father, one Hail Mary, and one Creed. Kiss the Cross.

Go to **St. Brigid's Cross**, on the outside wall of the Basilica: kneel, and say three Our Fathers, three Hail Marys, and one Creed. Stand with your back to *the Cross, and, with arms outstretched, renounce three times the World, the Flesh, and the Devil.*

Walk slowly, by your right hand, four times around **the Basilica**, *while praying SILENTLY seven decades of the Rosary and one Creed at the end.*

Go to the penitential cell or "bed" called **St. Brigid's Bed** *(nearest the bell-tower) but if there is a line take care to join it before going to the Bed.*

AT THE BED

(a)   Walk three times around the outside, by your right hand, while saying three Our Fathers, three Hail Marys, and one Creed.

(b)   Kneel at the entrance to the Bed and repeat these prayers.

(c)   Walk three times around the inside and say these prayers again.

(d)   Kneel at the Cross in the center and say these prayers for the fourth time.

The exercises are then repeated at six more "beds," named after saints Brendan, Catherine, Columba, Patrick, Davog, and Molaise.

What is the purpose of these repetitions? The Lord's Prayer (which always comes first) consists of words originally spoken by the godhead. He *instructs* his followers to repeat them. By doing so, they hope to establish his universal order on earth. Similarly the Virgin Mary is "encountered" by being hailed, while The Creed lays out the details of the Christian cosmic drama. Said together, the three prayers construct the myth of which they speak. That is why, for believers, they cannot be spoken too often.

During the all-night vigil that follows, the prayers of the four Stations are said aloud, and in common in the Basilica during the night of the Vigil. Between these Stations pilgrims may leave the Basilica, use the night shelter, and walk around the immediate vicinity of the Basilica only, taking care to keep their voices down.

Gradually, the space around the pamphlet fills up with the throb of an outboard motor, and an open boat approaches the mainland jetty.

BELOW *Station Island, seen from Ferry House. Every summer, tens of thousands of Christians cross to an encounter with the sacred on Station Island. The tip of its basilica is believed to mark the spot beneath which St. Patrick descended into Purgatory.*

A young man and woman leap ashore and run between the puddles of water to one of the parked cars. Their faces are animated by something more than the pleasure of release. Thoroughly shrived, they make off together at high speed, like Adam and Eve before the Fall, toward the garden of a new existence. Having secured his vessel, the boatman, dressed in yellow oilskins, plods up the ramp and into the Ferry House. He is old. He has been ferryman here all his life. Once in his youth he had cycled to the Croagh Patrick mountain pilgrimage in Co. Mayo, "but that was, oh . . . years ago. Will you be going barefoot?" (meaning on the pilgrimage) he asks.

THE MEDIEVAL PILGRIMAGE

One of the earliest surviving accounts of St. Patrick's Purgatory is to be found in Giraldus Cambrensis' *Topography of Ireland*, of 1186. He described "an Island, one part of which is frequented by good spirits, the other by evil spirits."

> *There is a lake in Ulster containing an island divided into two parts. In one of these stands a church of especial sanctity, and it is most agreeable and delightful, as well as beyond measure glorious for the visitations of angels and the multitude of the saints who visibly frequent it. The other part, being covered with rugged crags, is reported to be the resort of devils only, and to be almost always the theater on which crowds of evil spirits visibly perform their rites. This part of the island contains nine pits, and should anyone perchance venture to spend the night in one of them (which has been done, we know, at times, by some rash men), he is immediately seized by the malignant spirits, who so severely torment him during the whole night, inflicting on him such unutterable sufferings by fire and water, and other torments of various kinds, that when morning comes scarcely any spark of life is found left in his wretched body.*

Here the incoming tide of Christianity can be seen to split the world into a dualism of Good and Evil, with the newly divided self made visible in the form of a divided island. Previously, light and dark had been accepted as equally necessary and interdependent, like winter and summer, with the horror of "the Hag" regarded not as wickedness but another aspect of a totality presumed to be good.

Therefore Patrick was required to show the truth of his doctrine. On the island in Lough Derg, he attempted to do so; or rather he prayed there to his God to show him how to demonstrate the truth, and in response God immediately offered the saint a nocturnal trip to Heaven and Hell in the form of a dream. As Roger of Wendover wrote in the late twelfth century:

> *Whilst the great Patrick was preaching the work of God in Ireland, and gaining much reputation by the miracles which he there performed, he sought to reclaim from the works of the devil the bestial people of that country by fear of the torments of hell and desire of the happiness of heaven, but they told him plainly that they would not be converted to Christ, unless they first saw with their eyes the things of which he told them.*

In Giraldus Cambrensis' words, he procured by the efficacy of his prayers an exemplification of both states, even on earth, as a salutory lesson to the stubborn minds of the people.

RIGHT *St. Patrick, discovering the entrance to Purgatory on Saints Island. Fifteenth-century woodcut from Peter de Navalibus' Catalogue of Saints.*

·S PATRICIO

✛ PURGATORY ✛

The modern Catholic Encyclopedia defines Purgatory as "the state, place, or condition in the next world, which will continue until the Last Judgment, where the souls of those who die in the state of grace, but not yet free from all imperfection, make expiation for unforgiven venial sins, or for the temporal punishment due to venial and mortal sins that they have already been forgiven, and so, by doing, are purified before they enter heaven."

For Catholics, Purgatory was (and is) a kind of vestibule below the level of living, where the souls of the dead worked off their lighter punishments prior to the Last Judgment. At Lough Derg, access to Purgatory could be gained by *the living* through incarceration in an island cave; and from there also glimpses of Heaven and Hell, in repetition of St. Patrick's experience, might be had.

Scholars now say that St. Patrick never referred to Lough Derg in his writings, never visited the lake, and was wholly unconnected with it until several centuries after his death. This shows that myth can be more important than history, as does the unsubstantiated claim made in the current official Guide that the island has been a national shrine since the fifth century.

In fact, a group of Celtic anchorites (hermits) *had* settled on Lough Derg by the seventh or eighth century, to lead a quiet life, but on what is now Station Island, and knew nothing of all this.

ABOVE *A penitent attended by clerics entering the Purgatory cave; fifteenth-century illuminated manuscript. The cave, sited on Saints Isle, was renowned throughout Europe.*

ABOVE *Saints Island, Lough Derg, where Anglo-Norman monks established a Purgatory Cave in the twelfth century. It was transferred to nearby Station Island in the sixteenth century, into a pit previously held sacred by Celtic monks.*

The death of one of their number, Cillene, is recorded in the *Annals of the Four Masters*. They lived in beehive-shaped cells, whose outlines have been reconstructed to make the "beds" featuring in the present penitential perambulations. Among the carved stones from the eighth century is a Latin cross slab, now incorporated into the basilica wall, and two worn seventh-century inscriptions to St. MacNissi. Despite Viking raids, it is believed that this community of hermits was still there when, in the early twelfth century, St. Malachy of Armagh encouraged the canons regular of St. Augustine to found a priory on the neighboring Saints Island in the same Lough.

Observing that their Celtic neighbors incorporated a cave into *their* pattern of worship (which they associated with the name of their founder, St. Daveoc), the Anglo-Normans responded by "finding" a cave on Saints Island, and out-Daveoced Daveoc by announcing that *the original* Christian in Ireland, St. Patrick, had

been led to this newly dug cave by Christ, where the saint received his vision of Purgatory, Heaven, and Hell. This rivalry was part of a wider struggle between the Celtic Church, established in the fifth century, and the more recent Latin Church. At Lough Derg the Celtic community lost and was disbanded.

One of the most popular and eagerly copied books of the Middle Ages was Henry of Saltrey's description, written in 1185, of how he gained access to the dread cavern:

> *Patrick and his successors established the custom that nobody may enter without license from the bishop of the diocese of Clogher in which it lies.*
>
> *The bishop shall first implore the pilgrim to abandon such an undertaking, saying that many have entered and never emerged, . . . and diligently advise the pilgrim to try some other penance. But if he persists the Prior brings him to the [Saints Island] church, where he remains during fifteen days of fast*

✠ HEAVEN AND HELL ✠

St. Patrick's Purgatory is founded on the principle of mythic repetition, running in an unbroken sequence from the Son of God, through St. Patrick, to the individual. It was Christ's supernatural journey after Calvary that underlay the pilgrimage. "He descended into Hell, and on the third day he rose again from the dead; before ascending into Heaven." The canons announced that Patrick had enjoyed a modified form of this experience; he descended into Purgatory where he glimpsed Heaven and Hell, before re-ascending to mortal life. The medieval visitor, chanting the Apostles Creed, was repeating, at the human level, the journey that Christ made between Good Friday and Easter Sunday, a thousand years before; hence the "confusion" between Lough Derg and the Holy Land in the popular mind. The intention was to close the gap, and the gap was duly closed.

BELOW *Medieval man, Tawnamore, Co. Sligo dressed in his grave clothes. He wears new shoes for his walk across Magh Mhór, or Great Plain, which was believed to stretch beyond pre-Christian death.*

and prayer. Then, fortified with Holy Communion, and sprinkled with Holy Water, he is led to the entrance of the cave, with a procession of clergy singing a Litany. At the door a final warning is given, but if the pilgrim remains firm, the door is opened in the presence of all and the priests give him their blessing, and mark his forehead with the sign of the Cross. He enters, and the Prior closes the door.

If these precautions seem overelaborate, it must be remembered that holy places had to find ways to be taken seriously. Saltrey's account continues:

> Next morning the door is opened by a Prior. If the pilgrim is waiting there he is joyfully conducted to the Church for another fifteen days of vigils and prayer. If however he does not make an appearance he is abandoned as lost and the door is locked.

Lough Derg chose the Very Severe route to international publicity, and it worked. People flocked to take the ultimate test, and have flocked ever since.

OWEN IN PURGATORY

We can get through the door in Roger's version of 1153, in the company of a certain knight named Owen. Shut in by the Prior, he passed courageously along the cave until he was in total darkness. At last the light again broke upon him and he found himself in a twilit plain entering a pillared enclosure, like a cloister, where fifteen men in white garments warned him of the imminent approach of a multitude of unclean spirits who might destroy him, body and soul, unless he carried himself manfully, and called on the name of the Lord.

Left alone, the knight heard a noise around the building, "as if all the men in the world with the animals and beasts were making it, and after this noise came a terrible apparition of ugly demons, of which an immense multitude rushed into the hall." They advised him to return through the door by which he had come, to enjoy all the pleasures of the world and wait for a second meeting with them until he was properly dead. The knight held a contemptuous silence at this suggestion. Indignantly, the demons kindled a large fire and "seized the knight by his arms and legs, threw him into the midst of it, dragging him with iron hooks, backward and forward. When he first felt the torture he called on the name of Jesus Christ saying 'Jesus Christ have mercy upon me.'" At this name the fire was put out, so that not a spark remained. The demons then dragged the knight

. . . through a wilderness of black and dark, towards the place where the sun rises in summer, and he began now to hear lamentations as if of all the people in the world. Then he was dragged to another plain, filled with woe and calamities . . . full of persons of both sexes every age, naked, and lying with their bellies to the ground, with hot nails of iron driven into the earth. Sometimes in the anguish of their suffering they gnawed the dust, crying and lamenting "spare us, spare us, have mercy, have mercy upon us!" The demons coursed over these wretched beings, striking them with heavy blows.

In another place . . . the people were pinned on their backs and fiery dragons were sitting on some of them, gnawing them with iron teeth to their inexpressible anguish, . . . whilst fiery serpents coiled around others' necks, arms, . . . and fixed iron fangs into their hearts. Toads, also, of immense size and terrific to behold, sat upon the breasts of some, and tried to tear out their hearts.

The demons showed the knight a violent whirlwind from the north, which swept a large number of people into a cold stinking river. All were sitting naked, apparently awaiting in terror the approach of death. Eventually he was shown a stinking fiery well in the south, from which hot naked men were shot forth like sparks, before sinking again into the flaming pit. "That fiery well is the entrance to hell where we live." (All the torments he had so far seen were a mere foretaste of the real pains of Hell, lying beyond.)

The knight was then made to cross a narrow slippery bridge, dizzily high, over a flaming river.

At last he was released from demonic persecution and saw before him a high wall of wonderful workmanship, having in it a closed gate adorned with precious stones that shone brilliantly. When he approached it, it opened, and a sweet smell came forth, reviving him.

Then out came a procession of crosses, tapers, banners and branches of golden palms, followed by archbishops, bishops, abbots, monks, priests, and ministers of every ecclesiastical degree, all clad in sacred garments. With pleasing salutations and concerts of unequaled harmony, they led him within the gate in triumph. Two archbishops conducted him through most delightful meadows, adorned with different fruit and flowers and herbs. Darkness never fell in that region. Harmonious human choirs lauded the Creator of all things. No one felt heat or cold.

The holy pontiffs told him that this was the terrestrial paradise before the Fall, populated by those who had purged their sins by penance and hoped to reach Heaven. (This concept was eventually rejected by the Catholic Church at the Second Council of Lyons.)

Then the prelates led the knight to a mountain and bade him look upward; and asked him what color Heaven was, from where he stood. He replied:

"Like the color of gold that is red-hot in the furnace."
"This," said they, "which you now see, is the entrance to heaven and the celestial paradise. As long as we remain here, God feeds us daily on heavenly food." A ray of light [then] descending from heaven, covered the whole country, and the flame, settling in rays upon the heads of each, entered into the bodies of all. At that, the knight felt such a delicious sweetness pervade his heart and his whole body . . . but this feeling was over in a moment.

The knight was then told to return to the world. After visiting the Holy Land he returned to Ireland, where his vision of Purgatory continues to glow.

BELOW *Legananny Dolmen, Castlewellan, Co. Down, third millennium* B.C.E. *Morning gold in the pre-Christian underworld. In Ireland, there is an interplay between pagan and Christian forms, involving natural events.*

PURGATORY AND EARTH

Children attending Roman Catholic Confirmation classes in the mid-twentieth century were aware that the mythic journey described previously did not end in the Middle Ages but was everyone's inescapable destiny. On entering the Cave of Death, they too would be required to stride into the flames. "The best that my sisters and our friends could hope for, as we gathered in Mrs. Donaghue's front room to learn the truth, was that if we were good the certain terrors of Purgatory *might* not be followed by the eternal agony of Hell. Either way, it would be an unforgettable excursion and probably last longer than the Second World War, of which we could not recall the beginning, nor guess the end."

BELOW *Prelate and altar boy, Stuttgart, Germany, 1617; engraving. With sacred book and holy water they lead in a "St. Patrick's Purgatory" tableau (see p.25).*

Today, some Catholic authorities, adopt a slightly embarrassed tone regarding Purgatory:

The punishments of purgatory and allied topics are much more obscure than the question of the existence of Purgatory. All theologians hold that there will be some kind of purifying punishment there (from the very etymology of the word) that will cease with the last judgment, [but] a veil of mystery prevents any accurate assessment of the intensity of the pain [and] certain conceptions . . . stressing too much the horror and misery of purgatory are to be discouraged.

In the eleventh century, Irish belief in Purgatory was so strong that it was thought that purgatorial fires might rise into the real earthly landscape in an Hiroshima-like event:

To wit, a flame of fire, swifter than a blast of wind, which will cleanse Ireland from the Southwest. And that is the fire which in the twinkling of an eye will burn up more than four fifths of the men of Ireland, men, women, boys, and girls, without communion, without confession, without sacrifice . . . black ashes will be made of their bodies, and the color of the coal [will be] on their souls therein.

Although attributed to Adamnan, Abbot of Iona, who died in 704 C.E., this forecast was written in 1096, only a few years before Patrick's Purgatory was instituted. It continues:

. . . the men of Erin have again followed Heathenism as it was at first, before beliefs and before Patrick's advent . . . they perpetrate wizardry, dealing in charms, philters, and enchantments, and fidlanna [wooden staves, carved with magic signs used in divination], so that every harm is ripe to come, both scamach [cattle mange] and murrain, and blight of fruit, and hunger, and famine, and mortality.

A new link between heathenism and all these perils, especially fire, was provided by the Viking raids on Ireland of the ninth to the eleventh centuries. Up the Irish estuaries and navigable rivers, the Apocalypse became a matter of fact, and the wives of the Viking warriors conducted heathen rites on monastery altars, as at Clonmacnoise.

"The sea spewed forth floods of foreigners over Erin," recorded the Annals of Ulster for 820, "so that

no haven, no landing place, no stronghold, no fort, no castle might be found, but it was submerged by waves of Viking and pirates." These newcomers were "heathens who have never believed, with a devil's nature in [their] body."

By 840 the most important ecclesiastical center in the country, Armagh in Ulster, founded by St. Patrick, had fallen. Churches and abbeys were turned into temples to Thor, and many Irish soldiers, who became known as *Gall Gaedhil*, or Foreign Gaels, joined forces with the pagan Norse.

The establishment of St. Patrick's Purgatory in the twelfth century was a clerical reaction aimed against *all* pagan beliefs. Another effect was the attempt by monks during and after this period to portray the surviving pagan Irish deities as mere historical characters, so robbing them progressively of mythic power.

In the long run, it could be said that the Viking onslaught gave the Church another chance to complete a project begun in the fifth century – the eradication of the mother of the gods, Ana, and her replacement by Mary, the virgin mother of a celibate god.

This was to be the key act in the proposed de-sexualization of the Irish landscape. The pagan "Land of Woman" as an Otherworld ideal and standard of earthly perfection, was to be obliterated by abstinence, and by the concept of Original Sin, while the former life-giving orifice of spring and the maternally sheltering cave were to be experienced ideally as the many mouths of Hell's vestibule. Purgatory was, in the first instance, a negation of the pre-Christian earth goddess – the new religion had denounced the feminine from Eve in Genesis to the Whore of Babylon in Revelation.

THE FEMALE GLEN

ABOVE *Tullaghan, Co. Sligo. St. Patrick chased The Devil's Mother, Caorthannach, to the top of this mountain, before driving her from Ireland for ever, according to folk belief.*

Ever since the first people arrived on its shores, Ireland in its entirety had been regarded as a female deity, identified by many names, including Banba, Fódla, and Ériu. From Ériu, the modern Eire is a conscious derivation. To pagans and Christians alike, Ériu-the-Island was a living divinity, but whereas *the people* more or less continued to regard her as the source of wonder and the sustainer of human existence, to the clergy she became a hostile erogenous zone, harmful to spiritual health, from which they tried to escape through prayers of renunciation, and by rejecting her proffered fruit.

In clerical writings the new pornography of place became centered on the image of the deep valley, where the natural vulva of the land goddess was redefined as the mouth of Hell. This image was playfully echoed by James Joyce, in his decision to rearrange the place-names around the Wicklow Mountains so that the Anna Livia (Liffey) River could be said to rise from Devil's Glen:

> *But first of all, worst of all, the wiggly livvly, she side slipped out by a gap in the Devil's glen.*

As various folktales, colored by Christianity, make clear, it was the Devil's *Mother*, sometimes in the form of a wide-jawed serpentine monster, who was the *genius loci* of such places; for example, at Tullaghan in Co. Sligo, where St. Patrick pursued her into a springhead. He alone had the courage to drive her from Glen Tachair in Co. Donegal, as O'Donovan recorded in 1835:

> *Yesterday we traveled through the deep and romantic valley of Gleann Tachair . . . to its very head, where is to be seen a stone exhibiting the impression of the Crozier of St. Patrick, which remains in it since that Saint destroyed Tachar, the serpent or demon, that presided over the valley.*

Similar calls on the mythical St. Patrick's attention came from every corner of Ireland except the southeast. He alone had the strength to replace a national goddess, Ériu, with a new god for the whole nation, and the audacity to lie on her thousands of traditional "beds," the stone mounds and barrows by many a spring, to neutralize their potency, without himself becoming contaminated.

No wonder that Station Island was treated with a sense of awe, for there an entire mythic system was grounded. Yet in *being* grounded, it was compromised from the outset and threatened from within, because the Purgatory cave itself had been inherited from a denigrated goddess.

Drawn to attack the image of her life-giving orifice as a rival to be overthrown, Christianity converted the very threshold of her love into The Crack of Doom, to be used as a punishment hall prior to Last Judgment. That this was a dangerous policy from the Christian viewpoint may be judged by the accounts of some medieval pilgrims, who emerged from incarceration in bewilderment, recounting visions of beautiful women who had proffered invitations to their banquet. Beneath the floor of Purgatory still lay the pagan Land of Women – an alternative buried dream, rising unbidden into the hearts of Christ's pilgrims and expressed in song by the minstrel Tuileagna Mac Torna, who called Lough Derg "Eire's Pilgrimage . . . the Paradise of pleasant waters . . . with its soft-sounding shore . . . a quiet calm-gray fairy lake . . . supreme Paradise of Tuathal's Land."

In the year 1517, a visiting Papal Nuncio reported that the Purgatory Cave was known as The *Well* of St. Patrick, and that the cave was roofed by rock like a millstone, whose echo when struck gave rise to many fables. These features of the cave hint at the oracular power and fecundity of an earth mother still in possession, secretly protecting the eternal spring of Nature's holiness from the doctrine of Hell-fire lit around its brim.

BELOW *Noon's Hole, Co. Fermanagh, 250 feet (76 meters) deep. This, the deepest pothole in Ireland, was associated with the earth goddess Crón. She was a personification of the abyss, and a great swallower.*

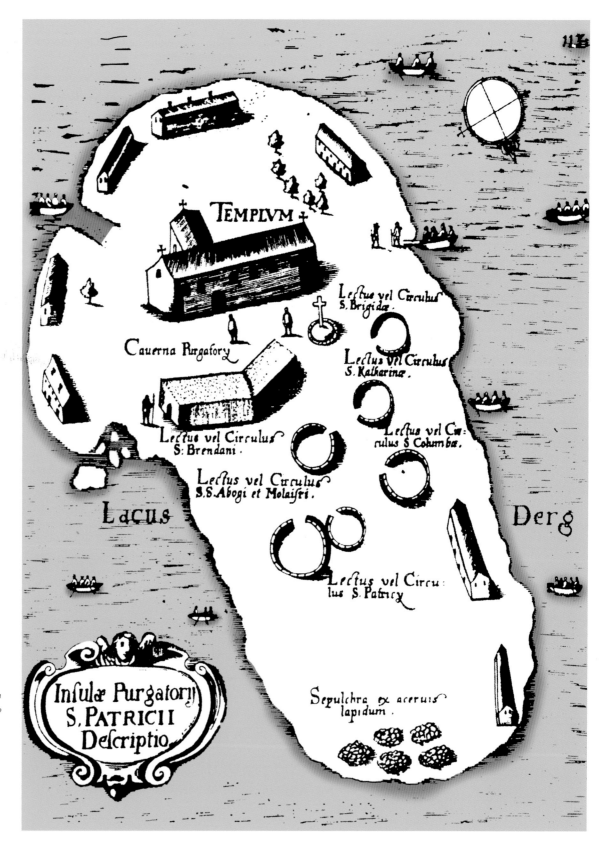

TEMPLVM

Cauerna Purgatory

Lectus vel Circulus
S. Brigidæ.

Lectus vel Circulus
S. Katharinæ.

Lectus vel Circulus
S. Brendani.

Lectus vel Circulus
S.S. Abogi et Molaisri.

Lectus vel Ci-
rulus S. Columbæ.

Lacus

Derg

Lectus vel Circu-
lus S. Patricy

Insulæ Purgatory
S. PATRICII
Descriptio.

Sepulchra ex aceruis
lapidum.

RIGHT *Station Island in
1666, with (from top to
bottom) dormitories of
the four provinces, the
church, dog-legged
"Purgatory," circular
remains of pre-Norman
monks' cells, and rock
"bones" of the
Caoranach monster.*

LOUGH DERG
AND THE REFORMATION

After the Reformation, and the sixteenth-century decline in foreign pilgrims, Station Island came to function as a microcosm of Ireland. Pilgrims were housed according to which of the four provinces they came from, in one of four provincial dormitories. These lay in an arc on either side of the landing place, to correspond to their geographical location in Ireland. This arrangement persisted till at least 1625. Likewise, neat subdivisions of the sky were incorporated into the ritual pattern, for, as J. Richardson found in 1727 and recorded in *The Great Folly, Superstition* and *Idolatry of Pilgrimages in Ireland*, the Stations were repeated daily three times – namely at sunrise, noon, and sunset. By these means the ideas of Heaven and Hell were reunited with sensual experience, so immensely strengthening their popularity.

In 1701 Archbishop Hewson described the "beds" as six circles of stone, above a foot high, and five or six feet in diameter, with a gap in the side of each, put together carelessly, and with rocky uneven floors. In this they closely resemble their 1989 appearance. In Archbishop Hewson's day those shut in the Purgatory Cave, which was by then a dog-legged dark cabin, were given water and tobacco, but denied sleep, on pain of being carried off by the Devil. Richardson (1727) found the cave to measure 22 feet (6.5 meters) long, only 25 inches (63 cm) wide, and a mere 3 feet (89 cm) high. "It hath a bending within six feet off the far end, where there is a very small window to let in some light and air to the pilgrims. There is little or none of it underground, and it seems never to have been sunk deeper than the rock. It is built of stone and clay, huddled together, covered with broad stones, and all overlaid with earth."

The last chance any mortal had to enter the Station Island Cave physically was in 1789, for in that year the much disputed bunker was filled in by order of the Catholic prior, because the pilgrims were in danger of suffocation through overcrowding, the medieval discipline having long since broken down. From then on, the extraordinary chamber could work only as a spiri-

LEFT *St. Patrick and the Devil at St. Patrick's Purgatory. Medieval woodcut.*

✟ A NEW PURGATORY ✟

During periods when access to the Station Island was completely prohibited by the Calvinists, one response of the faithful was to recreate the Purgatory Cave in their own parishes. A microcosm under stress may hop sideways to one of the many other possible locations within the macrocosm.

For example, at the Chapel of Monea in Clogher diocese, a "large hole was made in the Chapel floor and filled with water as a representation of the holy lake (of Derg), and at Coronea, Co. Cavan, circles were cut in the Chapel floor, and figures chalked on the walls in imitation of the beds and crosses of Station Island. A prompter to the company repeats at each set of prayers: 'Now we go round St. Bridget's Bed, now we go round St. Ann's circle.'" These activities were reported with disgust by Philip Dixon in 1836. Disgust was (and still is) a common reaction of rationalists to the Lough Derg phenomenon.

tual metaphor, especially after Father Matthew Kelly, having reviewed all the evidence in 1848, reluctantly announced that St. Patrick "probably never visited Lough Derg." Many priests accepted this verdict,

including Father Maguire of Inniskeen. "God has no need of our lies; neither has St. Patrick," he retorted.

Yet, as the 1990s pilgrims demonstrate, it is the mythical rather than the historical St. Patrick whom people follow. As Aristotle remarked, this serves to show that Poetry rather than History is the chief vehicle of enduring truths. By the same token, fiction is preferable to fact, being more resilient before the unpredictable blasts of discovery. As fiction, "St. Patrick" has achieved a scope that would have been impossible for an individual set in fact, on the narrow heels of a single lifetime.

Similarly, when the Purgatory Cave was lost in fact, it quickly reincarnated as idea, embodied in a newly substantial thing – the basilica, completed in 1931. Its pinnacle is positioned exactly over the center of the former cave. In this way, Purgatory was elevated onto the surface as a volume of national prayer, uttered by hungry, exhausted people, who afterward flop gratefully onto hard bunks and in the morning drink tea.

PART ONE

ULSTER 2

the Caoranach

In Ireland little is lost; mostly, things get rearranged, in a remarkable conservation of mythic energy. What is not converted hovers on, in an altered yet still recognizable version of its original form. So, at Lough Derg, the guts of a pre-Christian monster, named Caoranach, were pointed out to J. Richardson in 1727. Turned to stone, they stood as a heap of large natural boulders at the northernmost tip of Station Isle. As recently as 1932, people were pointing to "the enormous knot of stone, visible in the rocks off Patrick's Island, as a morsel of the bones of the Caoranach."

The creature's grip on the pattern of worship was such that her offshore rocky remains, known as The Altar of Confession, were visited at sunrise, noon, and sunset, at the conclusion of every station. "Here pilgrims go into the water, and go round the stones thrice, saying five Paters, five Aves and one Creed, and then they lean upon the corner of one of the stones." Finally, they waded to another stone close-by, called Leac na mbonn, or footstone.

Lying less than a yard below the lake's surface, this "flat stone . . . hath a singular virtue of curing bruised and wounded feet of pilgrims." There the pilgrims said three prayers. The stone was smooth, and had a hole in the middle of it, in which there was another stone. This suggests the form of a *bullaun*, associated with goddess worship, and especially of Brigid. Bullauns are found throughout Ulster. (They in turn are related to the *yoni* and *lingam*, female–male

OPPOSITE
Glenballyeamon,
Co. Antrim, in winter.
Like the battle of the
seasons, Christian and
pre-Christian forces
fought over Lough Derg.
Yet as clouds turn to
rain, or snow, or ice, so
every myth is a different
version of the same story.

LEFT St. Brigid's Stone
in Killinagh, Termon,
Co. Cavan. Until recent-
ly large pebbles resting
in the hollows of this
bullaun were turned to
promote fertility or to
strengthen a curse.
Whether as a saint or a
goddess, the outcome
rested in Brigid's womb.

imagery of the completed cosmos, reintroduced to Britain in the Hindu temples of recent immigrants, but known to the entire Indo-European tradition for at least 4,000 years.)

Of Irish holed stones, W. Frazer wrote in 1896, "They are still popularly considered to exemplify that worship of generative power which prevails to the present day in India. In Ireland they are regarded as helpful to women in obtaining successful childbirth, and influence men in securing progeny . . . beliefs which are far from extinct." Such perforated stones are also considered to cure infantile diseases, and the maladies of cattle — convictions "firmly accepted in many districts."

Referring specifically to Ulster bullauns — horizontal boulders or rocks with artificial or natural basins — I. R. Crozier notes that they are often found by the side of lakes or near Megalithic remains, and that they "played an important role in surviving pre-Christian rites, especially at Beltane and Lammas," when they were sought out by childless women. W. F. Wakeman maintained in 1875 that many Christian churches were erected close to bullauns, in order to share in and redirect their potency.

The water that lapped so gently in and out of the *Leac na mbonn* cavity was called The Wine of St. Brigid, and drunk by nineteenth-century pilgrims, as hot as they could bear, from a cauldron. They were proud to show off the blisters so received. In the figure of St. Brigid, or Brigit, Christian and pre-Christian realities coalesce. She has a foot in both myths.

From her rocky "chair" on the south shore, she gazes across the lake of her own wine-blood, called Derg (Red), though in her Christian guise her mildness sits incongruously on the visceral coils of the pagan goddess of the lake — the monstrous beast Caoranach, whose airborn self was heard in the cry of the featherless corra bird.

ABOVE *Votive Iron Age bronze sheath, Co. Antrim; a version of the Caoranach monster.*

In Irish, "Corra" means Female Fiend, and the Devil's Mother. In her pre-Christian role as the Great Swallower she is wellknown in Ireland. Flying from Lough Corra in the Galtee Mountains, she swallowed Cliach, while he played on the nearby stream harps, while as chieftainness of the demon birds it was she who had assailed St. Patrick on the holy Mountain of Croagh Patrick, in Connacht. There, on her white quartz harvest hill, he had thrown his silver bell at her. She blackened it, and turned it to iron. In the pre-Christian cycle, Croagh Patrick was the supreme expression of the White Goddess-in-harvest, the western peak of the year, after which a rapid decline to the northwest, and winter, was inevitable. Echoing this theme, several oral accounts say that Patrick chased the Corra from Croagh Patrick to Lough Derg, a distance of 95 miles (152 kilometers) as the crow flies. The link is strengthened by an alternative name of Lough Derg, namely Lough na Corragh, as Otway discovered from a guide in 1839. At Lough Derg, folktales say, Patrick killed the Corra, and so turned its waters half red with her blood.

ABOVE *A vision of the Corra,* Book of Kells, *fol. 124r, eighth century* C.E. *St. Patrick turned Lough Derg red with her blood.*

OPPOSITE *Croagh Patrick, Co. Mayo. From this mountain, St. Patrick is said to have chased the Corra or Female Fiend, alias The Devil's Mother, to Lough Derg.*

ABOVE *Finn McCool's Finger-stone at Killibeg, Co. Fermanagh. Sandstone, 22 inches (56 centimeters) tall, with cup marks. By sucking his finger or thumb, Finn acquired the secrets of his earth mother's generative power and underworld forms.*

Both Corra and Caoranach are closely related, etymologically, and as mythic partners. Having struggled with Corra, the pagan energy of the air, it was inevitable that the saint should then confront her submarine equivalent in Caoranach, for as the original advocate of Ireland's first monotheism, "Patrick" was set the task of destroying all other gods. Corra is to air, mountain, and island tree, what Caoranach is to lake and shore. The Irish word *Corr* means "stork," with childbirth associations, and "mountain peak," while reaching its long neck downward, to see its partner, in a third meaning, of "well or pool." In a story told in Co. Galway in 1935, the Lough Derg Caoranach features as a gigantic eel that was killing all who passed around the lough, till St. Patrick spent two days and nights in the lake bravely fighting her with a sword. At last he found the vulnerable spot in her side and killed her.

Although the rocks on the north end of Station Island were regarded as her petrified backbone, many believed, according to C. Otway in 1829, that Caoranach was not dead, but fastened alive to the bottom of the lough, "where in times of storm amidst thunder and lightening, the serpent rises, and takes its sport on the surface, and can be seen when men pass that lonely water." They see her "riding the waves like a wild horse with a flowing mane, the froth boiling away from its sides, and all is terrible entirely."

On these occasions her long body, rearing from the water, appeared as islands. Therefore both Station and Saints Island can be claimed as parts of her anatomy. Equally, the whole lough can be regarded as the maw of the female swallower. Some oral beliefs may imply that she also swallowed the sun and moon into her underworld, so converting it into a Realm of light – an event reenacted by a ritual fire, lit in the sunny province of Munster, according to a story recorded in 1935 by the Irish folklore Commission, from the Arigna Valley, Co. Leitrim, which says that before being chased to Lough Derg from the *south* of Ireland, "she used to have a grand light lit in the mouth of the cave at night, and anyone that saw that light was dead in his grave that time twelvemonths . . . she had a grand place inside this cave and she had a good way of living too, for anything she'd lay her eyes on she brought it by witchery."

At Lough Derg, set in northern darkness, the Caoranach reached her most ferocious development, in keeping with the winter demands of an annual nationwide cycle. J. Richardson recorded her actions.

This monster [of Lough Derg], called by the natives Caoranach, would suck men and cattle into its mouth at a Miles Distance, and becoming by this attractive quality so very pernicious to the Country that no one durst come near the Lake: at last . . . they obliged themselves to send a certain Number of Cattle to be devoured by it every day, [so that] almost all the cattle in Ulster were destroyed; [then] . . . they were forced to send to Leinster and Munster for supplies.

Thus the tribute in kine of the eastern province of spring and prosperity, and of the southern province of noonday, music, and song, poured down Caoranach's throat, as she sat on Crock na Cunny, a hill half a mile (800 meters) east of the lough. Cunny, or Cuinn, may mean "of Conn," offering another possible link with Croagh Patrick in Connacht, and so reinforcing a sun-wise annual narrative into northwest Ulster. In this drama, due north was (and is) the nadir and the central axis between every sunset and sunrise.

✛ MYTHIC DIRECTIONS ✛

The waters of Lough Derg drain due north, via the Derg River, to Lough Foyle, on Ulster's north coast. The Irish language word *tuaisceart*, "north," is enmeshed in dangerous qualities. It can also mean "awkwardness, rudeness, and left-hand side," while *tuais* means "arrogance, vanity, and pride." *Tuaithe* is "a negative magic charm or spell." *Tuairech* means "forebodings," *tuairse* – "remnant, remainder;" *tuaicthe* – "anguished hearts," and *tuaircnige* is "hammering, beating, smiting."

Gaelic embodies a mythic view of reality where "abstract" directions are unknown. Instead they are a vehicle for and an expression of the daily and yearly myth. Language is no neutral bystander. Situated in the northern quarter, the fearful role of Lough Derg is partly the outcome of the verbal associations that make up the fabric of its provincial location.

FINN CONAN AND THE WHITE WORM
∽

In many folktales it is the "Gyant Conan" (son of Leinster's sunrise demigod Finn McCool) who puts the Caoranach into Lough Derg. In one version of the story Conan finds that he has a little white worm stuck between his teeth, which he throws into Lough Derg, and is amazed how it grows. In another account, told by James Ryan of Tamlaght, the worm crawls out of the shin-bones of Finn's mother; these bones were all that remained of her after Finn had carried her across country on his back to the shore of the lough. Seeing the worm, Conan says: "If that worm could get water enough it would come to something great." With that, he, or his companion, threw it into the lough, where it soon turned into the monster.

In pre-Christian terms, the lake was sacred because the phallic worm of the new year, doubling as the necessary maggot that had fed on the decomposing wreckage of the old year, was weaned in its waters. Originating within the shin-bone of Finn's mother who was a goddess from the *síd* of Almu in the province of Leinster, the worm carried the seed of her hidden easterly dawn underneath the dark waters of Ulster, and illuminates them (Lough Fion) with a hope disguised in horror.

LEFT *Finn McCool and Conan, his son. Conan is said to have thrown a white worm into Lough Derg, which had previously wriggled from the shin-bone of Finn's dead mother.*

True to the demands of mythic repetition, the folk mind also insisted that St. Patrick had to repeat Conan's traditional journey into and out of Caoranach. And so he did, according to nineteenth-century folk belief, where the Lough Derg serpent is sometimes called Big Bolaun – "big as a round tower," in a version told by a Mr. O'Connor of Athlone.

St. Patrick pursued the beast of Lough Derg and watched from the main shore as it swam to Station Island, and coiled up there. The two adversaries gazed at each other across the water, till Patrick suddenly stripped off his clothes. Then, crozier in hand, he dived into the lough and thrashed out toward the island. Seeing the saint approach in a little storm of white water, the serpent opened its great mouth and made at full speed toward him. They met, head to head, and in an instant the holy man was gulped down.

For St. Patrick, there must have been an overwhelming sense of *moral* revulsion at being reenmeshed in the physicality of the feminine, which might explain why this particular storyteller, out of consideration for the saint's feelings, refers to Big Bolan as "he." Whether it was the Devil or the Devil's Mother, the saint slashed his way out, using his crozier as the sword, grateful to end the nightmarish reenactment of his nine-month journey as embryo and fetus, from the depths of his own mother.

ABOVE Sweat-house near Blacklion, Co. Cavan, 1889. Many such "saunas" were in use until c. 1850. Here "Purgatory" is both useful, and a version of the sid, or dwelling of the old gods, under the hill. It is also a version of the earth goddess' belly and womb.

In his naivety, the wise fool Conan is instrumental in reactivating this most perilous sequence of events, and is transfixed in terror as the monster Caoranach, undulating above and below the water, makes towards him at furious speed.

It is Conan's destiny to be swallowed by the Caoranach. Ancient texts describe the swallowing as his *turas* or pilgrimage. This holy journey took the demigod into the fire of the lost winter sun, deep in the gut of the mother goddess – an alternative "Purgatory," which by no means died out with the coming of Patrick.

Conan was swallowed by Caoranach and carried in her belly under the lough. Eventually he managed to wound the monster in the side and cut his way out with his dagger. He swam to shore, having lost his skin and hair by the heat of her entrails, for which reason he was afterward called Conan Muil, "Bald Conan." The monster immediately died, and Conan, having cut off its head, threw it on the shore of Station Isle, where the stones have been colored red ever since (though J. Richardson believed this effect to be due rather to a mineral spring).

RIGHT Rock-carving on a Neolithic tomb, Lough Graney, Co. Clare. The Christian "Devil's Mother" was the pre-Christian Mother Earth, with her divine engendering power.

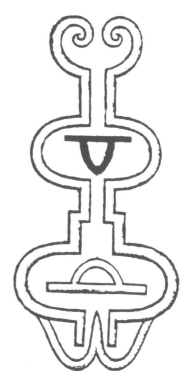

DAVEOG

∽

In the minds of the pilgrims who came to Lough Derg after 1150, Conan, Patrick, and Caoranach required and received sincere propitiation. If the people's response was "two-faced," it was because they were confronted by a two-faced reality — two intertwined universes, equally real, derived from a single physiological root. Spiritual and physical survival depended on learning to play a correct part in each.

Polytheistic tolerance came easily to the people, much to the dismay of their priests. Often ridiculed as undiscriminating and muddle-headed, the popular loyalty to the Caoranach stories was the necessary concern of a farming people for the drama of the annual cycle. Today the pluralism of the folk voice gains long-overdue intellectual respectability, since its instinctive chords are now being echoed by the discoveries of cosmologists and nuclear physicists regarding the multiple worlds and parallel structures of physical reality.

A good example of what modern physicists call *superposition* (the existence of two realities coexisting at one point) may be seen at Lough Derg in the figure of St. Dabheog, that most obscure personage, venerated by the Celtic community on Station Island, prior to the Augustinian invasion. Christian hagiographies have nothing to say about him — a reliable sign of pre-Christian sanctity granted the token blessing by a new authority. On Station Island, the cult of Dabheog was centered upon the cave, or underground chamber. What pre-Christian significance this had is unknown, but it might have been regarded as a *davoch; dabhoch,* or *dabchach,* variants on a single word that in Gaelic means "a vat, a mashing vat, a large tub," from Old Irish *dabach.* It also means "large stomach," as applied to men, and "a huge lady." The immense appetite of Caoranach comes into view, along with the possibility that the offerings of cattle made to the lake from Leinster and Munster (where east and south recognized the just claims of north) were symbolically and actually put into the Station Island stomach — the

BELOW *Human fetus, from the eleventh to the sixteenth week of pregnancy. The St. Patrick's Lough Derg Purgatory experience may be seen as echoing the nine months spent in the maternal womb, but reinterpreted as a punishment or defilement.*

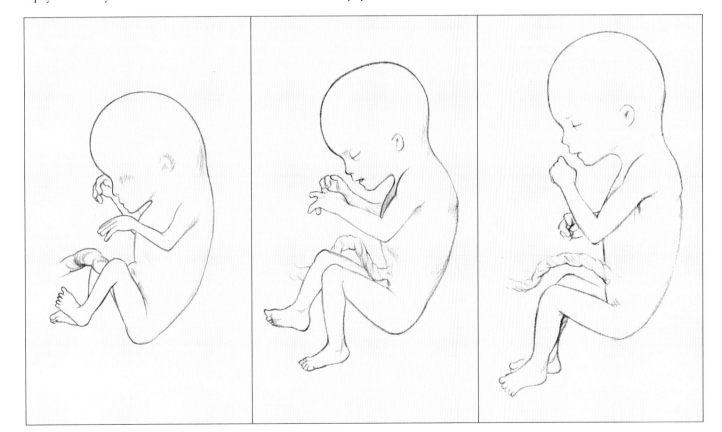

mashing vat of the giantess. The festival of Daveog was celebrated on January 1st – the day on which women in the Hebrides, whose culture was largely Irish, gathered around the Knockin' Stanes for the ritual pounding of barley with wooden mallets. This communal ceremony was focused on a hollow in the Knockin' Stane boulder. The stane and Daveog's cave were two versions of the fertile interior of the goddess.

Liquor for the vat could have come from the spring reputed to lie beneath the cave. This might also explain why so many claims concerning Caoranach's fossilized bones are associated with Station Island. The bones of the great monster naturally lie near her former "stomach-womb," whose site is now sealed beneath the center of the basilica.

The "-og" ending of the name *Daveog* (which as O'Donovan noted in 1835 is always a feminine ending), means that the "saint" was female, or perhaps a water-monster goddess, access to whose womb could be gained on Station Isle.

RIGHT *The "Female Fiend" as enthroned goddess, about to give universal birth. Sheela-na-gig carving, Caherelly Castle, Lough Gur.*

Both the ordeal of those incarcerated in the Station Island Purgatory, and the modern Night Vigil in the basilica, evoke the Great Night prior to Creation. M. Eliade produces massive evidence to show that primordial Chaos is involved in every ritual regression, prior to rebirth. Such chaos is the "Cosmic Night" of the universal mother, the "in the beginning" state, where germination and hope of renewal attaches itself to the uterine wall, eventually to emerge, born into appreciation of existence as a sacred gift of the gods. Therefore, this second visit to the womb destroys the "taken for granted" quality of infant and childhood profanity, and replaces it with adult responsibilities toward sacred truths, previously ignored. Thus the second birth introduces the adult to the solemnity of culture, whereby he or she assumes the need to nurture the cosmos. From now on, Nature is known to be a supernatural force.

By repeating these adventures in ritual, the pilgrim achieved a similar moment of cosmogonic or macrocosmic identification. That is why, to this day, Lough Derg pilgrims are required to *stay awake* throughout the black night of their spiritual rebirth, which has to be known in body and mind, as distinct from the automatic processes that befalls a baby prior to parturition.

A good place to watch this happening was "the Chair of Daveog," a natural rock seat on the mainland overlooking Station Isle. O'Donovan described the chair as lying "in the townland of Suidhe Dhabheog (Seeavog), where, in the living rock, some impressions of elbows are shown, according to oral tradition, which maintained that Daveog was a woman who died during the *turas*, or pilgrimage walk, and was revived by St. Patrick. Then, having reached the rock called her chair, within sight of Station Island, she died again, and was interred on Saints Island."

In this pattern of birth and resurrection, devotee and deity are happily confused – a right and proper merger, since anyone who chooses to sit on Daveog's Chair with serious intent is shaped by, and so *becomes*, the supportive deity on whose knee he or she rests.

In 1652, Colgan reported that Dabheoc's feast was celebrated on July 24th, as well as on January 1st,

suggesting a pattern of harvest-birth veneration to match the midwinter swallowing. To this day, the "Spa Well" on the lake shore, lying between the Chair and Station Isle, flows all the year round.

On leaving the Lough, as Philip Skelton observed in 1786, each pilgrim was given by the priest as many holy pebbles out of the lake as he or she cared to take away. Such stone coins were legal tender in the currency of the two traditions. These stones might evoke the Easter Saturday communion host and the vertebrae of the indestructible monster of the lough. So the pebble in the hand represented two sacred narratives, both rising from beneath the surface of the mundane, in order to tell the hidden truth.

ABOVE *St. Brigid's (alias Dabeog's) Chair, Lough Derg. Nineteenth-century print. Pilgrims flocked to sit on the stone "lap" of the most effective female saint in Ireland, situated 300 yards from Ferry House.*

ULSTER 3

the Cailleach and Bith

The chief female of the Ulster underworld is the Cailleach, the aged goddess and primal mother of the province. Her body and living presence was, until recently, seen in one of the major third-millennium B.C.E. passage graves of Ireland, the south cairn on Slieve Gullion, Co. Armagh.

In 1789, Charlotte Brooke heard that the tomb was locally called Cailleach Birrn's House, or The Old Lady's House, in which it was said Finn McCumhal (McCool) was buried. Thus the solar hero lies timelessly in the womb of the northern province in a stone chamber shaped to evoke the maternal image. The roofing slabs rise in height from entrance passage to main chamber. The surrounding cairn is 95 feet (29 meters) in diameter and 16 feet (5 meters) high.

A well-beaten track joined this Cailleach monument to a circular pool close by, where there was another cairn. In Ulster, there is an interplay between womb-lake and architectural effigies of the mother.

As late as 1938, it was believed that Cally Berry (as she was then called) had thrown a white stone from Slieve Gullion to the Dorsey Ramparts, several miles away, where it is still to be seen, and was whitewashed every year by local people.

From the Creggan parish, T. G. F. Patterson recorded the following convictions:

Do you know her house on the mountain and the lake beside it? Well, if he [Finn] was fleet of foot and strong limbed, well sure she was stronger still in spells, as if she did not entice poor Finn into it. And he went in fresh and youthful, and came out a done old man, and they had a high time making him right again. Often I started up the mountain to see the lake, but I could never tread the whole road, I was so afraid; for you know, a wedding party went into Cally Berry House once and they were turned into stone. Her house goes down and down, and in the very bottom chamber sits the Cally herself, to this very day, and will, maybe till the end of time.

In Irish tradition, the Cailleach is infinitely old, and has many lovers. Her veil (*caille*) barely hides the fact that she is the great goddess of pre-Celtic and Celtic times. As recently as 1927 the folklorist Eleanor Hull wrote that "In Ireland, the goddesses are held to be both more numerous and more powerful than the gods . . . and still regarded as the builders of mountains, the impersonators of winter, and the harbingers of spring."

OPPOSITE *Oats harvest, Toome, Co. Antrim, before 1914. The very last tuft of the crop to be cut was known as the Churn or Hag. It personified the Harvest goddess on the verge of winter. The family hurled their sickles at "her," in a ritual of severance.*

LEFT *Stone A, Knockmany chambered tomb, Co. Tyrone, c. 2400 B.C.E. The goddess Áine-as-hag, flaps her wings, mouths a worm, and regards the four quarters. She also conceals the big summer sun in her lower winter hide.*

ABOVE *Oats harvest at*
Toome, Co. Antrim,
before 1914. The grand-
mother embodies the
hag-goddess phase of
human life. After her
meal of bread, butter,
and milk, she will con-
tinue to arrange the
sheaves into stooks. She
is the Cailleach, the
eternal "Old One."

Ulster, as the Northern nadir of light, was the natural home of the Cailleach, although of course she was acknowledged in each of the provinces including Munster, where her chief stronghold was on the Bheare peninsula.

In Ulster, the *cailleach*, or *caillighe*, was the eternal mother. Figured in prehistoric monuments and white-washed stones, she also appeared as the hag at the end of harvest, when she was severed from the earth out of which she had sprung in a sickle-throwing rite.

An old man from Ballymoyer recalled in 1944: "I saw the Cailleach cut by the scythe only. It was afterwards taken into the house and put around the woman of the house. It was always put about the neck of the woman of the house. That was the right thing to do."

Neolithic-chamber-standing-stone-oat-sheaf-housewife: the mythic chain joining the first harvest wife to the most recent was completed every year. The cailleach sitting on the woman's neck was an awesome sight for all. Then the goddess was hung above the table during the harvest feast.

THE TOMB OF BITH

From the archaic strata of Irish myth concerning the original settlement of Ireland, as recorded in *Lebor Gabála*, the first man and woman to land were Adra — "The Ancient" (alias Ladra) — and his sister Cesair, with their father, Bith, together with a number of subordinate women.

Bith traveled north through Ireland from the Munster landing place and then died at Slieve Beagh, on the Ulster mountain named after him. There, the

"seventeen magnificent maidens" who accompanied him on the journey to the northern province buried him under the mountain-top cairn they constructed, the Carn Móre or Great Cairn.

The Irish word *bith* means "cosmos, world, eternity, everlasting, being and existence." Thus his name, his body, and his cairn carry the load of the entire universe. He brings a truly cosmogonic myth to the southern fringe of Ulster.

An alternative name for Ulster is Uladh. *Uladh*, as a language word, reveals "a monument, a hoard of hidden treasure, a stone tomb, a charnel house, and a pile of bones." In these senses, Uladh (Ulster) is synonymous with Bith's tomb. Uladh is where the personified Cosmos drops into the dream of northern night, prior to its recreation by the next wave of conscious envisagers, the next generation, as they voyage into awareness by cutting themselves free from the coils of oblivion. Like Cesair, Adra, and Bith, they too are survivors of The Flood – that amniotic ocean that fills the entire horizon of every unborn child.

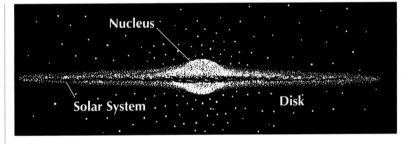

In 1894, Canon O'Connor reported that the cairn was being undermined by quarrying, a fate that seemed to symbolize the collapse of an entire cosmology. For Bith was Cosmos, and regarder of Cosmos, the universal idea, beholding, and so creating, the Universe. Thus Carn Móre embodied the merging of subject and object, of interior and exterior worlds, of thing with action. It stood for integration of body with spirit. From its lost summit the mind–body split of Christian Lough Derg would seem unnecessary. Yet however overgrown the track over Bith's grave has become, he nevertheless stands for the underlying unity of Christian, pagan, and scientific myth.

MUNSTER

inherited words

People first landed in Ireland nine thousand years ago and watched the sun climb to the top of its daily arc over what is now Munster, Ireland's southern province. This repeated event helped to establish the sun goddess Áine and her sister Grian as Munster's chief pre-Christian deities, while they were worshiped in some form throughout the country. Áine was also known as An, Ana, Anu, Dana, and Danu. Cormac in his *Glossary* called her *mater deorum hibernensium* – "the mother of the Irish gods," adding "it was well she nursed *deos*, i.e. the gods." It was in Munster, the southern quarter, that her power stood highest, both in the sky and in terms of human response.

Since myth is primarily a verbal affair, Áine's proper name was also an Irish-language word, *aine*. Áine the goddess lives on as *aine* the word, meaning: "Delight, joy, pleasure, agility, expedition, swiftness, play, sport, amusement, music, harmony, melody, experience, truth, veracity, brightness, glow, radiance, splendor, glory, brilliance, wit, and drinking up."

The name of a deity is a godhead's first expression and last resort, and often tells what the deity does and *is*. In the Irish language, *aine* and related words are, like sunbeams, now largely separated from their divine solar source. Yet they still shower down through a space rapidly turning neutral, to animate Munster life.

The switch from Irish to the English language that has occurred in most parts of Munster during the last two hundred years has all but killed off the use of *aine* words, and for the same reason there has been a change in the perception of "south." Whereas in English, "south" is a largely transparent word, used to, establish an abstract geometry, its equivalent in Irish *dess*, or *deas* – reinforces and overlaps with Áine's southern persona. *Dess* meanings include "south," "right hand," and "being to the right of a person facing east."

As W. Stokes noted, the Irish, "like the rest of the Indo-Europeans determined their orientation by looking at the rising sun." Therefore south was *lam des*, the "right hand," which was considered more propitious than *lam clc*, the "left hand," cognate with Welsh *cledd*, "north." With *dess* firmly attached to the ascending side of a sunrise greeting, its "south" was never a neutral zone, but a subjective condition, from which many positive qualities flowed, as further meanings of the word *dess* reveal: "right, just, meet, agreeable, well-arranged, fine, neat, precise, correct, pretty, elegant, decent, and dexterous." This is the legacy of the Munster quarter.

OPPOSITE *Sunrise, Munster. In Munster, the dawn goddess is Áine Cli, "Áine of the Light." She is equally at home in the sky, on earth, and under ground.*

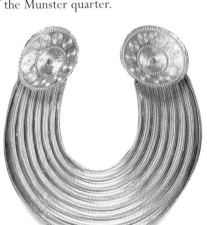

LEFT *Gold collar, engraved with "solar disks." Glensheen, Co. Clare, 650 B.C.E.*

RIGHT *Munster
comprises Counties
Cork, Kerry, Limerick,
and southern Tipperary
in southwest Ireland.
In Limerick, a hill near
Lough Gur called Cnoc
Áine is said to be the
sun goddess Áine's
main home; it is also
known as Deise Beag
or "Little South" where
Munster is said to be
replicated in miniature.*

A specific solar connection is found in *dessel* – "direction of sun, sunwise," and therefore "lucky, favorable, and propitious." This leads via *deisceart*, "southern quarter," toward Áine's regional characteristics in *desse* – "seemliness, comeliness, beauty, pleasant aspect" – echoed in the golden *deasac*, "ears of corn."

"Ah yes, Áine Cli, that's Áine of the light, the Beautiful," explained Tom Harnon to an officer of the Irish Folklore Commission in 1972, for in the neighborhood of her principal Munster *síd*, Cnoc Áine, she is still recalled with affectionate respect. The territory around this 528-foot (161-meter) high, sickle-shaped hill in Co. Limerick, was known as Deise Beag, "Little South," and stood for Munster in miniature, where the vast and varied province overseen by An was represented on a more intimate scale and inhabited by Áine. In this way, *dess* and sun goddess came together at their provincial headquarters – a coalition emphasized by an alternative name for this part of Co. Limerick, in use till 1690, "The Seignory of Any."

CNOC ÁINE

Áine's sanctuary hill, Cnoc Áine, and the nearby sacred lake of Lough Gur have a central place in Munster's mythology. Ceremonies held annually at Cnoc Áine on St. John's Eve (June 23rd) marked the summer solstice and were vividly remembered in 1879. "Every St John's Night, men used to gather on the hill from all quarters. They were formed in ranks by an old man called Quinlan, whose family still lived on the hill in 1876," wrote D. Fitzgerald.

Reports spoke of bunches of hay and straw, tied upon poles. These "cliars" were lit and then carried in procession around the hill, and around the little moat on the summit. Afterward people ran through the cultivated fields, and among the cattle, waving the cliars, which brought luck to crops and beasts for the following year. The torches showed that Áine had visibly climbed to the top of her annual axis and highest solar achievement of the year, which was also the start of her annual decline. The June 23rd gathering therefore combined triumph with sadness, and some accounts, such as that from Manannán mac Lir, even speak of the ritual as her "funeral," at which "the good people" or fairies emerged "from every lios [enclosure] and rath [hilltop earthwork] throughout Ireland," and they all trooped to Cnoc Áine bearing lighted torches in her honor. These Otherworld multitudes may have been matched in former days by human pilgrims, drawn islandwide, and enjoying the opportunity to mingle with the supernatural legions.

When, one year, out of respect for the death of a local man on June 23rd, the torches in the human procession remained unlit, those in the supernatural phalanx were seen to burn with exceptional brightness. "Áine herself was observed in the front, directing and ordering everything."

Áine was sometimes seen on Cnoc Áine as a *cailleach*, or old woman, comparable to the Ulster hag of Knockmany. Those who accepted her modest

✛ ÁINE AND THE FAIRIES ✛

In the nineteenth century, many families living around the hill, including the O'Brien's, Dillanes, Creeds, Laffins, O'Deas, and Fitzgeralds, claimed direct descent from the goddess Áine. They spoke of her in near-human terms as "the best-hearted woman that ever lived," yet on occasions she reminded them of the difference in kind between her supernatural pantheon and common humanity.

For example, on one St. John's Night a number of girls had stayed late on the hill, watching the cliars, and joining in the games, when suddenly Áine appeared among them. She thanked them for the honor they had done her, but said she now wished them to go home, since her Otherworld friends wanted the hill to themselves. Some of the mortals then looked through her ring, whereupon the hill appeared crowded with fairies previously invisible to them.

BELOW LEFT *The sculptured stone at Áth An Charbaid, Co. Kerry, is perhaps a full-length portrait of the Sun-Moon deity.*

BELOW CENTER *Síd Áine, Áine's cairn on the summit is now destroyed. The other barrows are associated with her father (Eogabal), her brother (Fer Í), and Uainide, "The Green."*

BELOW RIGHT *Map of Cnoc Áine (Áine's Hill), Co. Limerick.*

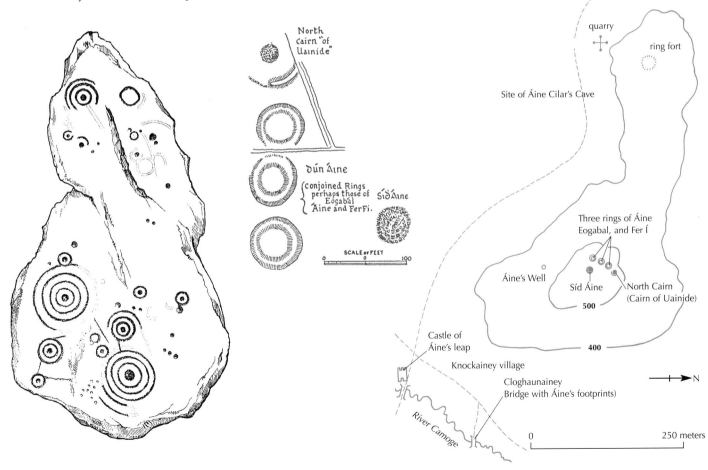

North Cairn "of Uainide"

Dún Áine
(conjoined Rings perhaps those of Eogabal Áine and FerFi.

Síd Áine

SCALE of FEET
0   100

quarry

ring fort

Site of Áine Cilar's Cave

Three rings of Áine Eogabal, and Fer Í

Áine's Well

Síd Áine

North Cairn (Cairn of Uainide)

500

400

Castle of Áine's leap

Knockainey village

Cloghaunainey Bridge with Áine's footprints)

River Camoge

N

0   250 meters

PREVIOUS PAGES *Cnoc Áine, Co. Limerick. A twelfth-century text says that this hill was given to the goddess Áine "till the end of the world" and was "the abode of kings and queens." It was "the best hill ... both ordinary and extraordinary that stood on Irelands wondrous land." The picture is overlaid with an Irish gold dress fastener, c. 700 B.C.E., engraved with solar circles. From Áine's sunny breasts the land-milk flowed. Ireland's landscapes are divinely imagined.*

RIGHT *By tradition, Irish women used to colour their hair to honor Áine's sun-gold locks.*

demands enjoyed good fortune. If they slighted her or exploited her, difficulties soon overwhelmed them. The need to observe the divine balance by means of an exchange of gifts is the theme of these anecdotes.

Mr. Harnon of Bruff recalled his grandfather saying of the Dunworths who lived on the hill during the famine of the 1840s:

> One night a knock came on the door of their houseen, and a little old woman was there. And they asked her in, to come to warm herself. She could not delay long, she said, as she sat by the fire . . .
>
> Then she left, and thanked 'em, and she said they would not regret it. She wasn't gone too long when they heard, as they thought, another knock on the door. So they went out. "My goodness," they says, "What now?" She couldn't carry on, the old woman said, so she came back and she stayed, and into the kitchen walked a nice sheep. The family were in an awful state over the sheep, for in that time people used to be hanged for stealin' a sheep, if it could be proved, or even if the skin of a sheep was found in a peasant's cottage you were hanged immediately and

especially on the O'Grady estate! In the mornin' old Dunworth went . . . to Kilballyowen House, to the oul' O'Grady, and told him about the sheep. Oul' O'Grady sent his herdsman out, and all the sheep were intact in their pastures and paddicks. "No," he says, "the sheep don't belong to us."

Dunworth then went to Oul' O'Grady again and asked him what would he do with the sheep. "What'll you do with him?" he says, "He's yours. Keep it!" And he did keep the sheep. Right, the sheep grew up, and she had two lambs. Those two lambs grew up, and had two lambs, and they had two more lambs.

And then the next was, they got the idea that the sheep was getting old, and that they'd take her to the fair of Hospital to sell her. The night before the fair, a knock came to their door, and the little woman came, and . . . she asked, "Are you goin' to the fair with your sheep tomorrow?" "I am." "Let me give you advice, and keep that sheep, and don't go to the fair!"

Well, they went to the fair the next day and they sold the sheep, and from that day on their luck changed. In fact, within a week all the sheep were

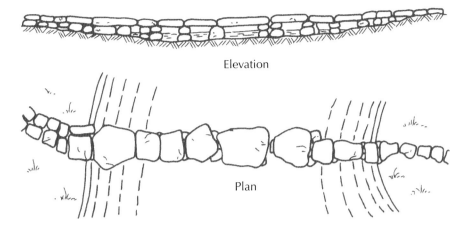

Elevation

Plan

LEFT *Cloghaunainey,
Áine's Bridge, near Cnoc
Áine. Demolished in
1930, it was believed to
have been built by Áine,
and to carry the impress
of her feet on its slabs.*

dead. That was the Dunworths'. They came down in the world again, and they became just as badly off or even worse than they ever were. The remains of the houseen might still be there, for all I know now. On up above David O'Grady's . . . up beyond the quarry there, at the sunset end of the hill.

Just east of the village and hill of Knockainey runs the little Camoge River, over which Áine was said to have built a primitive stone bridge, Cloghaunainey. It survived until 1930, when it was demolished, along with the locally revered impressions of her footprints, said to be visible on its broad flagstones.

According to a local belief, it was on the bank of the Camoge River that Áine conceived the mysterious Geároid Iarla, the male phantom who haunts nearby Lough Gur. The story tells of the violent meeting of the first Norman lord in the area (the Earl of Desmond) with the regional deity. In Irish myth, overlordship or kingship depended upon the male claimant making love to the territorial goddess. By that means he therefore won his legitimacy, as described in Fitzgerald's transcription of a folktale current in the district:

The first Earl of Desmond led very much the life of a libertine, and walking one morning along the river's edge, he saw a beautiful woman seated by the water, combing out her long hair after bathing.

Her cloak lay behind her on the grass. The Earl, whose name was Muiris (meaning Great), advanced noiselessly on her from behind, knowing that if he had but possession of the cloak, he would have her in his power; and he seized it before she was aware of his approach.

The beautiful woman was Áine-n'-Chliar her-

self, and she told the Earl that he could never have had his will with her, had he not seized her cloak. She told him further that she would bear him a son, Geároid, whom he was to bring up with all possible care, like any other gentleman. One caution however she gave her love: he was not to show surprise at anything, however strange, his son should do . . .

The boy grew up from year to year to manhood, and excelled in the accomplishments of his age and rank. But one memorable evening it happened that there was a gathering of great ladies and gentlemen at the castle of the Earl of Desmond, which still stands in Knockainey village. There was dancing, and of all the ladies none could vie with a certain one among the guests. The grace and the endurance of this young woman were however beaten, everyone said, by those of the young Earl Gerald himself. When the dance was ended, this lady engaged him in another contest, for while all were seated at the supper-table she suddenly arose, and at one leap cleared guests, table, dishes and all, and then leaped back again. The old Earl of Desmond turned to his son and said "Can you do anything like that?" "No," said Geároid. "Well, stand up and try. Don't let yourself be beaten by a woman." Thus commanded, Iarla rose to his feet, and making a spring from where he stood, leaped right into a bottle, and then leaped out again. There was great admiration at this feat; and with the rest the Earl of Desmond looked in the greatest astonishment at his son, saying he never thought he had such power. "Were you not warned," said the young Earl, "never to show wonder at anything I might do?"

By his public show of amazement, the old Earl unintentionally cast his son out of the normal world, for once people had identified Iarla's feats as Otherworldly, he became classified as a demigod and could no longer sit wholly comfortably in the mundane, but was now bound to follow her into the supernatural. "Now you have forced me to leave you," were his last words to his father.

Iarla's jump takes us into the supernatural realm.

THE TUATHA DÉ DANANN

A collective term for many of the nature gods, coined in the Middle Ages, was the *Tuatha Dé Danann*, the people of the goddess An, Áine, or Danu. They were the Neolithic and Bronze Age pantheons of gods which Áine was credited with founding. As we have seen, belief in her has not yet died out, while in the manuscripts of Christian clerics, her "people," the pagan gods, "are fully recognized as such till the late tenth or mid-eleventh century," and called "unfading . . . whose duration is perennial."

It was recorded that the boy sun god, Cúchulainn of Ulster, had let a drunken raid of the Ultonians to Cnoc Áine. They reached the hill in winter and set up pillars to shelter their horses from the snow.

In a peace treaty recorded in the twelfth century, each province is allowed, through their gods, a share of Cnoc Áine — an arrangement confirmed by the monuments on its summit.

Throughout Ireland, Áine was known as the wife of Manannán the sea god, from whose bed she climbed every morning. She was also said to be the wife of Echdae the sky horse. By leaping regularly from one spouse to the other she joined sea and sky together and landed at Cnoc Áine within the summit monument, Síd Áine. This much-disturbed mound is placed on the eastern end of the hill, and is balanced by the traditional site of her "cave" (destroyed c. 1900 by quarrymen), which lay at the western or sunset foot of the same sacred hill.

The Irish word for fairy is *sióg*, or *ben síd*, literally "woman of the síd." Fairies were the army of the hidden goddess, or versions of the gods in her pantheon, seen much reduced in size and power, yet persistently

working for the neglected values of a goddess submerged by Iron Age warrior patriarchy, Christianity, and modern materialism. They symbolized an endangered vital relationship – the cohesion of Culture-in-Nature, and the sense of a sacred whole.

In rural Ireland, fairies, or "the Good People," were taken seriously, at least until the arrival of television. Appearing at dusk, they displayed something of their former divine powers, and resisted the process of genteel emasculation which was their fate in nineteenth-century England.

The deities and fairies of the Tuatha Dé Danann found allies in the poets, or *fili*, who were collectively known as *aes dana*, "men of arts, servants of the goddess Dana" (Ana-Áine). They moved freely through tribal areas and across politico-social boundaries, and were especially well represented in Munster, the province of poetry.

Poets were specialists in liminality; they operated at the thresholds, between categories of space, time, or identity, in dangerous, "frontier" conditions, among uncomfortable truths. These they shaped into harmonious knowledge on behalf of the community.

The poets were expert in native learning – legal tradition, history, genealogy, and the science of natural phenomena – all were viewed as aspects of the divine myth, and realized in verse form. Because myth is repeatable, the poets claimed to possess the ability to predict the future pattern of events, and were the bridge between the mundane and the supernatural spheres.

But as the folklore of the Cnoc Áine district makes clear, access to the divine was not restricted to poets. Rather, almost the entire human population of Munster could claim direct descent from pre-Iron Age stock, and so held to an unbroken thread of identification with Áine, reaching back to the Neolithic. In this sense they were collectively "the folk of the goddess Dana or Áine."

MYTH AND THE FOLK VOICE

Irish folklore resounds on a mythic frequency. Traces of the primary sacred narratives permeate its apparently inconsequential scraps. This is because these folk tales represent a collective wisdom and speak with an open voice, unconstricted by the claims of excessive individualism, and so are relatively immune to disruption by personal mortality. Instead, by word of mouth, folklore opens a free passage between the generations, a route confirmed at intervals by parallel written records.

In Ireland, the literate and oral traditions have remained unusually close together, for, as MacCana explains, "while the native men of learning, the *fili*, did not eschew the use of writing, particularly in the post-Norman period, the fact is that they inherited something of the druidic preference for the oral mode, both in their teaching and in their composition.

"Consequently, the Irish oral tradition embraced the literature of greatest social prestige as well as the common lore of the mass of the people.

"Thus Irish literary tradition is ideally the manifold *oral* tradition which in a sense had no beginning – and has hardly yet ended in the Gaelic-speaking areas of Ireland and Scotland."

✠ IRISH FOLKLORE ✠

Irish folklore is pluralistic (it works by inclusion), and polytheistic (gods are often disparaged in the stories, but rarely turned away). Its world is made from the merging, conservation, and recycling of all available sacred insights. "Move up!" the storyteller cries to his assembled divine characters, "I hear another god at the door. It may have come to destroy us all, but I will talk it into some kind of accommodation." This is both a habitual gesture toward mythic comprehensiveness, and, on a political level, the art of compromise of a much-invaded people, living in an ancient land. Thanks to such tactics, the spirit of the old gods managed to survive, and continued to join people and place together.

Irish folklore tends to be open-ended partly because it has no holy book. Consequently its earliest deities have interbred with later gods, historical characters, and monotheistic saints, in the interests of overall synthesis and continuity.

BELOW In Ireland, gods speak to the people, and the people speak of the gods. An oral tradition, passed from remote antiquity, is sustained by a continuing love of story-telling and conversation.

Conversations with people in mid-Limerick in 1989 and 1990 suggest that traditional attitudes to Áine are fast declining, but have yet to disappear.

In the summer of 1990 Pat MacNamara of Lough Gur, near Cnoc Áine, favored me with a monologue on neighborhood traditions, delivered in a rapid, matter-of-fact tone, as though it was his duty to repeat *everything necessary*, like a St. Patrick's Purgatory pilgrim doing the stations. His repertoire has eluded death by Bronze and Iron Ages, incineration in one and a half millennia of Christian Hell, incessant tribal warfare, Norman invasion, English settlement, Protestantism, rationalism, famine, emigration, mechanization, television, and at least one change of language.

Around Cnoc Áine, anecdotes passed thus between the generations have stretched the communal horizon toward the primeval. What was heard prepared the mind of the local listener for the re-emergence of the archaic as a contemporary event. In other words, the doings of the gods were known initially through listening to older people in house or inn, and then *experienced* as walking apparitions, if and when conditions were favorable.

Because they were so valued, accounts of supernatural events were often withheld from strangers, as T. J. Westropp discovered in 1917:

> *Knockainey's ancient observances were in full force within the last forty years, [but] a suspicious feeling in the present inhabitants prevented my learning whether the rites are not, still, performed, but certainly the ancient goddess and her brother Fer Í [Fí] are still remembered.*

Fortunately other collectors have been more successful than Westropp, including David Fitzgerald in the mid-nineteenth century, and Canon Lynch c. 1900. In the 1930s, the newly established Irish Folklore Commission gathered more material through a local schools survey, and in 1971 Daithi o'Hógain of the Commission, a native of the town of Bruff, conducted many tape-recorded interviews with older members of the community.

The typical Folklore Commission interview is an exchange of mutual trust and a shared passion for a Past erupting as Present.

In collecting these stories, the rhythms of the speech are usually transferred directly from tape recorder to manuscript, in the same way as a musical score contains a symphony.

However some contributors, like Tommy Hannon, fell silent when the tape was switched on. *He* had not received the relay of ancestral confidences through a machine, and would certainly not agree to pass them on by that means!

In Ireland, the Divine is nourished by conversation. At its best, Irish talk retains a sacramental quality and so needs no other justification. Like any creative act, or rather like *The* Creation of the gods,

"the crack" is understood to be a primary event. In its stream, idea, emotion, and thing combine in whirlpools (whose equivalent in traditional Irish music are jigs and reels), alternating with placid stretches and furious falls. At times, submerged cargoes, long supposed lost, rear up, waterlogged yet intact, to bump and nuzzle in the ceaseless flow. Such supernatural talk is no mere description or illustration of a parallel reality. It *is* the Other, returned to life – a life made between speaker and listener (who exchange roles, turn by turn), and where eye and gesture contribute like the glitter of sunlight on a wind-stirred lough, to the business of serious delight.

ABOVE *Lough Gur, Co. Limerick, looking south from Knockfennel over Garret Island. The tip of the bigger Knockadoon island is visible.*

PART TWO

MUNSTER 2
Lough Gur

Two and a half miles northwest of Cnoc Áine a group of rocky limestone hills spring from the plain. Among them lies a sacred lake – Lough Gur. Before its eastern side was drained in the nineteenth century C.E., its broad reaches formed an approximate square around a large triangular island, named Knockadoon. Throughout the prehistoric era, Lough Gur appeared as an unbroken ring of water, over five miles in circumference, to which An the traveler was drawn, in the person of the goddess Áine.

"As all Munster knows," wrote Fitzgerald in 1879, "Lough Gur is enchanted . . . in the past, no minstrel, piper, or poet would willingly spend a night within a mile of its shore, such was its fearful reputation and potency. Even to fall asleep in daytime on its banks was considered among them to be reckless folly." The sense of danger arose from the belief that the original poets of Lough Gur were either descended from, or *were* demigods, like Geároid Iarla, able to draw human poets out of their depths.

Oral tradition places Lough Gur under the aegis of the goddess Áine who made it. "The old people used to say that the sky was widest over Lough Gur," reported Tommy Hannon in 1972. As sun goddess, Áine looked at its gray waters, caused them to sparkle, and so made her entry into another element.

Flickering traces of Áine Cliar, The Bright, may explain why the night air around the lough is sometimes seen to be filled with unearthly fire.

Around the lough, Áine can appear as an old woman, a young princess, a mother, and a mermaid. Nineteenth-century reports claim that "Áine is frequently to be seen, half her body above the waters, on the bosom of Loch Guirr, combing her hair." Áine, Danu, or Anu, the principal pre-Celtic, Celtic, and modern deity of Munster, is the constant traveler who yet sits still, the feminine in the man, and the embodiment of world as a woman. An account of how the lough was formed from Áine's urine was given by Ned Hynes in 1971:

> *Do you know how the Lake came there? St. Patrick came around Ireland, didn't he? He came to Patrick's Well. But he passed Lough Gur. But there's a well in the Avenue. And he came along, and there was a poor oul' woman makin' her water, in pardon to you. And he said: "God increase you!" And she kept on makin' it away until she made the Lake. And the Lake was comin' all around her.*

Another Lough Gur story relates how Geároid encounters a young woman on the shore of the lough. He points to a ring on a stone, and when she picks it up, the waters of the lake rise up red, like blood. When she screams and puts the ring down again, the lake subsides. This emphasizes the immediate effect on the environment of Áine's slightest action. The lough is her divine blood, the world is her extended body.

The belief that the lake sprang from a young woman's failure to replace the lid of a well that overflowed is also still held in the area and is another means whereby the bodily fluid of the land, as a living entity, is connected to the actions of a representative female, who is both human and divine.

LEFT *The enchanted Lough Gur, Áine's water-home. In and around its shores, she may appear to people in many guises.*

EEL, TREE, AND HORSEMAN

Every human state has corresponding apparitions, which are its supernatural equivalent. This also applies to the human corpses, rotting in the lakeside graveyard at Grange on the western shore of Lough Gur. Fitzgerald was told by Mr. M. Whelan in 1877, who had the story from an earlier generation, that the graves of this ancient burial ground used to be found every morning:

> . . . all bored with holes, and as it was thought that this was the work of dogs, a neighboring gentleman directed two of his men to go to the place provided with guns, and watch during the night. To their amazement they saw a great eel rise from the lake, and coming ashore, roll on and on over the ground, till she had worked herself into a church-yard. Then she began to bury her snout in the soil over a grave, and was fast making her way into it to feed on the people, when the men fired and hit her. When they came up they found her lying motionless, seemingly dead. In this state they carried her to their master's place and threw her down in a corner of the kitchen where she lay all next day. The following night, the mournful cries of another eel were heard about the lake.

"T'adhg a bhí im lorgsa!" said the eel in the corner, raising herself up. "Tadhg that was looking for me."

"Go to Tadhg, in the name of the Devil," cried one of the astonished onlookers, and the creature glided through the door, rolled herself towards the lake, and there disappeared.

Tadhg is an Irish word meaning poet. At every stage in her lifecycle, Áine required him to sing her praises and to offer physical companionship. At Lough Gur Tadhg was given a poet's dirty work to do — sucking words through collapsing coffin walls in lakeside graveyards, where the flesh of ancestors is arranged in death sentences that must be joined to the mute hopes of the yet unborn. Supernatural skill is needed for the task; that is why the best poets were often demigods, like Tadhg and Oisín, son of Finn.

In the nineteenth century, Lough Gur was believed to disappear by magic once every seven years. At these times, as an old woman from Askeaton asserted in 1879, a supernatural tree was revealed, growing from the bottom of the lough. This tree might be regarded as another appearance of Áine's treetrunk father, Eogabal, united with his green foliage brother, Uainide. Both "men" had traveled from Uisnech, Ireland's central sacred hill, to confirm Cnoc Áine and

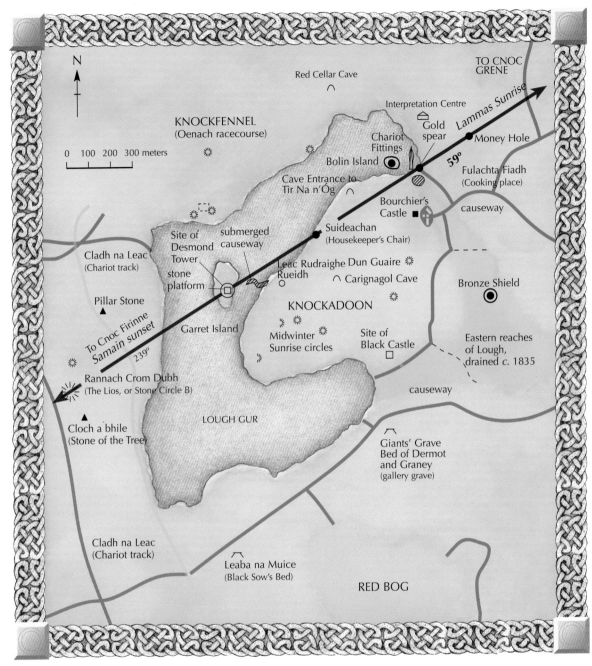

Lough Gur as Munster's provincial equivalent of a national *axis mundi*. In Lough Gur, a version of their Tree of Trees was rooted into the lake bed, and so drew several layers of reality together. Eogabal + Uainide = *axis mundi* = World Tree, the mythic synthesizing vegetable, which brings the worlds of the gods and humanity together. It stands, like the Christian Cross, at the center of many European cosmologies.

The Lough Gur tree stands for a divinely renew-

able prosperity. It is envisaged in poetic form because poetry is the language of the gods. Especially when sung, poetry takes us beyond categorization and allows us back into the primordial forest where the tree of life is synonymous with the tree of knowledge.

The exchange between the under-lough tree and the surface world is reiterated by the standing stone named *Cloch a bhile* (Stone of the Tree). This megalith, described by Ó'Ríordáin as "a large upright stone,

ABOVE *Cloch A Bile,*
"The Stone of the Tree,"
6½ feet (2 meters) tall,
perhaps the stone stump
of the magic tree
revealed at seven-year
intervals from below
the lough, which could
engreen the whole earth.

measuring seven feet by four feet at ground level and six feet high," is sited close to the west shore of the lough, and southeast of the great henge monument, erected c. 2500 B.C.E., at Grange. The stone, now dappled with green moss and gold lichen, may have served as a solid reminder to those in the real world that the phantom tree beneath the lough, the ideal tree, was also substantial, and would be seen again. Equally, the Cloch a bhile was itself an outpost of the sacred, where treetrunk and Áine's female trunk merged into one effigy, cosmological axis, and living force in the land.

THE GIANTS' GRAVE

Around Lough Gur, Otherworld voices are heard crying out in alarm, when their hopes of eternity are plundered. For example, Tom Harnon recalls the 1938 archeological excavation of the Giants' Grave, a Neolithic tomb, standing close to the south shore:

Giants' Grave: they excavated that. They took the bones, put 'em in a bag and brought them here to the castle. I worked with them. But I believe, — I've been told it by several people, that if every bean sí in Ireland were ever clanned together that night, that the greatest keening and crying was heard all around the lake, and through the hills, and even farther on, away even into the bog, the Red Bog, and across even to Knockdere.

The *bansíde,* as the name implies, are the queens of the *síde* or underworlds and led by the goddess Áine. She was greatly upset by the desecration of the Giants' Grave monument, which until then was the house of living spirits, including her own, so the banshees of Ireland united to mourn the death of a five-thousand-year-old tradition.

The locally used Gaelic name of Giants' Grave was *Leabthacha Dhiarmada is Ghráinne* — "the bed of Dermot and Graney," where the youthful Dermot had lain with the sun goddess Gráinne (Áine's alter

There are grounds for regarding the Giants' Grave in its entirety as an effigy of the goddess Áine/Grian, with the west chamber (one stone now fallen) as her head, and the outer walls of smaller megaliths her hair. When Dermot entered her main chamber he was entering her body. Though outwardly a mere mortal from Finn's war band, once inside, he grew in her proximity to reach a matching gigantic length and set an example that young men in every locality were happy to follow.

ego), below the level of the horizon, in a night of lovemaking, as described in the Finn Cycle of poems. (By the twelfth century the scribe had reduced the goddess to a woman, and Dermot to a hero in Finn's war band.)

O'Rahilly writes of "Grian, the sun goddess and her double Áine," and around Lough Gur both modes of the goddess are represented by hill sanctuaries, with Grian's, or Gráinne's, being at Cnoc Grene, a hill near Pallas Green, 7 miles (11 kilometers) northeast from Lough Gur. Knockgrean, as it is sometimes called, was named after "The Lady Grian of the bright cheeks." (The Irish word for "sun" is *grian*.)

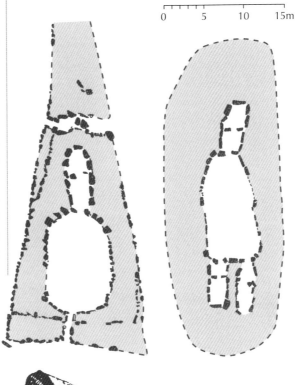

LEFT *Neolithic tombs of Creevykeel and Deerpark, Co. Sligo, designed with heads, eyes, bodies, and even legs. Underworld deities often took architectural form.*

BELOW *Giants' Grave, or Bed of Dermot and Graney, c. 2600 B.C.E. This ruined gallery grave, excavated in 1938, yielded remains of at least eight people, and many bones of ox and hare. The "giants" were the god and goddess, whose combined bodies the tomb describes in effigy — probably Donn, the underworld god, and Gráinne, the sun goddess. They became Dermot and Graney in medieval romance.*

✠ NEOLITHIC TOMBS ✠

Throughout Ireland, Neolithic tombs continued to be used by human lovers, identifying with the divine coition as Wood-Martin reported in 1902:

Even in the present day "Dermot and Grainia's beds" are associated with runaway couples and with aphrodisiac customs. Cotton went in search of the Ballycasheen bed, in Co. Clare. He asked some country girls the way to it, and was heartily laughed at.

At length, the oldest girl of the group agreed to go, if certain he was a stranger, and if he told her his name. But the girl's conversation was in Irish (which he spoke not) and dragged on, and as the evening was growing late, he became impatient and very ungallantly rode away. A mile further, he made the same enquiry from a herdsman's wife. She said . . . it was the custom that if she went with a stranger to Darby and Grane's bed she was certainly to grant him everything he asked!

Borlase also found no fewer than twenty-two Megalithic tombs in Co. Clare alone, named after the divine prototypes.

Upon entering Gráinne's bed at the Lough Gur monument, Diarmaid discovered that he had a golden sword. The existence of this precious weapon within the tomb was affirmed in the neighborhood as recently as 1938. For this magic weapon the chamber provided the stone sheath.

In the Highlands of Scotland a comparable sword is known in oral tradition as The White Glave (sword) of Light. As told by John the Tinker of Inverary in 1860, it belongs in "the Realm of Big Women," or "behind the face of the sun."

The conjunction of Gráinne, a hero, and the golden sword at the Lough Gur tomb may be compared to the Excalibur-Arthur-Megalithic tomb ensemble that is so often found in Britain, where Arthur's claim to earthly rule derives from his association with the goddess Morgan le Fey.

DEAD HUNT AND SILENT COACH

Up and down, from zenith to nadir, the gods ran rings over and under Lough Gur. Their transit sometimes took the form of a hunt in the sky where the hounds of death pursued the individual.

People who live around the lough knew of the Dead Hunt. Tom MacNamara told me in 1990 that it passed right over him one night, on the east side of the Lough. He had Iain down in a cold sweat till it had gone. In Tom Harnon's opinion, "You never heard the hunt in your youth. That 'twas in your matured years that you actually heard it. When you were young, the older people in the household heard it, but you did not . . . But after that hunt there's always someone supposed to die on the following day in that locality."

The Dead Hunt explicitly links the Lough to the *síd* of Cnoc Áine, and associates human mortality with the sport of the gods. The person who is about to die, or to be buried, is the hunted quarry selected by the spirits of the underworld and pursued from one world to another.

Another supernatural event experienced by Lough Gur people is the passage of the *Coitse Bodhar*, or Silent Coach. Speaking in 1972, Ned Hynes described its

BELOW Horses grazing. The passion for horse racing in Ireland may be traced to pre-Christian sacred "sun sports."

LEFT *Gilded bronze disk, Lattoon, Co. Cavan, 4 inches (11 centimeters) in diameter, c. 600* B.C.E.

BELOW LEFT *Bronze horse, Irish, 6 inches (15 centimeters) tall, c. 300* C.E. *Apparently pregnant, the mare's fetlocks are pierced chariot attachments.*

BELOW RIGHT *Irish solar chariot (restored). In Old Irish, "chariot wheel" was* droch óir, *literally "hoop of gold."*

effect: "It is like you'd run a tractor down the road now, drawing all buckets after it." Is it dangerous? he was asked. "No. But you wouldn't hear it passin' you out" (as it drew close). Hence its "silent" name.

John Brien of Bruff, aged eighty-two in 1972, believed that the Coitse Bodhar ran along routes laid down in antiquity around the Lough, and still visible, as archeologists confirm. The remains of ancient wooden causeways across the Red Bog, immediately south of the Lough, were once part of the ancient road network and known to local men in the nineteenth century. "We've been diggin' and burnin' the ould piles for years," commented Paddy Regan, a laborer, to Mary Fogarty of Lough Gur. Ó'Ríordáin accepts the Cladh an Leac, running around the west side of the Lough, as "portions of an ancient road clearly visible, a sunken track bordered by boulders."

The owner and occupant of the coach was Áine, judging by a story related by Mr. James Butler in 1897. He told of a herdsman, Sean O'Shea of Knockfennel, whom she summoned to play his bagpipes at a ball that night, and he was "carried off in her carriage, sitting beside her." In this manner they passed down winding avenues of choicest fruit trees, evergreens, and sweet smelling roses to a grand mansion. Inside, a great ball was in progress, with good food, drink, and company.

The Coitse Bodhar may be seen as one of the wagons in which the North European mother goddess traveled. Tacitus knew of her in Denmark as Nerthus, or "Mother Earth." When not visiting her people in her sacred wagon, she kept it in a grove on an island.

FINN McCOOL AT LOUGH GUR

The trail left by Áine around the lough attracted mythic heroes in pursuit. Among these was Finn. "Finn McCool used to pass that way – he was after her," Tom Carroll affirmed in 1972. Finn was the demigod son of the warrior Cumhall, and of Muirenn his goddess mother from the *sid* of Almu in Leinster.

Finn's name means "bright," and he was bound to chase the sun goddesses Áine and Grian (Gráinne), since Diarmaid, one of his men, had eloped with Gráinne. Indeed, Finn camped on the summit of Cnoc Grene, as the name *Seefin* (seat of Finn) there makes clear. From Cnoc Grene he traveled to Lough Gur and arrived for the Oenach, at the start of harvest.

The twelfth-century *Duanaire Finn* states: "At the Hill of Doon, the rock above Loch Goir, the horses of the Fiana came to race at an Oenach [great festival] with the Munstermen." Cormac derived the word *oenach*, "religious festival," from *aine-ech* "delightfulness

of horses," and in 1911, Canon Lynch was told that the Lough Gur racecourse was on Knockfennel, the hill bordering the north side of the lough. Others recalled how people came from all quarters, for a First Fruits Ceremony at the start of harvest, or Brón Trogain, the month when the earth labors for her fruits. Compatible with this annual effort, the word *gur* means "keen and painful," as in *Mná re gúrlámnad* – "women in painful parturition," and *gure*, "pangs."

The event is inseparable from the divine birth. Lough Gur is probably Áine's birth-lake, hence it was known locally as "the hatching lake." What she gave birth *to*, was a horse. A certain black mare, belonging to a druid, Dil, won the three chief prizes of the Lough Gur oenach, "unto the rock over Loch Gair," and was presented to Finn by Fiáchu, the local potentate, who had obtained it from Dil, his druid grandfather.

There for thee is the swift black horse,
Said Fiachu to the prince of champions [Finn],
There is my famous chariot,
And there is a horse for thy charioteer.

This mare, a horse goddess born from the lough, was the perfect gift for Finn. She acquired extra value through being presented via Fiáchu and Dil. At Lough Gur the black horse passes from Dil the priest to Fiáchu the farmer, and thence to Finn the warrior. This represents a transaction that, according to G. Dumézil in 1958, might be expected of any Indo-European community from the Bay of Bengal to Co. Clare. It ritually united the three chief subdivisions of Indo-European society. The divine horse carried the secret of social cohesion, and Lough Gur folklore is seen to gallop with the orthodoxies of two continents.

A lakeside farmer, Edward Fitzgerald, knew of the Lough Gur horse in 1911, when "people had various tales of the wonderful black mare." Was this the horse involved in the attempt to snatch the cloth from the under-lough tree? If so, the fragments of one myth touch the remains of another, and the mare who produced political stability also engaged the vertical unifier, the tree, shared by gods and people.

ABOVE *The island of Knockadoon, seen from the west shore of Lough Gur.*

RIGHT *Croker's map of 1833 shows two relatively new causeways, yet Knockadoon still suggests the plump form of the international Stone Age deity, squatting in the birth act.*

FAR RIGHT *The squatting goddess has been drawn, sculpted, and perceived in landforms since the Paleolithic times. Silbury Hill and its lake in Wiltshire, England, were constructed c. 2600 B.C.E, when the stone circles of Knockadoon were being erected.*

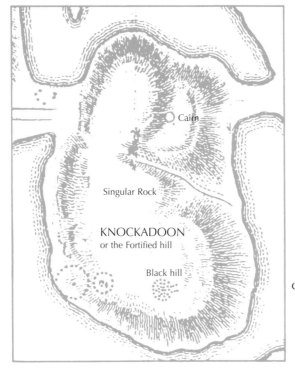

Cairn

Singular Rock

KNOCKADOON
or the Fortified hill

Black hill

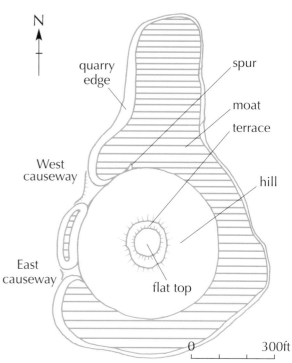

N

quarry edge

spur

moat

terrace

West causeway

hill

East causeway

flat top

0   300ft

✠ SUN WORSHIP ✠

As the returning sun goddess, Áine was probably driven around the Lough in a ceremonial showing at the summer festivals. Parts of bronze and gold votive models encapsulating such an event have been found in Ireland and are based on Bronze Age Scandinavian designs, notably that of the Trundholm sun chariot. A gold leaf sun disk, 5 inches (12 cm) in diameter, made c. 1000 B.C.E., and probably carried by a model chariot, was found at Lattoon, Co. Cavan. Two bronze Irish backing disks, similarly incised, and with loops for attachment to a model chariot and horse, suggest a nationwide tradition, while a bronze horse, 6 inches (15 cm) tall, with holes for axles and disk attachment, extends the practice into the late Celtic period.

KNOCKADOON
AND TÍR NA N'ÓG

After the charioteering and the harvest gathering on Knockfennel, the demigod Finn cast his eyes across the water of Lough Gur to Knockadoon, the large rocky island, rising in the middle of the lake. According to one medieval text, he then crossed the water with his men to visit "Dun over Lake," which O'Grady and MacNeill take to be the fort, Dun Gair, on the summit of Knockadoon.

Once there, he and his Fianna or military troop, "three score hundred" strong, enjoyed three days and three nights of feasting, according to the poem "The Headless Phantoms."

The meaning of this short journey may lie partly in a mythic rebirth of Finn by the Munster sun goddess, Áine, from the midst of her principal birth-lake.

Knockadoon is a picturesque intermingling of gray limestone cliffs and outcrops, with deciduous woodland and pasture. The remains of prehistoric habitation sites, and of stone circles, dot its hilly surface. These combine with folklore survivals to offer nearly five thousand unbroken years of a sacred economy, while the name *Gur*, being derived from "pangs," suggests that, mythically speaking, Knockadoon stands at the center of a birth process involving the lough-as-womb of the presiding goddess.

ABOVE *Knockadoon, summit. After his Knockfennel horse race, Finn and his men are said to have visited Dun Gair (fort over lake) Knockadoon's summit.*

LEFT *Bronze shield, found cloth-wrapped in a bog between Cnoc Áine and Lough Gur, probably a votive offering to the goddess, 26½ inches (68 centimeters), c. 800 B.C.E.*

ABOVE *A cave on the island of Knockadoon, in the middle of Lough Gur. This was one of many entrances to Tír Na n'Óg, "The Land of Eternal Youth," sought by Finn.*

✠ ÁINE'S BIRTH-LAKE ✠

As late as 1685 C.E., Knockadoon was still a true island. By 1833 it had been joined to the mainland by two wide causeways. After that, the east end of the lough was drained. Despite these alterations, it is legitimate to read the prehistoric island in its entirety both as a child of the lake, and as an image of Áine the mother of the gods, squatting in labor.

Throughout the world, Stone Age art is centered on the birth act, and serves to link human and divine parturition with sympathetic topographical events, such as the emergence of streams from caves, and of islands from lakes. The sight of Knockadoon, apparently rising up from a ring of water, was probably the underlying inspiration for the extraordinary concentration of monuments around the lough.

For all prehistoric peoples (and for Munster's rural community in more recent times), the features of the landscape are considered to be alive. At certain locations, favored because of their particularly evocative appearance, this background vitality takes on a supernatural intensity, and reveals the chief deity of the province. Thus Knockadoon *is* the goddess Áine, arising from her waters of parturition, just as the Paps of Anu, *Da Chíche Ánainne*, in South Munster, were recognized as those of the same goddess, and emphasized by the nipple-shaped cairns that were constructed on their summits in antiquity. At both

In 1910 a local man showed Lynch an entrance to the Tír Na n'Óg cave on the north cliff, and said that it was believed to have been occupied by "a mysterious old man and his wife." This may have been the cavern visited by Fitzgerald in 1826, and found to be twenty-two feet (6.7 meters) deep. Croker was told "that at various periods of danger, even so late as the year 1798, it had been used as a place of retreat."

So Knockadoon, an eminence thrusting up through water from the depths, reciprocally gave access to a hidden realm, and the dream of uterine return. In these terms, Knockadoon and all its many caves comprise "one of those unexpected landscapes which sometimes inspire a strange familiarity derived from pre-natal emotions, which the unconscious mind clothes in pictures of a fairy land. Strange yearnings of the heart, and fantasies of floating are associated with these prenatal 'memories'." In Irish culture, they are translated as the possibility of entering the mistress of eternity.

In Irish tradition, Tír Na n'Óg is sometimes accessible to the living. Instead of the gloom and pain of the Classical Inferno, those who traveled there found that living itself achieved perfection. Tír Na n'Óg is variously described in early Irish literature as the Land of Youth, of Honey, of Promise, the Wonderland, the Silver Cloud Land, the Land of Women, and the Land of Bliss. These were different names for a single, flexible, poetic realization, over which the figure of a "queen" ruled, and called mortals to her side. Entry was by invitation and enticement, or by courteous exploration of adult voyagers. In either case, human access was dependent on the poets, whose words were needed to carry the adventure over the threshold. To equip them for this task the Irish poet's traditional apprenticeship was spent in the dark, in underground chambers, where the rules of composition were taught, and poems committed to memory. As Edmund Spenser observed in the sixteenth century, even when poets emerged to hear their works sung by bards at social events, out of respect for the divine source of inspiration, they lay in darkness (facing the Tír Na n'Óg cave) as they had been taught to do while students of the art.

places, natural endowment and human response were mutually supportive. The synthesis also permeates the "art" of Áine, like the low relief of the goddess found just over a mile (2 kilometers) north of Knockadoon, at Caherelly Castle, where the limestone torso becomes a landscape of paradise.

In Croker's day, the south-west lobe of Knockadoon was known as Back Hill, perhaps this is because its shape makes the rump of a giant rock woman, facing north, whose vulva coincides with a cave regarded locally as the entrance to Tír Na n'Óg, the Land of Eternal Youth.

MONEY HOLE AND BULL

All traditions are liable to decay, and on Knockadoon that of Tír Na n'Óg has produced an offshoot, where endless joy may be sold off for cash. Local opinion now insists that there *is* something of value hidden under the island of Knockadoon – money. The Land of Women is prostituted in keeping with the rising commercial ethic.

The precise location of the Money Hole is disputed. Earlier this century Mr. John Hynes used to point out a large flagstone, about three feet high, in the fence of the old road between Knockadoon and Knockaroe Hill, which lies to its north. He maintained that a woman from Co. Clare had dreamed on three consecutive nights that a mass of golden treasure lay beneath the stone, and she led a body of Clare men to dig there. However, before they could find it they were attacked and driven off by local people, who later regretted that they had not delayed their response till after the gold had been located.

BELOW *Searching for the Money Hole. In the nineteenth century, Canon Lynch was told that its entrance lay beneath a Knockadoon stone circle, perhaps this double stone ring, c. 1000 B.C.E*

Yet Lynch was told that it was "located a short distance above the Black Castle on the *southern* slope of Knockadoon Hill [though] somewhat concealed now, as . . . it is situated in the center of a so-called grove . . . which consists of bushes and briars."

This Money Hole has been the rendezvous of many exciting efforts to discover the much coveted but hitherto unobtainable crock of gold that is believed to have been buried there long ago, by a Geraldine chieftain before going to battle. He compelled one of his soldiers to swear he would guard the treasure dead or alive. The chief then shot him and placed his body over the Hidden Treasure, and the soldier's spirit, in the form of an enchanted bull, still guards it.

In 1837 the eastern part of the Lough running up to Knockadoon was drained, and huge quantities of ox bones were revealed in the mud of the former lake bed, suggesting that ritual slaughter had been carried out, possibly at Samain, over a long period of time. (At Samain ritual slaughter and the practical need to cull the stock before the winter fodder shortage, worked together.) R. Harkness recorded in 1869 that, "More than one hundred cartloads of bones were removed, and sold to dealers in such articles. And later, during the potato famine [of 1845], the poor of the town of Bruff obtained a scanty living, by collecting and selling bones from this locality . . . the remains of *Bos Longifrons* [the most ancient type of domestic cattle], the heads of which almost all exhibited a fractured front, produced by the blow which had killed them."

In 1977, on a wet Sunday morning in September, the writer was challenged on the slopes of Knockadoon by an angry inhabitant who believed an attack on the Money Hole by metal detector was about to take place. Once satisfied that it was only a camera being carried, he explained that during the Famine the English landowner de Salis had dug from Knockadoon a great mass of old weapons and vessels. In fact, prehistoric bronze chariot fittings, shields, and axes *were* taken from the Lough. "There is scarcely a museum or a private collection in Great Britain and Ireland which does not include some object from the lake and its vicinity," is Professor O'Kelly's assessment.

In their starvation and despair, local people rightly felt that the embodiment of community values (their chief treasure) was being stolen, and with its disappearance, a framework of beliefs that had supported them for millennia was being dismantled. Hunger's bitterness was then complete, and those who had the strength to crawl to the emigration boats departed, truly bereft.

Yet in 1977 enough trace of the Money Hole remained for a young man to fly to its defense as a working proposition. If not indelible, the last version of Tír Na n'Óg is proving hard to eradicate.

FINN IN THE BRUIDEN

One way to approach the hidden Otherworld of Knockadoon is to follow the gods – to let *them* locate the entrance, and so slip across the threshold unnoticed at the rear of their party. We can tag onto Finn and his Fianna; but if the ride is free, it is far from easy.

Finn, the most volatile of demigods, is hard to pin down, but he *was* seen feasting on the summit of Knockadoon, as Samain, the Halloween quarterday, approached. Samain, Summer's End, was a zone of instability, being the void between one year and the next, in which feasting and sexual adventure merged with monstrous wintry images of disintegration.

Nothing better illustrates these perils than the Bruiden type of story, a tale connected with Halloween, where the god-hero is enticed into a magic house that *could* be in Tír Na n'Óg, but where he is unexpectedly abused, ill-treated, and often killed. He has been tricked. Too late does he realize that the banquet hall belongs to another type of supernatural realm, which is bound into the bleakest segment of an annual cycle. That is where the poem "The Headless Phantoms" takes us. These words, attributed to Guaire (alias Oisín), Finn's blind son (who was believed to have spent three hundred years in Tír Na n'Óg), slam shut behind his father, giving him no choice *but* to go downward.

THE HEADLESS PHANTOMS

∽

Both Guaire's descent into Tír Na n'Óg and Finn's entry into the Bruiden are widely known in Irish oral tradition. From that enduring source, one twelfth-century writer drew his material.

Finn had to be lured into the house of treachery at the start of each November. This also explains why Bruiden poems (whether memorized or read) were recited at Halloween, for on the words spoken and heard the demigod rode to his annual destiny on behalf of a fearfully grateful humanity. The words projected the deeds that *ought* to happen as between men and gods, with the demigod in the vanguard of the exchange. True to the incantatory mythic method, it is on lines of verse that he and his Fianna lower themselves into the chamber of the supernatural.

Near the entrance, the blind poet Guaire stands. (Has he ruined his eyesight, for a glimpse of the dark behind the Bruiden door? If so, that is a poet's fate.) Finn, meanwhile, confronting the Celtic New Year, speaks in terms of physical appetites. He wants shelter from the growing cold. He needs more food and drink for his men. In search of these commodities, The Headless Phantom verses send him on a rapid circuit of Munster. By telling the tale, under his *Guaire* pseudonym, Oisín drew the action toward Lough Gur, and to Dun Guaire on Knockadoon, the sum of its province, and therefore a good site for the nebulous and enchanted lodging that Finn eventually finds, with darkness descending.

Entrance to the magic hostel might be under the large flat stone close to the northwestern shore of Knockadoon, traditionally called Leac Rudhraighe Rueidh, connected in local belief with "Red Rury," a mythic, Charon-like ferryman. As named on the 1927 Ordnance map, the slab may mean literally "The Flat Stone" (*Leac*), "of long occupation" (*rudrad*), or "a searching groping sojourner, a darkening, and a dark gloomy countenance" (*rudhrach*), and going on "a great journey" (*ruidh*), with a "rush, a vault, a bound, and running jump, a throw or cast" (*ruid*), into the Bruiden. At the door stood "a gray-haired churl," a Giant. "My welcome, O famous Find [Finn], saith the Giant cruelly." The Giant quickly seizes Finn's horse and fastens the door with iron hooks. Finn and his men "sit down on the hard couch that has to rest us all at once; the log of elder that is on the hearth has all but quenched the fire."

The elder-log is a well-known emblem of the goddess-as-hag – Áine in her winter underworld, for example. The privation of the scene is reminiscent of the flea-ridden, smoke-blackened barn in the Welsh *Mabinogion*. The Book of Leinster version reads:

The Giant flings firewood of elder on his fire: it almost smothered us with smoke . . . A hag abode in the great house, with three heads on her thin neck: a headless man on the other side, with one eye protruding from his breast.

The churl urges the people of the house to rise up, and sing a song for Finn . . . Nine bodies rise out of the corner from the side next to us. Nine heads from the other side on the iron couch. They set up nine horrid screeches; matched in loudness, but not in harmony.

This is the birth cry of Chaos and winter dismemberment, complementary to the harvest birth, due to occur nine months later at Lughnasa, which has to be earned in the pit.

They are a screeching, wailing, shouting, and clamorous rabbly household.

That strain which was sung to us would waken the dead out of the mold. It almost broke the bones of our heads.

The Giant then lifts the firewood ax, and "deftly smites, flays, and destroys the Fianna's horses, but Finn tells his men not to complain, saying "Well for us if he grants life to us." [Finn knows, if his men do not, that they are no longer in control, but in the power of a different kind of sense.]

The giant then sets out 50 spits of rowan, but each came from the fire with the meat still quite raw. Finn rejects these: "Take away thy food, O Giant! For I have never devoured raw food; I will never eat it from today till Doom."

Rowan, in Irish belief, keeps the dead from rising, and for that reason was planted in graveyards. In rejecting the offer of raw flesh on rowan spits Finn

LEFT *Rowan, mountain ash. In Ireland it prevents the dead from rising, and so was often planted in graveyards. The rowan tree was seen as a supernatural being.*

was therefore declining the role of a supernatural corpse eel, which *is* allowed to eat the uncooked flesh of the Grange graveyard. Had he accepted the meat, he would have shifted the balance of his demigod status firmly toward the divine, and so spent the rest of his existence identified *totally* with the Knockadoon *síd* and with the Tuatha deities.

In refusing, Finn retains a grip on the human aspect of his double personality. He opts instead for a borderline role and the ability to move freely back and forth between worlds.

"If thou has come into our house," saith the Giant, "to refuse our food, it is certain that we shall go against yourselves."

Then fighting ensues, the fire is quenched, and Finn and his men are driven "into a dark, black nook, where they lay head-to-head till morning, till the sun lighted up the house." (At the same instant, in the Otherworld of the famous New Grange tumulus, Co. Meath, the sun pokes its golden wand at midwinter dawn through a stone roof-box leading to the central

OPPOSITE *In the Bruiden, the underworld House of Treachery, Marble Arch cave, Co. Fermanagh. Here the nightmare certainty of our own death is carved by the underground river of life.*

chamber, with a touch of hope.) Here, the smile of Áine may alight on the Fianna's distress and confusion. But instead, having declined her raw meat, with implacable logic her sunbeam strikes them with the spear of mortality. Consequently, "When the sun rose, each man falls hither and thither," and "A mist falls on everyone's head so that he was dead on the spot." Such is their welcome back into the world of mortals.

They are born dead; it is midwinter.

But this is not the end, for though the Fianna have opted for humanity, they are granted a special kind of *eternal* humanity. Thus: "For a short time we lay in our rest. We rise up, We are whole." Now conspicuously "human," the Fianna pay the price, for the fairy Otherworld immediately vanishes from view: "There the house is hidden from us. Everyone of the household is hidden." But mortal life goes on: "Thus arose Find of Inisfail, with his own horse in his hand. Whole were we all, both head and foot, every blemish was absent." Yet this is no robust return. Instead, like animals reemerging from long hibernation, "We fared thence wearily, feebly. Those we met in the real world, they asked of us tidings. We had no wish to deny it. 'We found,' saith Find, 'on our way Tribulation for our billeting.'"

Inside Knockadoon, his imprisonment may be connected with the cave known as Carrignagol, named on the 1927 Ordnance map. It means "Rock of Weeping, Wailing, and Lamentation" (*gol*), and stands close to the Leac Rudhraighe Rueidh. There he might reflect on *gola* – the pit, prison, or pre-Christian "Purgatory" from which he has escaped.

Through the mean days on the far side of winter, traumatized by his Otherworld treatment, Finn seeks a motive for the attack, and concludes: "Those that came against us, the three shapes out of Yew Glen, [came] to take vengeance on us for their sister, whose name was Cullen wide-maw."

Cuillen means "holly tree." Perhaps it was *her* burning, as an annual yule-log sacrifice, that stirred her evergreen sisters to avenge the incineration, by attacking Finn the fire god. ("Yew Valley" also evokes Áine's brother, known as Fer Í or Fer Fí, whose name means Man of Yew.)

LEFT *Knockadoon's Suideachan, or "Housekeeper's Chair." Áine sat on this lime-stone slab in order to give birth to harvest on August 1st, Irish* Brón Trogain, *when "the earth is in travail" for her fruits.*

SUIDEACHAN, THE BIRTH CHAIR

To witness the birth of Áine's child, we have to return to Knockadoon, where her birth chair is situated. There, "at the old edge of the lake, beyond the Western Circle of Knockadoon," writes Lynch, "is Suideachan, the little seat of the Housekeeper (*Bean tighe*)." Here Áine comes up from Tír Na n'Óg and sits to give birth, in the manner shown by numerous Paleolithic and Neolithic figurines.

The chair consisted of a small grassy mound, with the rock seat on the west side overlooking the lake. Other descriptions of the mound say that it was eight feet (2.4 meters) high, with a hollow in the middle. It is sited "just this [the north] side of Ash Point" according to Tom Carroll. Pat MacNamara calls it a rocky outcrop on the shore near the gravel pit, before Garret Island is reached, walking from the north. It was here that Sean O'Shea, a herdsman from Knockfennel, met Áine on a fine August evening.

Next morning his wife told him that she had had a bad dream, in which the starch for her Sunday cap had turned yellow as gold, and she then saw a fine lady in a carriage who was throwing up gold balls with one hand and catching them with the other. Worse still, this lady never ceased grinning at her, and mocking her, till she was wakened by the fright. (The "lady" was probably Áine, juggling with her solar self in miniature, the theme of so much of the golden "art" of Irish prehistory.) Sean, ignoring his wife's misgivings, then drove off with Áine to her mansion.

"Inside, a great ball was in progress, with good food, drink, and company. He then saw shoals of freshwater fish gazing in admiration through the windows of her enchanted banquet hall, for he was in one of the submerged palaces of Geároid Iarla. At the end of the night, the lady gave him a purse of gold, which on awakening he discovered contained only yellow furze flowers." This story was related by Mr. James Butler in 1897.

ABOVE *Birth goddess from Feltrim, Co. Dublin; tinned bronze with green glass eyes and swivelling "crown."*

OPPOSITE *Passage Grave, New Grange, Co. Meath; third millennium* B.C.E. *The underworld could take either cavernous or monumental form. Here sunlight at midwinter dawn enters via a deliberately designed stone "box," and illuminates the center chambers.*

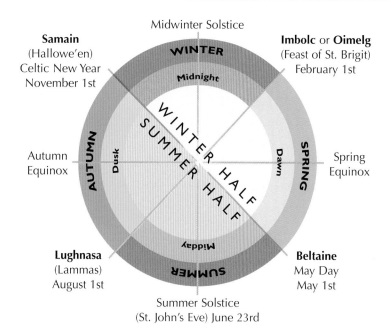

Midwinter Solstice

Samain
(Hallowe'en)
Celtic New Year
November 1st

Imbolc or **Oimelg**
(Feast of St. Brigit)
February 1st

WINTER

Midnight

WINTER HALF

SUMMER HALF

Dusk

Dawn

AUTUMN

SPRING

Autumn
Equinox

Spring
Equinox

Midday

Lughnasa
(Lammas)
August 1st

SUMMER

Beltaine
May Day
May 1st

Summer Solstice
(St. John's Eve) June 23rd

ABOVE *Time provinces in Ireland. Each season began with a quarter-day festival. Samain, marked the start of winter and a new year; Imbolc, spring; Beltaine, summer; and Lughnasa, harvest.*

OPPOSITE *Ireland's greatest stone circle, Rannach Crom Dubh, stands on the west shore of Lough Gur. It has 113 megaliths. Here the harvest porter-god, Crom Dubh, annually carried in the first sheaf of harvest.*

OVERLEAF
View of Lough Gur from the south.

In the 1870s Áine appeared at the Housekeeper's Chair to another local man, Mr. James Cleary. "She was every inch a queen," he told his friends. A few evenings later he was out on the lough in his curragh when it capsized and he was drowned. Her call, they concluded, could not be resisted. Anyone who saw her, it was believed, was driven insane by the spell of her beauty, or died shortly after. (Madness is a voyage to another reality, where "normal" behavior dies.) Both O'Shea and Cleary may be said to have enjoyed or suffered a *reverse* birth into Lough Gur, and a return to the divine as sacrificial victims.

In the mid-nineteenth century it was told how on one occasion Áine came up from the depths of the lake and sat on the housekeeper's seat to comb her hair with a golden comb, while in 1971, Tom Carroll affirmed that she *still* sits on the Suideachan, "combing her hair with a golden comb, and she'll continue to do so till her comb is worn out and her white hair . . ."

In Hiberno-Scottish tradition recorded by J. F. Campbell, solar-lunar suggestions play about "a fine golden comb and a coarse comb of silver; they are worth a deadly fight with a giant in many a story," while the pre-Christian Greek rites of the earth goddess Ge-Themis were centered on a comb (*kteis*), seen as synonymous with the female pudenda from which the earth goddess gave birth to sun and moon.

At Lough Gur, a man named Cuacaill, or Herdsman of the Island, coveted Áine's comb and

stole it. Afterward, misfortune befell him, and on the verge of death, he ordered that it should be flung into the lake, where Áine is sometimes to be seen, half her body above the waters, "combing her hair," as reported by Fitzgerald in 1879.

THE HARVEST BIRTH-LINE

Áine as mother-to-be appears in the word *ain*, meaning "in my womb," and "the period of fasting prior to a feast day vigil," while *guaire* (gur) can mean "on the point of parturition." With these words, the mother goddess sits on her *suideachan*, or maternity chair, at the eve of the harvest quarterday, Lughnasa (August 1st), and waits for the dawn birth of her son Lugh. Sunrise occurs at 59° and joins the Cnoc Grene *síd* of her solar "sister," Grian, to the Knockadoon birth chair. On the way, it passes over the Money Hole site nominated by John Hynes, and over the north end of the Lough. There, a Bronze Age spear with two gold rings and "sunbeam" gold inlay on the socket was dredged up in 1857, and presumed by O'Kelly to have been a votive offering. The same alignment passes from the Chair across a circular stone platform of Neolithic age on Garret Island (named after Áine's son, Geároid Iarla), and thence to the western shore of the Lough, where it enters Ireland's greatest embanked stone circle.

The one and only entrance to this monument is narrow, well-defined, and aligned precisely to receive the Lammas sunrise at 59° East of North. The enclosure is named Rannach Crom Dubh, after Crom Dubh, the porter-god of harvest, who in Irish folk belief carried the first sheaf, or *punnann*, from the goddess (its mother) to the people.

The Lughnasa dawn at Lough Gur threw a spear of light between Grian's *síd* and the birthday island of Knockadoon, where her sister Áine labored to produce the harvest child. Archeology, place-name evidence, topography, solar behavior, and folklore combine to recreate the most joyful day in the old Irish year, and to return the mythic narrative to the physical symbols through which it may become visible again.

ABOVE *Mowing corn with scythes, Toome, Co. Antrim.*

GARRET ISLAND
(occupied 3rd millennium B.C.E.)
The Island of Áine's child, Geároid

Desmond Tower

Prehistoric stone platform

RANNACH CROM DUBH
(The Staff of Crom Dubh)
Ireland's greatest stone circle,
built, circa 2500 B.C.E.
The single entrance to Crom
Dubh's stone circle, at 59°,
aligns with sunrise at the
August quarterday.

RIGHT *The entrance to Rannach Crom Dubh aligns with Lughnasa sunrise.*

LOUGH GUR

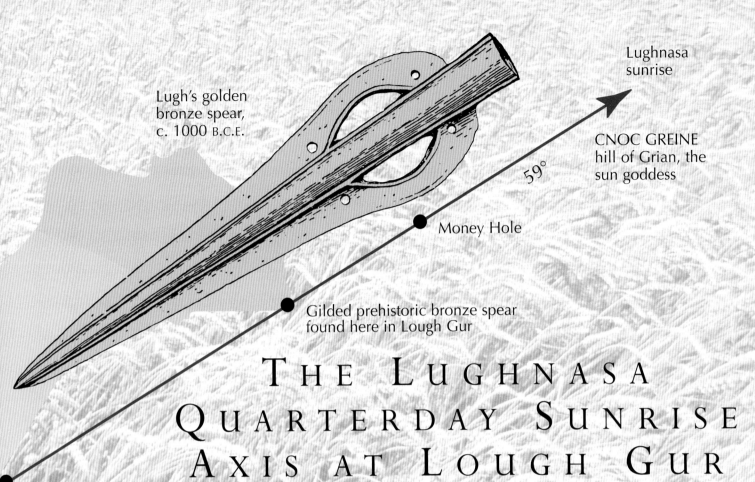

Lugh's golden
bronze spear,
c. 1000 B.C.E.

Lughnasa
sunrise

59°

CNOC GREINE
hill of Grian, the
sun goddess

Money Hole

Gilded prehistoric bronze spear
found here in Lough Gur

Áine's harvest birth-
chair, Suideachan,
Knockadoon

THE LUGHNASA QUARTERDAY SUNRISE AXIS AT LOUGH GUR

RIGHT *The stone
circle's biggest megalith
may represent the
sheaf-carrying god,
Crom Dubh.*

CROM DUBH

In her majestic survey of harvest folk-belief, MacNeill (1962) found a harvest god, Crom Dubh, spoken of in most parts of Ireland, especially in the provinces of Connacht and Munster, from Donegal Bay to the Dingle Peninsula. Crom Dubh, she writes "is a pagan deity" whose name means "the dark bent one." This harvest god is popularly regarded as the dominant God in the land till the coming of St. Patrick, and mid-nineteenth-century sources in Munster continue to refer to Crom Dubh as "the god of harvest." He was believed to emerge in most parts of Ireland at the start of harvest, on August 1st, midway between summer solstice and autumn equinox. In Co. Limerick the day was called Black Stoop Sunday. Crom stooped because he carried on his back the first great sheaf of wheat from the harvest, the inaugural and sacred gift from the Otherworld. He was dark or black because in order to find the wheat, he had been into the winter underworld of Gráinne-Áine's subsoil and *síde*.

That Crom Dubh and Áine were anciently linked together as harvest deities is made clear in a mid-nineteenth-century report from Co. Louth, which calls the festival *Domhnach Áine agus Chroim Duibh* (the Sunday of Áine and Crom Dubh).

Crom-the-giver complements Finn-the-taker, acting as farmer to Finn's warrior and as a darkness set against Finn's "bright." Wherever Finn goes, Crom follows, and vice versa, in a double act that is discernible at Lough Gur. So, Rannach Crom Dubh, the low-lying ring, complements Seefin, Finn's seat, on top of Cnoc Grene.

Subsequent to the Neolithic era, Crom was expected to carry extra loads imposed by centuries of cultural change, including the impact of bronze workers, Iron Age warriors, and attacks by Christian saints. Emerging as he did from the very foundation of Irish culture, all these challenges were loaded onto his shoulder for assimilation, on the assumption that, like an ox, he would continue working, whatever happened, and however low his reputation sunk in the eyes of clever newcomers, who needed him more than their abuse implied.

Both Crom and Finn can be seen as degraded versions of the high gods, Donn the dark one, and his dazzling opposite number, Lugh.

After reviewing a mass of folklore and early literature, MacNeill concluded that Crom is a version of Donn, "and that he can be regarded as identical with the pre-Celtic food-providing gods – Cormac, the Dagda, Elcmar, Midir, and Balor," all of whom were engaged in conflict with a Finn-Lugh opponent. Yet the outcome of these struggles was a joint affirmation; Lugh's spears came to hit their mark on Crom-Donn's shoulder as bundles of golden stalks, each tipped with a precious wheat or barley head. The spear was the staff, or *rannach*, of life, carried to the people by the dark god.

Crom brings the entire legacy of Neolithic goods from under the hills, including knowledge of plowing (his nickname, "Suicin," is probably a diminutive of *soc*, "a plowshare"). Grain, a granary, a feast, influence on weather, and (as we shall see) a bull, are also in his gift.

The sheaf that Crom brought to the feast on his shoulder was probably the golden grain child, Eithne. In folklore this girl is sometimes presented as Crom's fairy mistress, while the attempts of the god Lugh to wrest the sheaf from Crom is portrayed as a struggle to abduct the grain maiden, Eithne. The word *eithne* means "kernel" or "grain." Eithne (Anglicized as Annie in Ulster) can be regarded as daughter of Áine, and seen in "Maiden" corn dollies, and the astrological Virgo.

Her womanliness and long sojourn in Crom's underworld shows in *eitre*, "furrow." Eithne's November self is the new furrow waiting for the seed.

THE SAMAIN BULL RING

The opening of Rannach Crom Dubh at 59° for Lammas sunrise also admits its replica, the May Day sunrise, which falls along the same line. Moreover, if the 59° axis is projected *across* the ring to 239° East of North, an alignment with the complementary twin events of Samain and Imbolc sunsets is registered. B. C. A. Windle writes: "One thing is quite clear, when all [modern] obstacles were removed (such as Holy Cross cottages) a person standing with back to the entrance passage would get the sharpest possible sight of the sun going down [at Samain] through the notch between stones 67 and 68." The "notch" is the "V"–shaped space that the two stones (touching at their bases) offer as they rise to make a pair of tall stone horns, even though the tip of 67 has since been knocked off. They are now 6 and 7.5 feet (1.9 and 2.3 meters) high. Except for Stone 1, they are two of the tallest in the ring. The horns and the notch stand at, and make, the gate between the years.

According to Munster and Connacht folklore Crom's bull was believed to be immortal. By trickery St. Patrick once killed and ate it, and then ordered the bones to be thrown into the hide, whereupon the animal returned to life. Around Galway Bay at Samain every household skinned and roasted a bull in honor of Crom Dubh, and one may assume that Crom Dubh and the Bull were originally synonymous.

Both the pre-Celtic and Celtic annual circuits ended at Samain, Summer's end. The red sunset is therefore the blood-light of the old year, shed on the "gate-post-horns" of the new. Layer upon layer of organic debris, found immediately behind the horn stones, suggests that the annual bull was devoured as a roasted carcass on the spot, in repeated Samain feasts.

Evidence for sacred communal cooking places at, or attached to, Neolithic monuments in Ireland, is now abundant. Often, as at the Drombeg stone circle, West Cork, the tradition can be shown to have extended into the early Christian period. Now called *fulacht fiadh*, these "ox-cooking" sites are frequently associated with Finn and his Fianna, and probably derive from a Neolithic prototype exemplified here at the *Lios*, or "Enclosure" of Crom Dubh.

The *dubh* of Crom's name accordingly means burnt as well as dark. In Crom-the-Bull we witness the old year sinking to his knees, his huge weight falling, in fire and smoke, to the winter underworld. At Samain the monument became a bull ring. One meaning of "Lios" is cattle pound, which may explain its sheer and remarkably continuous inner wall of touching megaliths erected to prevent the bull's escape. At the Lios the third bull of a trinity bellows across the lake, to his mythic brothers, in the Red Cellar, and on Knockadoon.

The Samain human congregation desired to share in the bull's descent into the underworld, just as they craved for a crumb of Eithne, in the new Lammas loaf. For the same reason, they ate a morsel of the beef (*rann* means crumb *and* morsel). They reenacted the bull's downward journey into the underworld in their own digestive tract. Samain, as the start of a *new* year, was also the season of maximum virility, epitomized by the bull and emphasized in human liaisons. *Gam*

(November) was the month of weddings, with birth nine months later, at Lammas.

In terms of Áine's physical needs, the sacrificed bull can be said to enter her lake, and the body of her *síd*. The early twelfth-century account of Cnoc Áine specifically states that it opened at Samain to King Oilioll Olum, and Áine herself came forth, playing on a copper timpan or lyre, whereupon he violated her.

Another legend, which was current in the 1870s, says that when Áine emerged from the lake, she was accompanied by a red bull, and was then raped by the Earl of Desmond, and so gave birth to Garad (Geároid)! Bull, *síd*-opening, Áine, and fruitful coition are all clearly associated, in a mythic union at Samain, whose progeny was born the following Lammas, nine months later.

BULLS AND
✛ FACTION FIGHTS ✛

If Rannach Crom Dubh served to pen sacred bulls, it may have been the scene of ritual contests, ending in the death of a beast. In the early literature, a Brown Bull kills the Great White Horn of Connacht, and in Co. Limerick up until the mid-nineteenth century, contending human factions played out a battle of rival bulls (such as can be envisaged at the Lios), at the November Fair Field, beneath Cnoc Grene, situated on a Samain sunset alignment with the Lios.

Although in recent times the Bryanes and the Conways were the chief clans involved there, the rival teams were known as the "Three Year Olds" and "The Four Year Olds," implying a contest between beasts, perhaps bulls, with whom the people identified. The beastly origin of these team fights, with ash staves, is confirmed by many Co. Limerick people. Some say that two farmers disputed at the fair over their respective animals, while a more archaic tradition insists that it was the animals themselves that originally fought. Human injuries, and even fatalities were expected every year, imitating the annual instatement of a bull god and the deposition, in a trial of strength, of his rival. A hierarchy of contests is suggested by the Co. Limerick faction cry: "Parish against parish, county against county," leading to inter-provincial bouts.

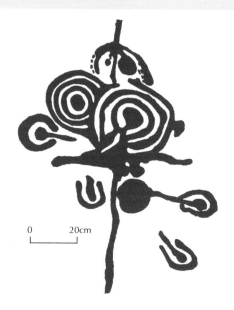

0   20cm

RIGHT *Prehistoric rock carving, Derrynablaha, Co. Kerry, involving a goddess-bullgod union.*

RANNACH, THE BURIED STAFF

The faction fighter's ash stave used in the team battles may have originally been regarded as allied to the magic staff of the Dagda, another form of Crom Dubh. Sealed under the yellow clay that was laid across the surface of the Lios at the time of its construction in 2500 B.C, Ó'Ríordáin found (but did not recognize) the Sama.in symbols of a Neolithic god and goddess. Made of stone on a gigantic and matching scale, these were the staff or walking stick of the god and the crescent new moon of the maiden-goddess. Both measured 119 feet (36.4 meters) from tip to tip, and came together close to the Samain horn stones. MacNeill's conclusion that Crom Dubh may be regarded as identical with the food-providing god called the Dagda, helps to solve the mystery of the buried "Staff" created from carefully arranged limestone rocks, since it was the Dagda's primary symbol of office, described in the ancient literature.

For example, with his double pronged staff "he cut the double trench of Lorg an Dagdae." He was known to have been active at Samain, as the Second Battle of Mag Tuired (the Plain of the Pillar) describes:

He trailed behind him a wheeled fork which was the work of eight men to move, and its track was enough for the boundary ditch of a province. It is called "The Track of the Dagda's Club" for that reason. His penis was uncovered. He had on two shoes of horse-hide with the hair outside . . .

As he went along he saw a girl in front of him, a good-looking young woman with an excellent figure, her hair in beautiful tresses. The Dagda desired her, but he was impotent on account of his belly. The girl began to mock him, then she began wrestling with him. She hurled him so that he sank to the hollow of his rump in the ground . . .

He looked at her angrily and asked, "What business did you have, girl, heaving me out of my right way?"

"This business: to get you to carry me on your back to my father's house."

Then he moved out of the hole, after letting go the contents of his belly, and the girl had waited for

LEFT *The contest
between the White Bull
of Connacht and the
Brown Bull of Ulster,
related in* Táin Bó
Cuailgne *has been
interpreted as the end-
less struggle between
night and day.*

*that for a long time. He got up then and took the girl
on his back; and he put three stones in his belt. Each
stone fell from it in turn — and it has been said that
they were his testicles which fell from it. The girl
jumped on him and struck him across the rump, and
her curly pubic hair was revealed. Then the Dagda
gained a mistress and they made love.*

This passage combines important Samain themes,
including the New Year's redefinition of land boundaries. Here the Dagda initiates the process on an
interprovincial scale with his club or staff, which has
a forked end.

At the Lios, "the wheel" is represented by the
circle of megaliths, incorporating the sunwheel of
the four annual festivals, spun by the goddess Áine in
her critical risings and settings, and encouraged by
the god's staff. This is not to claim that the *mechanical*
wheel incorporated into the Mag Tuired story, as
written down in the Middle Ages, was known in
2500 B.C.E., but that the divine digging stick helped
the year go around from the earliest phase of
Neolithic myth-making in Ireland. Gray considers

that the Dagda's staff is synonymous with his penis, a
combination confirmed in the word "*lorg*," since its
Old Irish usages include: "club, trace, mark, impression, track, trail, path, course, example, pattern
model, progeny, descendants, troop, company, wand
of office, and male penis."

One might argue that the Lios, like the entire universe, was generated by the *lorg* of the Dagda, in union
with the lunar crescent of the goddess, across whose
arc it runs. Concealed in the crypt of the temple,
which together they produced, their hiddenness
under the clay is a testimony to the strength of belief
in the Other, the unrevealed, beyond the reach of
sight, while harmonizing with the commonsense faith
of farmers who now, as then, bury things in the
ground, and hope.

The length of the god's lorg-as-penis gave rise to
heroic boasting among demigods and human heroes
on the same matter. Fergus mac Riog was said to be
"seven fists long in the penis, and a bushel bag wide in
his scrotum." At Halloween seven women were
needed to reduce him.

Halloween was also the time of year when hurling was played with staves resembling hockey sticks. An Old Irish name for the game was *Lorg ane*. Its purpose and origin was to mime in the play the union between god and goddess, which determined the prosperity of the year to come.

✝ FAIRY BATTLES ✝

In 1937 a priest was told by a farmer that every year a battle for the potatoes was supposed to take place in the fall between the fairies of Cnoc Áine, led by Áine, and those of Cnoc Fírinne, led by Donn Fírinne. The fight took the form of a cross-country hurling match and the victors carried the best of the potato crop to their side of the country. Donn is an alternative name for the Dagda, being a god of the underworld and of fertility whose hill, one of the most famous fairy hills in Munster, lies 13 miles (21 kilometers) southwest of the Lios on its Samain sunset side. The story certifies that the gods and goddesses of the hills around the lough enjoyed sporting relations, and that, in addition to its other functions, the Lios staff may also be regarded as a gigantic hurling stick.

THE NEW MOON

The other buried symbol at the Lios, the crescent moon, is a thick deposit of gray limestone rubble that runs from the Samain sunset gap (stones 67–8), through an arc of 85° toward the southeast. This deep deposit was immediately covered with yellow clay. Like the staff (the head of which comes to within 20 inches (50 cm) of the "moon"), it was intended to operate from underneath the clay.

Worldwide, the new moon crescent is understood to combine ox-horn, New Year, and young women references, and is equated with many a goddess held responsible for these matters. At the Lios, the head of the god's staff addresses the lunar crescent, as if bowing its head in worship, an attitude reflected in songs addressed to the new moon by young women in South Uist:

May thy light be fair to me,
May thy course be smooth to me,
If good to me is thy beginning
Seven times better be thine end,
Thou fair moon of the seasons,
Thou great lamp of grace.

LEFT *Poolnabrone Dolmen, Co. Clare, with moon. At Samain (November 1st), start of the Celtic new year, tomb spirits danced with the crescent moon, symbolizing the young goddess of renewal.*

From first-hand accounts, it seems that in Scotland as in Ireland the response to the new moon was one of a communal tenderness, which, like moonlight, drew things together and allowed the individual to walk into the domain of the gods. The new moon is more dark than light and sailed the black sky in a curragh no thicker than a fingernail paring, while returning in two weeks, with the same boat more laden with silver than a homewarding galleon. This recurring transformation was believed to affect many aspects of daily life, in addition to the behavior of the tides. The growing moon was written into the world's constitution, and at the Lios was set to rise to fulfillment from the clay.

✚ NEW MOON AND CATTLE ✚

Adoration of the new moon in Ireland was linked specifically to the well-being of cattle, as the seventeenth-century traveler William Lithgo confirmed:

> They also at the sight of each new moon (I speak it credibly) bequeath their cattle to her protection, obnoxiously imploring the pale Lady of the Night that she will leave their bestials in as good a plight as she found them, and if sick, scabbed, or sore, they solicitate her maiden-faced majesty to restore them to their health.

One function of the Lios crescent may have been to bless the herds at Samain, and Samain was a festival that was tied to a joint solar–*lunar* calendar. In other words, it fluctuated fourteen days either side of a solar Halloween, in order to follow the new moon's wanderings.

On leaving Rannach Crom Dubh, and pausing for a moment to view of the monument in its entirety, one sees how the criss-cross of quarterdays and sun and moon risings and settings make up the whole circle of the year. All around the enclosure, pots were found ritually broken and buried against the roots of the megaliths, probably in recognition of the enchantress "Áine of the Light," who shaped the world from shade to shade.

GEÁROID AND THE LOUGH

Patterns made by stories and monuments around Lough Gur are given physical and intellectual coherence by the water itself, and to the lake we should finally turn. It has claimed the attention and the lives of many. Among human remains found there were lower jaws of large size and heavy outline. If these were the remains of ritual drownings, they bring to mind similar acts in Britain. From Lindow, Cheshire, an Iron Age man, preserved by the sphagnum moss in the pool where he was drowned, now lies in the British Museum. He, like James Cleary, took the ultimate mythological walk into the sacred.

The tradition of a regular human sacrifice to Lough Gur survives in folk belief to the present day.

"The lake claims somebody every seven years. Somebody is drowned in it," stated Tommy Hannon of Bruff in 1972. Was it the seven-year sighting of the tree that drew these people from the shore? Perhaps the lake was dry for them, as they ran across the mud toward the knitter, committing themselves body and soul to an unfamiliar domain.

Geároid Iarla, Áine's son, is believed to have drowned in the lough. "He was in a boat, boating . . . and he got drowned or something. And he was seen [as a spirit] after that," says Mr. Carroll. Here folk belief parts company with historical record, for O'Clery's pedigree states that he died in his house of Caislean Nua (Newcastlewest) in 1399, while other authorities give Castleisl and Co. Kerry. This island seems his likeliest deathbed. But he did not rest there, for according to the Annals of Clonmacnoise "There was one earl, as they say, by name of Garrett, that was *by enchantment carried away* from Newcastle in Connellagh." By magic, he was conveyed to Lough Gur.

The magnetism of a sacred center pulls at what is historically dispersed and gathers further weight thereby. In this case, the historical fact that both the brother and nephew of Geároid were drowned (brother Maurice while crossing the Irish Sea in 1358, and his son Scan, in the Suir River) was pressed into service. These drownings were transferred to Geároid because as a poet, he was required to submerge into

LEFT Garret Island, Lough Gur. In folklore it is the Otherworld home of Geároid Iarla, Áine's Norman son. As a goose, his spirit still haunts the lough. "Goose of the Island" is his title. The barnacle goose was named gigrand because of its circular flight, following the arcs of the sun goddess, Gráinne. Its wing bones were found beneath a Neolithic Knockadoon house.

the muse of the birth-lake, for the benefit of society in general. (In Ireland, poetic truth tends to take precedence over historical fact because the benefits of poetry can be more widely distributed in time and space.)

Historically, Geároid was Geároid Mac Geárailt, the second Earl of Desmond, son of the first earl, Muiris, and born in 1338, who died (or disappeared) in 1398. His thirty poems in Irish are much concerned with Finn, Diarmaid, and Gráinne – appropriate subjects for a man who came to emulate Lugh's and Finn's roles at Lough Gur in joining the world of people to that of the gods.

Geároid, son of an invader, a foreigner, was taken to the heart of the Lough Gur myth cycle and installed there by local people as "an enchanted magician, a periodic rider, a lost leader whose return is awaited, and a feared king of the fairy host." "I am the son of the King of the Norman fairies and my name is Geároid Iarla" was a verse still sung in Co. Limerick in 1879.

Geároid's disappearance into the Lough had also to satisfy the demands of Christian myth. Accordingly, Tom Carroll was told that Geároid was banished under the lake "because he was working witchcraft. He was some kind of evil man." In this way the reunion of demigod with goddess is simultaneously represented as Christian punishment-by-separation.

The nineteenth-century population of Lough Gur attributed Geároid's "drowning" to Áine – the same old woman-knitter who sat under the mid-lough tree. She was out there, watching him.

She could have saved him when he called on her to do so, but she replied: "I'll not come at any rate till I put the needle in the back of the stocking," as knitters do, when coming to the end of a row they lay aside their work. That much delay ruined him, and the enchantment came on him.

Here the knitting needle is the equivalent of Excalibur, safely stowed.

Geároid's life-blade was a shared thing – a sword flung from generation to generation, via periods of immersion within the Lady of the Lake. Old Irish *colg* – "sword," also means "penis" *and* awn, or "grain-sheath of wheat." Thus the language itself urges Geároid to perform the role of a Neolithic vegetation god who must go under, for the sake of the next harvest. Local belief affirms that he lives on Garret Island, *and* beneath the lough in a bright city.

As if to complement his downward plunge, numerous votive offerings of carefully crafted objects were dropped into the lough in prehistoric times. O'Kelly lists 20 bronze axes, 12 bronze spearheads, 2 leaf-shaped swords, a rapier, several daggers, and 120 stone axes. To these Harkness adds "a great quantity of stone disks, about three inches diameter, and beautifully rounded in outline."

These sacrifices are still rewarded by visions of Geároid, reappearing to locals. Tom Carroll recalled:

There was a night's frost about nine years ago [1963]. There was a man skating on the lake. I saw him. He looked like an ordinary man – going up and down, and making all kinds of figures on the lake. There was only about an inch of ice there, it wouldn't hold a bird!

He was a black figure of a man with a cloak on him. A lot of people heard the swishing of him sliding over the lake. They say " 'tis him . . .'When the ice is thin, and on a bright night, you'd see him.

Tommy Hannon recounts how Geároid is

. . . supposed to go on hunts with the cavalcade. He leads them around the lake every midsummer night. It is dangerous to meet them. The oul' Geároid Iarla must be spoken to, to break the spell on him, but he himself can't talk till then. He gets very cross when not spoken to.

Midsummer night matches Áine's appearance at Cnoc Áine, and the belief recorded in 1839 by the folklorist Lady Chatterton that at the end of every *seven years* Geároid may be seen riding on the lake, mounted on an enchanted charger, fits the Lough Gur "World Tree" cycle.

THE GOOSE AND THE HOUSEKEEPER

In 1985 Lough Gur was declared a wild-fowl sanctuary and geese are now nesting in numbers on Garret Island. Among them is Geároid Iarla, the male spirit of the lake, one of whose folk titles is *Gé an Oileáin,* the Goose of the Island.

He had been transformed into a goose following the leaping match with Áine, held in the castle at Knockainey. Fitzgerald records the local belief:

He walked from the hall, his father and others followed him. He walked out onto the brink of the Camo'g [river], which almost washed the base of the castle, and they saw him step from the bank on the water. When he touched the water he was transformed into a goose, and in that form away he swam before their eyes.

Geároid's goosiness was applied to the Fitzgerald family as a whole; they were said to have webbed feet, and a song from Co. Waterford refers to "Gentle Áine Fitzgerald, close relative of a swan."

The right and left wing bones of a black and white barnacle goose were found beneath the floor of a Neolithic house on Knockadoon, and they may have been a foundation burial in honor of a bird whose annual migrations mysteriously seemed to join known to unknown worlds. The goose was a demi-god on the wing.

The otherworldly quality of all the geese on Lough Gur was appreciated by Tom Carroll as a continuing reality, in 1963:

Myself and Willy, we went in there to Charlie Hayes', one night, in there at Carraigin. Dinny Hayes was with us. He got in dread, you see. About 12 o'clock at night the geese came on down the lake, and they came right into us. Into the shade, you see, in the middle of the night. And we thought, you see, we were goin' to kill what was there of 'em. We fired 4 or 5 shots . . . I don't know . . . 6 shots at 'em. And we had a good dog, and he went out to 'em. There wasn't a stir at all after we firin'. I thought we had all the geese, the 20 geese killed. And the dog turned back in, and he started shakin' and cryin', and screechin', and the turned back in under my legs. We thought the hill was movin' away, and the next thing was the geese rose up out of the lake, like a flock of children . . . and they started laughin' at us like. But we got a woeful fright, didn't we?

The next night away we went again, and we went that night after them. And the geese came again at us and we fired again at them. And we saw a child, as we thought, or a young fellow, lifting his hand up and hitting the dog down on the head. And he turned then and left us.

The third night we went, and we went the third night, and the wind was gone this way. Comin' down from the east, you see. And they'd more of a shade, just inside here. And the gate opened inside there. Well, a man walked in the passage, with a pair of nail boots on him, and he was up against me. And I couldn't see him nor neither could Willy. Nor the geese took no notice of him. 'Twas as bright as 'tis now, with the moon.

RIGHT *Sword and sun. Irish Colg, "sword," also means "penis." Rock carvings at Östergötland, Sweden, c.1500 B.C.E.*

LEFT *Riverside swans, Co. Clare. In Irish legends, goddesses and people frequently exchange their human forms for bird shapes.*

Before dawn breaks, a goose wakes on Garret Island, opening an eye on the future. As the lough begins to polish its grayness, the bird slips into the water. With a rhythmic clatter, he pounds down the western reaches to rise and to swim in air. Secure in his new element he begins a slow circuit around the perimeter of the lough. The Knockfennel racecourse, the Red Cellar Cave, and the Money Hole pass in turn beneath him. On he flies, over the Tír Na n'Óg cave, and the Housekeeper's Chair. Beyond Ash point he goes, over the Giants' Grave, and St. Patrick's Well, to the place on the riverbank where the old earl raped Áine. From there, flying in a great arc over Cnoc Áine, he banks steeply and heads north again, to see the Red Bog and Black Sow's Bed gradually define in all their splendid detail. Down he glides over Cleadh na Leac, and with

ABOVE *Ballysodare Bay, Co. Sligo, homeland of W. B.Yeats, d. 1939, who gave new life to the sacred poetic tradition:"... a barnacle goose far up in the stretches of the night; night splits and the dawn breaks loose; I, through the terrible novelty of light, stalk on, stalk on."*

legs jutting, fizzles into the shallows of the still lough near Cloch a bhile and the Lios shore.

Then, the Goose of the Island witnesses Knockadoon float free from an eiderdown of mist, to become the embodiment of *ain*, and *aine* – words that in Irish and Scottish Gaelic still mean: "beauty, splendor, gladness, delight, reeds and rushes, oil, butter, music, harmony, heat, light, wisdom, knowledge, peace, and praiseworthiness."

Enthroned as the Housekeeper of these things and qualities, the goddess Áine was open to worship. She appeared when the ego subsided, allowing the freed spirit to enter the open house of two worlds. Then she was seen at her loughside, supervising the comings and goings of the generations, in myriad life-forms. In her role as protectress of the fetus and receiver of the corpse, she was the *bean tighe* and *bean síd* (banshee) in accordance with a natural order, supernaturally created out of chaos.

Today, a solitary goose skims across the water and perches on Suideachan, an empty lump of rock. He regards the spreading radiance of morning, stretches his neck toward the sun as it rises over Knockadoon, and barks to an elusive mate.

LEFT *Cathedral and graveyard cross, Kilfenora, Co. Clare. As at Lough Gur, the horseman tugs at a "cloak," but here he reveals Christ hanging on the world tree, surrounded by the magic birds of the Irish Otherworld.*

MUNSTER 3

from Lough to Province

The effect of a sacred center is not complete until it has driven the pilgrim away. Just as Otherworld voyagers eventually yearned to leave the magic island they had tried hard to find, so every satiated pilgrim is eventually happy to disperse the intensity of their experience along the ordinary roads that lead from it. Yet it must be admitted, that wherever one travels in the province the sacred is usually close at hand, since the entire Munster landscape retains something of its archaic sanctity.

A stream of sacramental invention keeps the land numinous in the present tense. By means of current activity the great resources of a divine past are tapped afresh, for though religious perspectives may differ, the sense of the sacred remains indivisible. Thus a prayer said for Mary breathes fresh life into the entire panoply of Irish deities, and the sign of the cross simultaneously hands tomorrow's dawn to the old sunwheel.

In Munster one is reminded that in Old and Middle Irish, there was no word "superstition." Whether embraced or not, *all* matters of belief were treated seriously. This attitude has often been characterized by foreigners as an abdication of judgment. Equally, it may be read as a declaration that every religious impulse keeps the entire issue of the Sacred alive as an idea — an idea that evades containment by sectarianism; for like water, once raised from the rock, the Sacred will run down the valleys of earlier long-lost habits, to confound the bigot and reunite the community with the ancestral spirits. For this reason Munster's world-renouncing Christianity goes to the land to affirm its truths, seeking out those very locations most beloved by other gods. Consequently an often unspoken reconciliation is achieved, below the level of dogmatic particulars, where the body of the land opens to all.

PAPS OF ANU, CO. KERRY

Áine-Anu held sway throughout Munster. Finn went into the mountain paps to sleep with her younger self, Créide. The poem says: "The couple slept in bed-espousal prepared by willing hands; and they spent seven days there, drinking and making merry." But Finn's attitude to the visit is ambiguous: "It has been fated for me to go there . . . to spend four days in trouble," adding ominously, "Wounded men, spouting heavy blood would sleep to the musical fairy birds singing above the eaves of her bright bower." On balance, Finn believes, he will have a good time: "It will be pleasant for me in her mansion, both in regard to bedding and beddown."

On the East Pap summit stands a 20-foot (6-meter)-high mound, with a large cairn on top. The mound is believed to be prehistoric, and a likely *síd* entrance. The West Pap also has a mound and cairn, with a visible chamber entrance. Between the two stand the threatening rocks known as Fiacla The Teeth. Finn sat down between the Paps on Halloween night

and they opened, and he saw a great fire in each, and he heard a voice from one of them which said. "Is your sweet food good?" "Good indeed" said a voice in the other fairy-knoll. "A question. Shall anything be

LEFT *Swan at Dungory castle, Kinvarra.*

taken from us to you?" "If that be given to us, something shall be given to you in return." Finn saw a man coming out of the knoll. A kneading trough was in his hand, with a slainsi pig upon it, and a cooked calf, and a bunch of wild garlic upon it; and as the men came past Finn to reach the other knoll, Finn made a cast with his spear, but did not know the outcome, till he heard a wailing and a chanting from the knoll.

The man carrying the pig was the Lord of the Otherworld Feast, in his typical guise as swineherd.

THE HARPS OF CLIU, CO. TIPPERARY

Fifteen near-parallel watercourses are gouged into the north face of the Galtee Mountains. "Here a man of the fairies made music, Cliach of the harp sweet sounding," according to the *Metrical Dindshenchas*. He played to King Black Marrow (Smir–Dubh), till "a loathly dragon that dwells in this place seized the harper."

This is a late variant on a myth where the Dagda comes from the *síd* to harp the seasons into being. His "finger breezes" play across the gulley "strings."

The five gulleys of the eastern instrument meet in a coomb called "Lyre" – meaning Fork (as one might expect of the Dagda) – separated by Glenageehy (Windy Glen) from a western harp of ten channels. The Harps

RIGHT *The stone heart of Latiaran, Cullen, Co. Cork, 4 feet (1.3 meters) Beneath this spot, the fire-carrying goddess Latiaran entered the ground at Lughnasa.*

epitomize the spirit of Munster as the province of poetry, music, and song – her natural and supernatural endowment.

LATIARAN'S HEART, CULLEN, CO. CORK

At the start of harvest it was customary for women in Cullen to curtsey to a heart-shaped boulder on the village green. It marks the spot where Latiaran, the youngest of three sister-goddesses, disappeared. A smith praised her feet as she was carrying hot embers in her apron. His remark broke her concentration, and so the embers burned through her apron. Crying out that no smith should ever again work in Cullen, she sank into the ground, to reemerge at the round well, a hundred paces away, below the modern graveyard.

In its present form, the myth shows Christian influence overlaying the conflict between the Stone Age population and Iron Age invaders, and the celebration by all of the start of harvest. Latiaran's Day is a Sunday in late July, when the Feis or festival of Latiaran, of traditional Irish song and dance, is still held. Today, the boulder remains as an abiding symbol of harvests to come, a gift to those who harvest the crops from the heart of earth.

LEFT *Roadside shrine, erected 1982, at Rath Luire, Co. Cork.*

LEINSTER

Leinster approaches

The eastern province Leinster, or Laigin, as it used to be called, faces the sunrise. Bursting with energy and confidence, the courts of Leinster's kings have sometimes aspired to national control – a pattern successfully followed by Leinster's and Ireland's greatest city, Dublin.

The Irish word for east, *oithear*, is filled with sunrise meanings, such as "beginning, forepart, future, and day to come" and "a day in the east," as well as "the façade or front of a house"; and the leading edge of the land is known as *oithir* – "the coast." Another form, Old Irish *air* – "east," leads to *airech* – "first," and *airechus* – "supremacy." The east, then, was called the chief or principal place, and the quarter from which the others were reckoned; hence *airtherach* is the perceiving intelligence, "the front part of the head." Head, home, sun, shore, time, and space came together in Irish "east" words, which were lit from within by the divine eye.

The *Laigin* is the old name for Leinster's inhabitants, and in popular etymology derives from *láigen*, "a spear," and so puts dawning sunbeams into the hands of warriors. The myth tells how they, like the rising sun, came across the sea from darkness, to conquer night's black territory, and were transformed as they advanced, with the broad blades of their spears taking on the deep-blue, green, gold, and silver hues of daytime experience. Laigin myths dramatize eastern-ness and incorporate dim memories of migrations to Ireland from that quarter. T. F. O'Rahilly cites movement of Celtic people from Brittany to Leinster in 300 B.C.E. as feeding extra material into a body of migration myth that also refers to settlement of Leinster from Britain. These intermingled memories and oral traditions, accumulated throughout Irish prehistory, are centered upon the desire to identify an ancestor-deity from the east. Early Laigin literature is "obsessed" with that issue, says R. O'hUiginn.

"When we *mean* and don't just *say* words," wrote L. Wittgenstein, "it seems to us as if there were something coupled to them." In Laigin that "something" is an ancestral god of sunrise, and his army of demigods, pointing their spears at the province of eastern opportunity. (The spear, transferred to civic hands, was thrown annually into the sea by the Lord Mayor of Dublin, to mark the limit of his jurisdiction.) Arriving out of night, sometimes they called themselves the Black Foreigners, or *Dubh Gael*; 2,200 strong, they carried their lances over the sea from the Continent. They were led by Labraid Loingsech, meaning literally the Speaker-Mariner, or Sea Rover.

OPPOSITE *Dublin Custom House, completed 1791. Many waves of invaders have landed on Ireland's east coast each bringing stories of deities in their boats.*

BELOW *Labraid Loingsech, or "Speaker Mariner," was a horse-eared sun-god, arriving from the east in a horse-headed sun-boat. Rock carving, Östfold, Sweden c. 1000 B.C.E. (top). Bronze Age engraved sun-boats, Östergötland, Sweden (bottom).*

Leinster myth may be said to begin with the first word that this Speaker-Mariner uttered. His founding proclamation created a province later renowned for its agricultural prosperity, for he spoke his grandfather's name, Ugaine. To the virgin forests of Leinster, he probably brought Ugaine's knowledge of farming, which undoubtedly *did* come to Ireland from the Eurasian continents lying to the east. Ugaine may well be a corruption of *ugaim*, "plow traces"; and of "horse harness," or "harnessing" – *ugmaim*.

Descriptions of the Speaker-Mariner emphasize his solar, superhuman quality. He is "Gold, brighter than the sun . . . he slew kings . . . he overcame men and gods" (says a sixth-century panegyric), and was himself a god – son of Áine, the goddess whom we have met in Munster. He was also known as Moen, from the word *moen*, "mountain," miniaturized as *moin*, "a heap of sods, or turf." "The one god is Moen, cried the poet, as Labraid came to earth, and was identified with a symbolic heap of Leinster soil, so founding the province.

But rather than simply exchanging a solar for an earthly habit, archeological evidence implies that the king-god of the province brought the two aspects together in a fire-mountain ritual, dating back to the third millennium B.C.E., nearly two thousand years *before* the Celts arrived, and confirmed in later literary accounts, which suggest that each new king of

Leinster burned his predecessor to death. Moen himself (despite being the *first* king!) is said to have avenged his father's "murder" by burning King Cobthach ("Whirlwind") at Dind Rig, on the southern border of Leinster.

On a rough night crossing by ferry boat from Anglesey, it can seem as if Ireland will never come. One suspects that she has quietly slipped moorings, and headed off into mid-Ocean, determined to retain her status as an elusive Otherworld when approached from Britain or the European continent.

She is "the high ship Ériu, Ériu lofty, very green" referred to in poems attributed to Amergin of the Sons of Míl, c. 500 B.C.E., in which Ireland is also called "the mighty lady Ériu."

> I seek the land of Ireland,
>
> Coursed be the fruitful sea,
>
> Fruitful the ranked highland,
>
> Ranked the showery wood,
>
> Showery the river of cataracts,
>
> Of cataracts the lake of pools,
>
> Of pools the hill of a well,
>
> Of a well of a people of assemblies . . .

The most important sacred ship, coming to Ireland from the east, was the sun boat. It carried the sun, led the sun, and was synonymous with the sun. It was carved on the wall of the west recess of the New Grange monument, facing the northern border of Leinster, c. 3100 B.C.E. The idea remained popular in Bronze Age Scandinavia, from where so many cultural influences continued to flow westward into Ireland.

The famous gold ship, made around the first century C.E., and buried one mile from the eastern shore of Loch Foyle, shows the continuation of the cult. A gold boat hook, mast-yard, steering oar, a miniature grappling iron, and two oars were found with the boat in 1892. Other parts of its riggings were sold to a jeweler and lost. Did he also purchase a crew of gods?

The sacred boat moved easily from sea to land; Borlase believed that most prehistoric Irish burial chambers were intended to represent ships, with the dead being conveyed across the Otherworld ocean. The physical ocean flooded people's imagination.

The religion in which Ireland now sails – that of St. Columba – has perpetuated the ship symbolism. Christ is viewed by the congregation from the nave (Latin *navis*), so called because it represented the ark, or ship, of the Church. Incense was held in a navicula, later called an incense *boat*, whose function is to erect a sail of perfume from the world ocean to the deity above the crow's nest.

LANDING

Dawn, and the night ferry approaches its destination. On the port side are the fanciful silhouettes of the Wicklow Mountains, and to starboard, the peninsula of Howth Head, with Lambay Island beyond.

A cheer goes up, and smiles are exchanged between total strangers. Returning migrants pass the names of their counties and small towns around, like cigarettes, to be briefly inhaled by others – so many destinations, lying beyond Dublin Bay, with tables set for homecomings.

Then, from somewhere astern, a fat new sun pulls itself above the horizon and rolls a red carpet across the waves, inviting us shoreward, as we pass between the now *pink* lobster claws of Howth Head and Bray Head, toward a Dun Laoghaire anchorage.

Beneath wheeling sea birds, and tiers of blue mountains, poke church steeples. Villas display their pilasters and cornices amid voluptuous gardens, which run down to eau-de-Nil and apricot terraces, lining the palm-fringed esplanades. Everything is agleam in the scintillating air.

At the Bay's center two red and white spears, or *láigen*, rear skyward, the chimneys of the power station beyond Ringsend. As if suspended by invisible ribbons from these poles, the entire panorama combines in one of the great urban dances of the world. A multinational babble of sound goes down the gangplank, passes through a perfunctory customs check, and along the Leinster shore.

PART THREE

LEINSTER 2

Dublin, the real dream

The incoming tide of tourist voices merges with the world language devised by James Joyce. He reclaimed Dublin on behalf of myth. After piratical raids on many languages, he brought to his native shore the intermingled treasures of a verbal ocean, thereby restoring the province to the state of Total Life that it had enjoyed in antiquity. Together with Yeats and other Leinster poets of our century, he worked toward a new day in timelessness, called modernism.

Unlike the nineteenth-century Romantic taste for ruins (remote in time and space), modernism and the archaic concur in their shared fondness for an eternal now, an ever-new light of "East."

During the last hundred years writers from Leinster have led the country and perhaps the world in "attempting to raise the archaic sacredness of language itself from below the horizon of consciousness to an *Autem generatio* of all the gods and their works," according to Davenport. Their hope was to turn the explicitly Christian words: "In the beginning was the word, and the word was with God and the word *was* God," into an affirmation applying to every divinity ever known, with new forms of the divine being continually reborn on the human tongue. Leinster was the setting for a project of total re-creation.

This enormous task suited Irish and Anglo-Irish writers, since of all Europeans they had inherited from antiquity a peculiarly primitive concreteness of expression and imagery, largely undisturbed by theoretical Greek thinking. Recently orphaned by the death of the Irish language, Leinster writers brought their collective habits of mind to bear on the emergent International Modern Movement that, according to B.R. Gluck, sought to "give back to language its prelogical functions," and "set the imagination in search of

a fabulous word." The writer Patrick Kavanagh maintained that there were never less than 10,000 poets living in Ireland. Many of them converged on Dublin.

Joyce carried with him the belief that "all language originated from the human effort to arrive at the meaning of the divine thunderclap." In his *Finnegans Wake*, the rumble reverberates above and below Dublin, like all the deities in the world speaking together. They talk of "multiple stratifications reaching back millions of years . . . related to the entire history of mankind, past and present, and brought to the surface with the hallucinatory eruption of images in the dream, the day dream, the mystic-gnostic trance, and even the psychiatric condition."

But Joyce's endowment to Leinster only yields its full dividend if it stimulates readers to recreate the "province-as-cosmos" in their own terms. (The labor of digesting *Finnegans Wake* is nothing, compared to the tasks that it invites us to undertake.) Alas, there are no free rides to mythic Ireland, the passive paradise isle vanishes as soon as it is touched. To find it again, one has to walk, and in a mood of informed innocence, toward *Magh Mhór*, the primary plane of being. But at least Joyce shows that such a Great Plain still exists, and exists in contact with the mundane world. He habitually used the pun as a bridge between the two

LEFT *Ha'penny Bridge, Dublin. Dublin is a robust, imaginative construct, suspended between the elements, where words and images contend with their opposites, and change in the process.*

states, old and new, so that in a word or phrase, "a
street full of traffic is also a panorama of prehistoric
places and animals."

To a peculiar degree, Joyce the novelist invites
each new reader to collaborate in remaking his novel,
and the city – a process unimpaired by the physical
demolition of many of the buildings he describes.
Rather than imposing a set of architectural preservation orders, his legacy to Dublin was a self-renewing
mythic methodology.

He advocated myth-making using whatever materials and circumstances came to hand. *Any* Dublin
could have served his pattern-making from cross-
references, as the life-work for every generation.

Should the tunnel vision of road engineers, or
some other self-isolating system-builder dissect the
city, the task would be the same; namely to draw this
new material, however intractable, into a wider
network of relationships.

But even for a man of Joyce's energy, the perfecting
of the method within a literary framework took a lifetime. From the picaresque descriptions of *Dubliners*
(1904), through the transposed heroic saga of *Ulysses*, it
was not until *Finnegan* woke in 1939 that a new myth
arose. With that work he touched the heart of an a-his-
torical "All-life," lying beyond the clutch of chronology.

LIFFEY RIVER

The most permanent thing in Dublin changes all the
time – the Liffey River. Its self-purifying motion
became for the author of *Finnegans Wake* a symbol for
the regeneration of the spirit as a cyclic female
process. The river begins and ends his last novel,
written between 1921 and 1939.

He envisages the river as she – Anna Livia
Plurabelle, incorporating the Irish Magna Mater, Ana,
or Anu, coupled with Life and Liffey (Livia), but as a
goddess of a thousand names (Plurabelle). This com-
posite being runs through Dublin into Dublin Bay to
meet the sun-god hero, Finn, whose head he identifies
with the Howth promontory. The novel begins in
mid-sentence stream: "river run, past Eve and Adam's

RIGHT *Map of Dublin.*
A Beltaine sunrise
—Samain sunset line,
drawn annually across
modern Dublin, joins
the deities of summer,
living on Howth Head,
to the dark forces of
winter, gathered in the
mythic bruiden of
Bohernabreena.

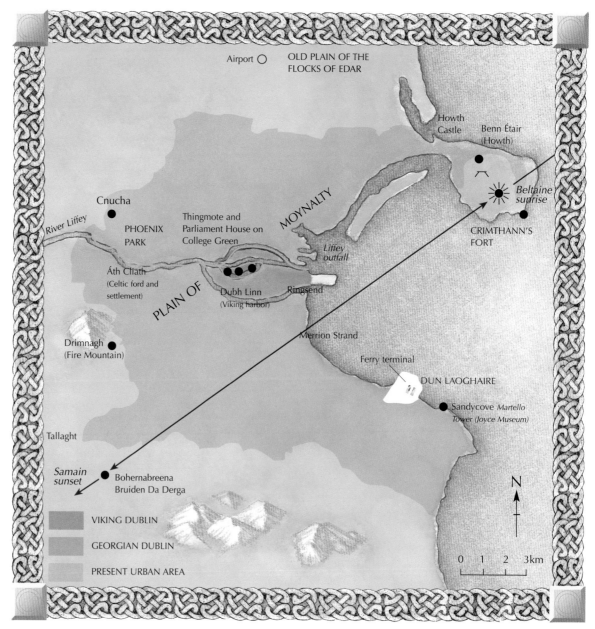

from swerve of shore to bend of bay, brings us by a commodius vicus of recirculation back to Howth Castle and Environs." It ends, six hundred and twenty-five pages later, with Anna Livia slipping Finn, her lover, in again, as she enters the bay at Ringsend.

So soft this morning ours. Yes. Carry me along, taddy, like you done through the toy fair! If I seen him bearing down on me now under whitespread wings like he'd come from Arkangels, I sink I'd die down over his feet, humbly dumbly, only to washup. Yes, tid. There's where. First. We pass through grass behush the

bush to. Whish! A gull. Gulls. Far calls. Coming, far! End here. Us, then. Finn, again! Take. Bussofthee, mememormee! Till thousendsthee. Lps. The keys to. Given! A way a lone a last a loved a long the...

And so back to the first word in the book. Three years after Joyce had begun his great work, the poet Yeats wrote: "Our 'natural magic' is but the ancient religion of the world, the ancient worship of nature and that troubled ecstasy before her, that certainty of all beautiful places being haunted, which it brought into men's minds." He referred to: "Men who lived in a

world where anything might flow and change, and become any other thing; and among great gods whose passions were in the flaming sunset, and in the thunder and the thunder show."

Joyce found urban existence equally dramatic, and showed that we need not choose between two worlds, since the imagination can turn them into one. In his work, "the end product is always fusion, rather than fragmentation." Everything comes together in the river.

HILL OF HOWTH (BENN ÉTAIR)

Of the Hill of Howth, overlooking Dublin Bay, the mariner St. Columba wrote:

> *Delightful to be on the Hill of Howth,*
> *After coming over the wide-bosomed sea;*
> *To be rowing one's little coracle,*
> *Ochone! on the wild-waved shore.*

The Gaelic name of Howth is Benn Étair, named after the mythical hero whose cliff head confronted the ocean and protected Ireland from attack. With a view

ABOVE *The Hill of Howth overlooks Dublin Bay. Its sea cliffs are named after Étair, the demigod who protected Leinster from attack.*

over comings and goings, Étair (or Étar) was *alive*, a living supernatural being, as the *Dindshenchas* makes clear: "Étar forehead to the flood . . . the gray sea roars against his shoulder."

The word *etar* means "great." As the living headland, Étar of Benn Étair looks east, with the Dublin rivers Dodder and Liffey, or Ruirthech, to his south:

> *His right shoulder fronts the Dothra (Dodder)*
> *the Ruirtech dashes wildly against his side,*
> *onset of the flood-tide, wave of the ebb,*
> *furious are the seas against the shore.*

This defensive stance is revised in the prose version, which makes Étar the son-in-law of Manannán, the sea god, by marriage to Áine, said to be Manannán's daughter. Land, water, and sun thus are brought into family relationship at a critical point. As a wedding ring, Étar's wife "puts a golden chain about him, [so that] the sea should not drown him while he wore it, nor should sharp spear points pierce him." Sunlight on the surf makes this ring around the head, to the narrow land neck on both sides.

The completed union dissolves the sexual divide, and Étar then becomes an androgyne, able to appear as female. "She" is "Étar softly-bright, splendid and stately, of the royal harbor." (George IV built massive harbor walls on the north side of the headland, in the early nineteenth century, hoping to make it the Holyhead terminus, but it silted up and is now used only by shallow-draft coastal vessels.) The text implies Étar was a primordial if not prehuman figure, who introduced the act of dying of grief for one's husband.

By way of balance, the male Étar was said to have died for love of Áine, "and his grave was dug on yonder peak," again, at Howth. At Howth, the front door of Ireland, and its point of morning arousal into consciousness, the myth-makers established that the task was not merely the *reconciliation* of opposites, but their complete integration in androgyny. In many religions the androgyne is an image of wholeness and of an original state of being. Howth shares in that international perception, through the dual sexuality of Étar.

Over Howth, Boeings glide down to land at Dublin Airport. From Manchester, Amsterdam, Rome, and Athens, flocks of planes descend on *Mag n'Elta Edar*, "The Old Plain of the Flocks of Edar." This was "the first plain in Ireland," says *Lebor Gabála*. On it, "birds settled to sun themselves, for never did branch or twig of a wood grow through it."

DUBLIN'S MYTHIC FOUNDATIONS

Not until the late ninth century C.E. did invading Vikings establish Ireland's first urban settlements. Of them all, Dublin, facing Britain and Europe, prospered most and was made the chief city by the Anglo-Normans, who followed them ashore. If, as Rose asserts, Irish "east" comes from *airech*, "first," Dublin has obliged by growing to urban preeminence.

The founding of a Viking town or city was essentially a mythic affair; at the outset humanity sought the advice and approval of the gods for the new enterprise.

College Green is considered to be the center of modern Dublin. There, where today's Church Lane and Suffolk Street meet, the Vikings constructed their *thingmote*. It was an artificial conical hill, 40 feet (12 meters) high, made as a place of assembly and justice, with a seat on top for the king, above tiers for his sons; and noblemen, according to rank. Standing stones and carved stone balls placed on the summit connected these Viking monuments to the cult of the earth goddess, in whose soil previous kings were interred below the summit, as at Uppsala, in Viking Sweden. Wherever they traveled, the Vikings took with them a belief in the divine ancestry of kings. Dublin's Thingmote, which survived into the seventeenth century, as Speed's map shows, was nothing less than a creation mound, combining the tomb of the traditional order with the womb of a new reality. Around it were constructed other burial mounds, between which the population practiced archery and throwing games, in imitation of the wars between the pantheons of Aesir and Vanir – which reproduced the Irish Sons of Míl versus Tuatha Dé Danann encounter, by other names. In both cases the weapons included sunbeams, thunderbolts, and flint arrowheads. (Neolithic flint arrowheads, regarded as "fairy darts," were *the* prototypical missiles, and in nineteenth-century Ireland and Norway they continued to be revered.)

The Dublin Thingmote, or Haugen, was leveled in 1682. Shortly afterward, a new world mountain arose close-by, in the form of the coffered dome of the Irish Parliament House begun in 1728. This was modeled on Hadrian's Pantheon, erected in Rome in 126 C.E., as a temple for all the gods, dedicated to the planets, and intended as a simulacrum of the universe.

LEFT *Statue of Hibernia, topping the Bank of Ireland, College Green, Dublin. The Irish Repbublic's economy is currently growing faster than that of any other European country.*

THE MISSING AUGUR

ABOVE Phoenix Park, Dublin, where town and country meet.

INSET The Templum of the Sky. Sixth century C.E. Quartering of the sky and earth together was achieved by the augur-priest, addressing trees at the cardinal points, in a city-founding ritual.

The future of Irish mythology increasingly depends on Dublin. More than a million people now live in its conurbation, compared with 1.8 million for Leinster as a whole, and 3.5 millions for the entire Republic. Late twentieth-century urbanism, a worldwide phenomenon, has transformed Ireland from a largely rural to a city-orientated country.

Two fifths of Eire's people now dwell in her capital city and are searching for new roots beneath sidewalks, where most of the pipes and cables run horizontally, rather than up and down. Without roots, the city may prove more ephemeral than the gathering of tents at the old *oenachs*, since *they*, like annual flowers, grew from fresh seed every year. By contrast, a city, claiming to be *perennial*, needs to find purchase in the subsoil, as the founders of cities in antiquity knew.

It can be said without exaggeration that the future of Dublin, as of modern urbanism everywhere, depends on some form of mythic reengagement, if a drift toward psycho-physical triviality is not to end in disaster. This is the very issue that, one way or another, will be resolved in the city, on behalf of the province and the country.

The founding of a Roman city required the services of a priest-surveyor, known as an augur. In him, "practical" and "sacred" coalesced from the outset. His first task was to ask the gods for guidance in choosing a propitious site. An important aspect of his prayers was careful observation of natural phenomena in the district – the flight of birds, the movement of stray animals, thunder, and the motion of clouds. Then the liver of a sacrificed ox was examined for portents.

Had a Roman augur ever stood on the Old Plain of Etar, in 100 C.E., among the mythic flocks and herds of creatures sunning themselves, he might well have decided to mark out the site for modern Dublin precisely where it now is – across this primal fruitful plain – on the grounds that humanity should follow the instincts of other species. By sheer chance and good fortune, without the assistance of an augur, the sprawl of modern city of Dublin represents and recapitulates a zoological creation legend. If farmyard, wilderness, and zoo have mainly negative connotations for today's urban sophisticate, Dublin's location nonetheless suggests a reconnection of jumbo jet with bird, car with horse power, and Phoenix Park (the largest urban park of any European city) with the original field of praise.

According to Varro, a Roman writer born 116 B.C.E., the augur stood at the center of the proposed city site, holding his curved wand, and scratched around him on the ground a diagram called *The Templum* (from Greek *temenos*, "sacred enclosure"). The design was always a cross within a circle. The direction of the augur's eyes followed his gestures, and by viewing the proposed town site together with the country beyond, he contemplated it, and "united the four quadrants or templa into one great templum by sight and gesture," which simultaneously "marked out the space in the heavens" into quadrants. Livy says that the first stroke was engraved toward the east, while Varro makes clear that this was a qualitative process, "*contueor*," involving "mature pondering, caring, and guardianship." The eyes, and "the vision of the heart," *cortumio*, were engaged together. This primary measuring was an act of devotion, acknowledging every aspect of the *genius loci*, or spirit of place.

The templum symbolized the integration of sky, earth, and underworld. Prosperity on the land-surface depended on a collaboration that also revealed the sky over the future city to be the temple of Jove. (In Dublin, "Jove's" domain had in deed, but not in thought, been brought to land, in the dome of the Parliament House.)

Then the four divisions of the templum (divided and reunited) were transferred to the proposed street pattern of the city. The main east–west route, the *decumanus*, crossed the chief north–south future thoroughfare, called *cardo maximus*, in an enlarged version of the templum, whose outer circle became the *sulcus primigenius*, or "first furrow," cut along the foundation line of the city walls. For this, a white male ox and a white cow were yoked to a bronze plow. Once again, links with nonurban ways are emphasized. City-making is regarded as a special kind of agriculture, an urban field, visualized as an intensification of the natural order, rather than its betrayal, and deliberately placed "at the intersection of the coordinate axes of the universe."

The templum ritual secured the union of sky, land, and underworld. The drawing was accompanied by the correct verbal formulas, which, in the city of Rome, ran: "Temple and wild lands be mine in this manner, up to where I have named them with my tongue in proper fashion."

Existing trees were invoked, one on each quarter, around the augur at the center of the pattern. The trees were a reminder of the primeval wilderness, denoters of chief quarters, and the vertical links between sky, earth, and underworld.

The augur's anxiety concerning the correct form of words arose because the templum was bounded by the words of incantation, by *verba concepta*, which drew a magical net around the landmarks that he named. It was this naming that actually fixed the boundaries of the city. By word and gesture, the priest hoped to "open up" the normal passage of time to allow the *primal* time of the deity or mythic ancestor (the time of perpetual Beginning) to slip into the urban foundations, so ensuring that the future city would enjoy divine favor.

MUNDUS AND BYZANTIUM

At or near the spot where the augur stood, a pit was dug, called the *mundus*. Into it were cast "first fruits" and "good things," along with earth from the settlers' home country. Conversely, some of the virgin earth *from* the hole would be taken for incorporation into homes to be built along the new streets. The cavity was consecrated to the infernal deities called the *Manes*, meaning The Good Ones. Their stone, the *lapis manalis*, was laid on top. It was regarded as a gate to the underworld, and was drawn back at seasonal festivals both to allow extra gifts to be deposited and to enable the hidden deities periodically to reenter the city from below.

Regarded as the navel or umbilicus of the city, the Roman *mundus* can be compared with the national navel stone of preurban Ireland that was set up at Uisnech in Mide.

Essentially the same idea – that urbanism cannot long be sustained without a recognition of the hidden core (or *síd*) values on which it is based – has returned to haunt the late twentieth century. But one of our difficulties concerns how to fit a Joycean language of mythic expression within a largely technical frame of reference. In the last thirty years, the Dublin solution (as with other cities) has been to ignore the problem. The city engineers and the poets have been working in different departments.

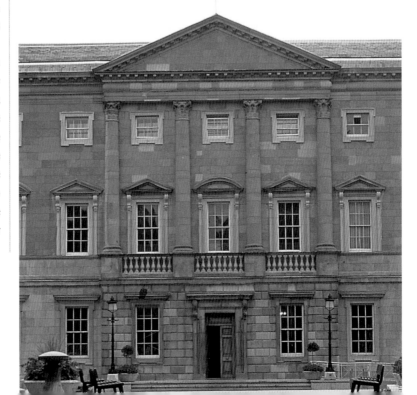

BELOW *Leinster House, Dublin; built 1745 in the classical style, now houses the Irish Republic's* Dail, *or parliament.*

For the ancient classical city, *mundus* digging and ritual filling constituted the birth act. Only then did the settlement come alive and receive its name, or names. (Normally there were three given; one public, one used by priests, and one never uttered. The secret name of Rome is believed to have been that of an androgynous god of harmony, Amor, and the secret name of Dublin might be borrowed from the androgyne Étar, of nearby Howth.)

The inspired search undertaken by many Dublin writers during the last hundred years for their "city-within-the-sacred" may be seen in every sense as a Classic preoccupation.

Collectively, writers in and around Dublin have constructed the divine city of Indo-European tradition on the banks of the Liffey. Sometimes they have used the method employed by William Blake (who built Jerusalem in industrial England), by consciously turning to Continental exemplars.

Yeats' poem, "Sailing to Byzantium" (1926), written in Dublin, offers Constantinople as a model and infuses Dublin with his dream. He explained that in the eighth century C.E., "Byzantium was the centre of European civilization, and the source of its spiritual philosophy, and I symbolize the search for the spiritual life by a journey to that city . . . There religious, aesthetic, and practical life were one. Architect and artificers spoke to the multitude and the few alike." Artists, he went on, were almost impersonally involved in their subject matter, which was 'the vision of a whole people." Yeats reimagined the coordinates of city planning as "the artifice of eternity," toward which the individual soul might gravitate. Although, as an old man in the new Irish Republic, he felt half-inclined to sail off to Constantinople, the effect of his work was to leave his idea on College Green.

Comings and goings across the Irish Sea, real and imagined, have brought Dublin to life. Joyce chose exile in Paris, in order to create his universal urban language from fragments of foreign speech, mixed with the humus and first fruits of the bilingual Leinster he had fled. He then offered the whole deposit to the city that had inspired his endeavor. So Dublin achieved a long-delayed mythic birth, despite its inclination to distrust the poet-midwife.

Thus "Finn again," as another Leinster sunrising man-god, shines down the unintentional "decumanus" of Nassau Street, across College Green, and westward along Dame Street.

DUBLIN AS MACHINE

Recent pessimism concerning the future of the city tends to represent its problems in technical terms (pollution, congestion), and to advocate "social engineering" regarding crime and drug abuse, without reference to a mythological base, or its absence. Yet this oversight is the problem from which all others flow, for without a mythological structure a city is unlikely to enjoy good health.

In the vacuum, anxiety, alienation, and apathy often replace the communal coordinates of god-given location, and The City, which once brought Nature's sacredness into focus, now exhibits an intensification of the absurd. This predicament is articulated with uncommon power by the Dubliner Samuel Beckett.

Following a walk along the Dun Laoghaire harbor wall on a dark and stormy night, he embarked in his novels and plays, from 1938 to 1985, on a courageous voyage to the dead heart of a city whose patterns lack spiritual purpose. He reopens the *mundus* and finds only a void – or the housing for a machine on the verge of disintegration. In his play *Endgame* (1957), Hamm, the chair-bound master of a dying Iron Age, expresses contempt for ancestral wisdom by setting his parents in trash cans.

The image of City-as-Machine (the rotation of spiritless matter) has its philosophical blueprint in Descartes' dualism and in Newtonian positivist science. Early twentieth-century optimism regarding the mechanical city gained further support with Walter Gropius' rational urbanism (a Cathedral of Reason), and Le Corbusier's designs for La Ville Radieuse.

The need to redesign cities around the automobile added further momentum to the mechanistic tendency. Across the Irish Sea came the influential Buchanan Report (1963), which recommended for Leeds (half the size of Dublin) thirteen radial highways built through the inner suburbs, with six of them eight lanes wide, and a series of highway cross-links varying from four to six lanes wide, and all "free of such obstructions as cross-roads and roundabouts." "Beyond all question there will have to be a great deal of urban road building in British cities," wrote Buchanan, and

LEFT *James Joyce. In his* Ulysses *and* Finnegans Wake, *he created a version of Dublin from river sounds and vernacular speech, combined with a host of other languages and mythic fragments.*

within two decades cities on both sides of the Irish Sea, have been transformed accordingly.

Yet from the outset, Buchanan himself admitted that "We cannot hold out any hope that this . . . vigorous programme of urban road-building . . . will go very far towards solving the problem [since] . . . each new motorway built to cope with existing traffic seems to call into existence new traffic sufficient to create a new congestion." Nevertheless, in Dublin, as in so many other cities, a ruthless highway-building program is now decimating the urban fabric.

But why, if the twentieth-century cult of the wheel is so harmful, are the cults of the Bronze Age gold disk with spokes, or Mug Roth's Leinster wheel, to be preferred? Is not a wheel a wheel in any age? The difference is that the first two were designed to roll *between* categories. They were the vehicles in which the cosmos was delivered. They drove out from the sun and back, enabling free transportation through the poetry of godhead. Consequently they were a civilized enhancement, and *realization* of Nature, rather than a means of its destruction, careering out of control, and turning medieval Dublin into a wasteland. Most of the former inhabitants have been bureaucratically dispersed to low-density new suburbs, "so that they should not talk to one another," as C. Toibin has half-jokingly remarked.

OPPOSITE *Phoenix Park, Dublin. At Cnucha in Phoenix Park, the solar powers of East and West fought. Here Aed ("fire"), demigod of the West, killed Luchet (*luchair, *"bright") of Leinster; but Aed lost an eye in the battle, and so became Goll, "one-eyed."*

ÁTH CLIATH AND ATHERNE

The city of Dublin is named after the *Linn Dubh*, or Black Pool. This was the tide-flooded mouth of the little Poddle River, which debouched into the Liffey River immediately south of the present Dublin Castle. Used by the Vikings as an anchorage from 838 C.E. onward, the pool was eventually drained to become the castle gardens.

Prior to that, Dublin did not exist, but there was a Celtic settlement, a "proto-town" just west of the castle and straggling along the ridge now occupied by High Street and Thomas Street. It overlooked a ford across the Liffey. In the early Middle Ages the river was broad, shallow, and tidal, and subject to flash floods from its mountainous headwaters. The ford, *áth*, was about 985 feet (300 meters) long, and was composed of wattle hurdles, or *cliath*. These made a roadway of rafts, staked to the riverbed, which were weighted down by massive stones. Its precise location has yet to be ascertained.

Áth Cliath Cualann (*Cuailin* meaning "bundle" and *cual* meaning "fagot") was a wholly Irish settlement – an irregular cluster of huts, perhaps bounded by an earthen ditch and bank. The name remained in use till at least 1368, by which time *Baile Áth Cliath* referred to the walled medieval town that had grown on top of the Celtic settlement.

The *Dindshenchas* says that the Leinstermen made the hurdles of wattling for the Áth Cliath ford, at the command of a greatly feared roving poet, Athirne the Importunate, who wanted to drive the sheep that he had rustled in South Leinster across the river to Dun Étair (Howth). Linked in this way to the critical eastern headland, Áth Cliath arrived on the national mythic map, long before it became a city. Athirne's (or Atherne's) walk had been undertaken on behalf of Connor of Ulster, who lived in the first century C.E.; yet the poet's task was essentially a mythological circuit of Ireland.

At his King's command, this "hard, merciless man" went at first left-hand-wise about Ireland [from Ulster] till he made the round of Connacht. Then he went to the King of the midst of Ireland between the two Fords of Hurdles [that is to say between Áth Cliath, and its counterpart in the far west, called Áth

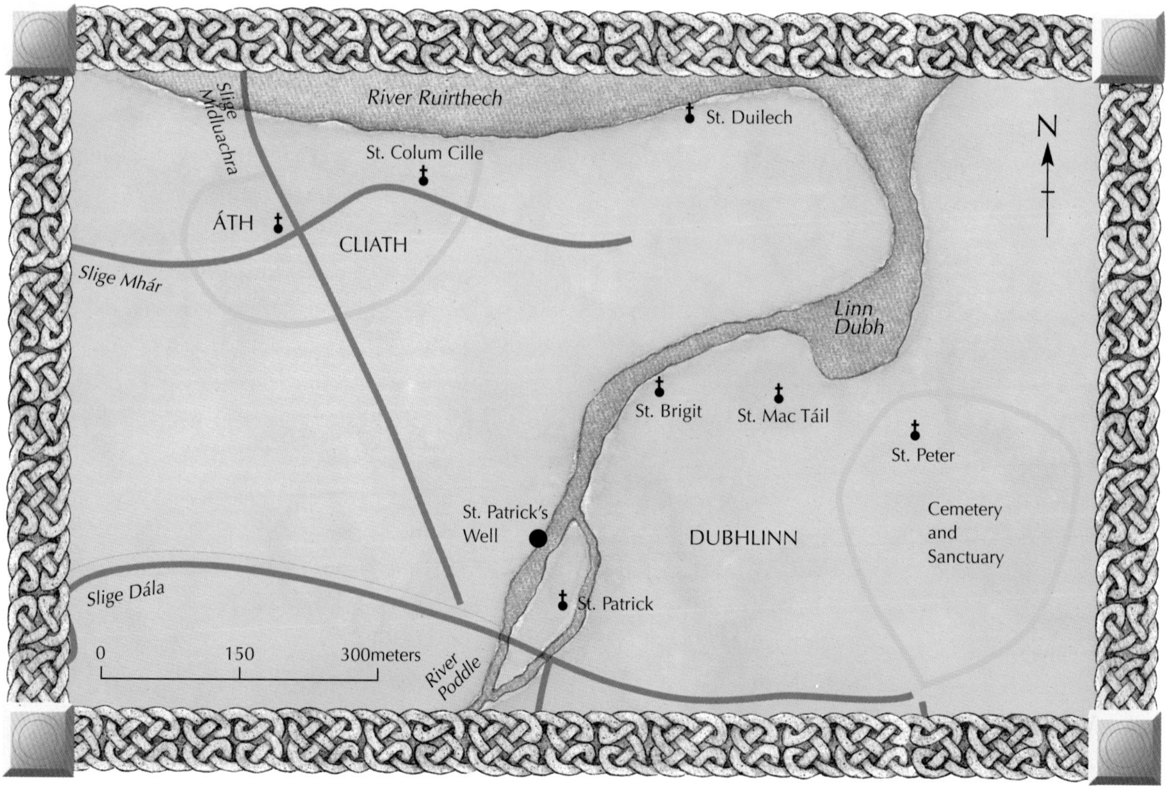
River Ruirthech
Slige Midluachra
St. Duilech
N
St. Colum Cille
ÁTH
CLIATH
Slige Mhár
Linn Dubh
St. Brigit
St. Mac Táil
St. Peter
St. Patrick's Well
DUBHLINN
Cemetery and Sanctuary
Slige Dála
St. Patrick
0
150
300meters
River Poddle

RIGHT *Map of Gaelic and early Viking Dublin. From* Áth Cliath, *"Hurdle Ford," the settlement became* Dubh Linn, *"Black Pool," where the Viking longships moored.*

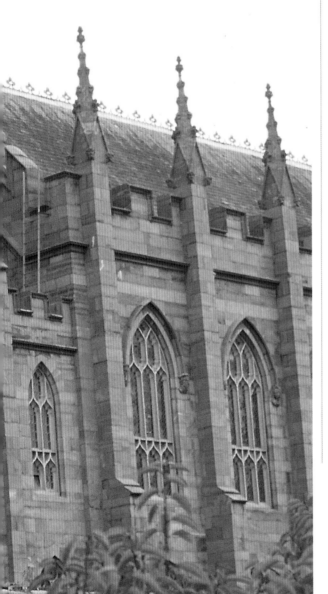

Cliath Medraige]. The King in the middle was Eochaid, who reigned at Lough Dergderc, on the North-South river axis, the Shannon. There Atherne "robbed Eochaid of his eye."

Then he traveled south, into Munster, and demanded to sleep with the queen of the province "or the honor of the men of Munster should be lost forever."

Continuing his round, he moved northward into South Leinster, where he deliberately insulted the population, inciting them to kill him, so that Ulster would gain a pretext for attacking Leinster. He therefore took "thrice fifty queens of the wives of the princes and nobles of Leinster, and drove them across Áth Cliath, along with the sheep and cattle he had stolen, and took them all to the Benn Étair headland." (At the center of a national road and rail network, modern Dublin, which stretches to Howth, makes a comparable sweep of the country.)

Áth Cliath, the pre-Viking proto-Dublin, grew around the zeal of Atherne. His ruthlessness is found in the Old Irish word, *aithe*, "sharpness," and shows a poet's weapon in *aith*, "tongue," and victory in *aithin*, "knowledge." His powers of prognostication, especially regarding the siting of settlements, is also conveyed in *aithin* – "the liver" (much used for divination throughout Indo-European lands). His theft of the

ABOVE *St. Patrick's Day parade, College Green. The March 17th journey of the national saint brings land and people together, including these shamrock-hatted revellers.*

LEFT *Dublin Castle, Record Tower, from 840 to 1014 the Vikings controlled Dublin (Irish* Dubh Linn, *"dark pool"). After the Norman invasion of Ireland, King Henry II established English rule here from 1171 to 1919.*

RIGHT Book of Kells, *Chi-Rho page, c. 800 C.E., Trinity College, Dublin. Created by Irish monks on Iona around Christ's initials, Irish sacred journeys can be labyrinthine, yet firmly structured.*

solar eye is possibly reflected in "firebrand," *aithinne.* These solar connections were inherited from his father's brother, who, riding a sky horse, landed in Munster and threw up a great sod. Only Atherne noticed a brooch of four-score ounces of red gold lying beneath the hoofprint and claimed it by ancestral right. It symbolized the golden wheel of the sun's route, emerging from the underworld, and was the counterpart of the jewels at first offered by King Eochaid (*eochaid* – "horse"), of the Shannon, before his eye was plucked out.

Gold was found again in the profusely flowering *aiteann*, "furze or gorse." This common bush was burned ceremonially at the February quarterday and used as May Eve torches or firebrands.

In this guise, the poet walked back into Áth Cliath, Linn Dubh, and Dublin. He was still flaring through the streets on May Eve in the eighteenth- and nineteenth-century versions of those festivals. Throughout the country, wherever Atherne went, *aiteann* bushes could be found hanging from house rafters and were changed annually for luck.

Atherne was a poet who earned his keep, for when his furze thorns were crushed he became winter fodder for the cattle, and as fuel for the hearth he showed his practical side again.

Etymologists derive *aiteann* from *ote*, "furze," in Basque – the most ancient language in Europe. This suggests that Aiteann's arrival in Ireland, as a mythic character, may have predated the first waves of Indo-European-speaking settlers, c. 2500 B.C.E. If so, Dublin could hardly ask for a more archaic, prickly, yet eternally vigorous founding father.

THE SIEGE OF HOWTH

The Ulstermen, led by their young sun god Cúchulainn, came south to Benn Étair to help Atherne defend his booty from the enraged Leinstermen.

The Leinstermen besieged Howth, so that the Ulstermen for nine watches, were "without drink, without food, unless they drank the brine of the sea, or unless they devoured the clay."

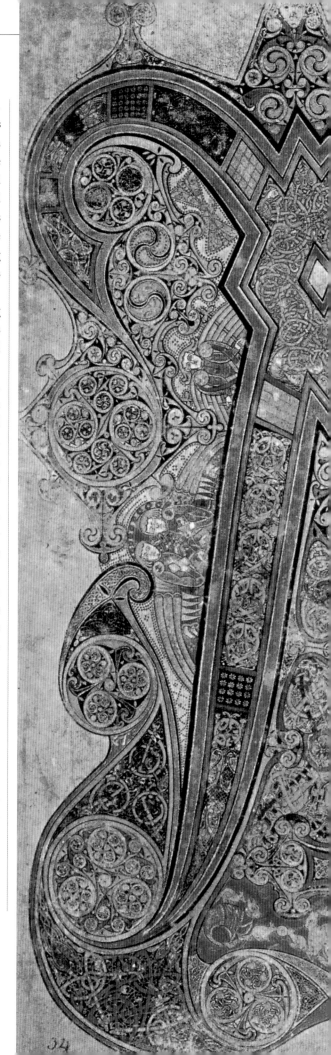

And of the seven hundred kine that Atherne had brought, there was not a boy or man of Ulster who tasted the milk, but the milking was cast down the cliff, so that of the Ulstermen none might find out Atherne's food to taste it. And the wounded men were brought to him, and he would not let a drop go into their mouths, so that they used to bleed to death alone.

King Connor was prevented from starving by a slave girl who came daily from his Ulster citadel, carrying food. Her feet and knees pointed backward, but she could travel around Ireland in a day and knew what was happening throughout the land. She was obviously the denizen of a Northern Otherworld.

The entire description has the ring of an archaic rite, spoken with the accent of a later warrior society. The widdershins, or antisolar, direction taken by Atherne, as a northern agent, suggests the stirring of subterranean forces, orchestrated from that nadir to promote a nationwide sacrifice on Howth, the point of eastern promise, as the prelude to a new round of prosperity in the upper world.

As a poet, Atherne was allowed by law to move freely around the provinces, demanding hospitality. On this assignment he is concerned with more than one kind of existence. His snatching of the solar eye from the head of Eochaid of Dergdec is an attack on the material world *per se*, with the aim of restoring it to an original chaos, a program that reaches its climax in the inversions and madness at Benn Étair. (As Mary Douglas has shown, such seasons of misrule act as a cleansing process in many societies.)

At Howth, drinking sea water (a recipe for insanity) is balanced by pouring milk (a crazy surf) down the cliffs, and while men eat clay, the only "real" food is delivered by an uncanny creature who walks backwards in another form of inversion. (Her elevation to king's confidante is, moreover, disruptive of the established social order, since she was the child of slaves, yet born in the king's bedroom!)

Finally, with the booty of Ireland assembled at Dún Étair, Cúchulainn set his foster son to guard the east door of the fort. Three hundred Leinster heroes (presumably spear-men) beheaded this guard, Mesdead, son of Amargen. His war cry, uttered at the point of death, caused general collapse. "It is the sky that crashes or the sea that flows, or the earth that quakes." That is how Cúchulainn interpreted the sound, while acknowledging that it betokened the death of the divinely appointed individual, whose solitary cry shattered the macrocosm, as did Christ's on the cross, prior to resurrection.

Howth was an ending and a beginning, a last shriek, *and* a first light. Above all, the siege was a point of exchange between the uncanny and the real.

BRUIDEN DA DERGA

The view southwest from Benn Étair across Dublin leads to a myth, first written down in the eleventh century, called the Bruiden (or Hostel) of Da Derga. At this magic Hostel, built over the Dodder River at Bohernabreena, 2 miles (3 kilometers) south of Tallaght, Leinster's natural and supernatural forces were attacked from the sea by the god Midir of the Northwestern Otherworld.

Seen from Howth, the fireball of Samain sunset goes down over Bohernabreena. Its Bruiden story, set at Samain, probably complemented the death of Mes-dead on Howth at Beltaine. The paired events make the mythic threshold between summer and winter halves of the year, just as their respective sunrises and sunsets lie at 180° to each other.

At the Beltaine festival Mes-dead, facing north-east, had to die to inaugurate May-day sunrise and the summer half. At Samain the forces of chaos came in from the sea and sent scouts to the top of Benn Étair to spy out the land. They identified the magic Da Derga house, selected for destruction, in the blue haze of the middle distance. It was crowded with revelers, including, as described in Stokes' translation of *Da Derga's Kostel* "a one-eyed man, asquint with a ruinous eye. A swine's head he had on the fire, continually squealing . . . blood has been spilt at every feast at which he has been present." He came from the great *síd* of the south, Slieve Femin.

Also present was the hag Cichuil, perhaps named after *cicul*, "cycle, or astronomical cycle." Cichuil was

RIGHT *Sunset over Dublin. In Leinster myths, the* Laigin *(sun-beams) attempt to push westward into the province of Goll, the one-eyed sun-god of Connacht.*

ABOVE *Stone
mace-head, Knowth
passage-grave, Co.
Meath, c. 2400 B.C.E.
By word of mouth,
divine speakers deliver
whole worlds out of
the dark.*

PREVIOUS PAGES *The Liffey, Dublin. The name Liffey is derived from Livia, deified wife of the Roman Emperor Augustus. Ruirthech, "The Impetuous One," was its Irish name, alluding to the flash floods common before embankment.*

"bigmouthed, huge, dark, sorry, hideous . . . though her snout were flung on a branch, her lower lip would reach her knee."

Then another ghastly giantess is reluctantly admitted – a lone woman, coming to the door of the Hostel after sunset, with pubic hair reaching to *her* knees, and her lips on one side of her head. (The Irish word *toth*, "female pudenda," is thought to be derived from pubic hair, and in the Neolithic goddess imagery of Ireland and continental Europe, her open orifice, sometimes fringed by luxuriant hair, is found engraved in tombs.)

As if to match the cosmic disorder attending Mesdead's end, the noise of the enemy fleet running ashore in Dublin Bay at Fuirbthe Strand (near Merrion Gate) shakes Da Derga's Hostel, "so that no spear nor shield remained on the rack therein, but the weapons uttered a cry, and fell all on the floor of the house." An inmate cries out: "I know nothing like it, unless it be the earth that has broken, or the Leviathan that surrounds the globe and strikes with its tail to overturn the world."

The built-up area of Greater Dublin now stretches from Howth to Bohernabreena, and so the paired myths of Howth and the Bruiden may be said to underlie every home in the conurbation. Each stands on mythologically prepared ground, where construction and destruction, being and nonbeing, are weighed against one another. The Bruiden alerts us to the contingent nature of the modern city itself, as it now confronts the prospect of self-induced desiccation in a purgatorial greenhouse.

In this respect, the site of Greater Dublin invites general alertness, being precisely balanced on the Howth-Tallaght beam, between the Beltaine and Samain junctions, which were the danger points of the traditional year. These were annually tested by mythic "fire drills," where, at the twin festivals, the poems were recited, and the contingent nature of surface life was made plain.

The purpose was to find communal security on the far side of whatever divine turmoil and human cataclysm had to be endured. So, for example, following the massacre of those within the Bruiden, Mac Cécht travels around Ireland, searching for one golden cupful of water to give to his dying king. But all the lakes and rivers turn out to be dry. At last, Mac Cécht, who acts like Sir Bedivere to King Arthur, is led to water by a wild duck. Then, with a renewed capacity for admiration of Nature, he cries:

> *That is splendid, O wild duck*
> *The lake water that spreads under thy breasts . . .*
> *O speckled little, red-bellied bird,*
> *a drop of gold water from thy wings!*

In this appeal, Mac Cécht is reassimilated into the natural order, via the supernatural order. The red duck is another "goose of Lough Gur," an intermediary who will lead humanity back to the sacred spring believed lost, yet preserving the water necessary for cultural rebirth.

Then Mac Cécht "turned throughout all the well, to bathe himself therein," and said: "Cold fountain . . . surface of strand . . . sea of lake, water of Gara: stream of river: high spring-well: cold fountain."

Thereafter "he took the full of his cup out of it . . . and reached the Hostel before morning, and poured the precious water down the decapitated king's throat."

✛ GREEN POETS ✛

Today, the men in the Greenpeace dinghy who challenge the dumping of radioactive waste into the Irish Sea perform one of the tasks of the ancient poets. They alert a complacent population to the fragility of what is taken for granted. So in Leinster, Mug Roth, personification of the great wheel of harmony, where all spears function as contributory spokes, is aware of another possibility. "It seemed to him almost as if the sky had fallen on the surface of the earth, or as if the fish-bounding blue-bordered sea had swept across the face of the earth, or as if the earth had split in an earthquake, or as if the trees of the forest had all fallen into each others' forks and bifurcations and branches."

Both then and now, the ability to imagine Doomsday is essential to the maintenance of reality beyond the myopia of complacent individualism.

ANNA LIVIA

Joyce proposed in *Finnegans Wake* that Finn lay beneath the soil with his head at Howth, with his feet at Castle Knock (the Phoenix Park Cemetery), and that Finn's Dublin was inseparable from the living natural water-scape of Anna Livia Plurabelle. She is the Liffey River Liffey, whose recurring history he told from source to sea, so inviting Dublin to take full possession of its soul and to become rooted in its province as never before. With Joyce's Esperanto (the talk of all nations, and of none), the augur's words were belatedly spoken along Liffey's quays, and people around the world heard that still-born, centerless, cities might be revived, that towns that had demolished their Thingmote might find it again, and that at any stage the City can open a new testament with the environment, if only the *civitas* (citizens) are inspired to do so.

Poets and novelists of every generation imply that all reality is an act of imagining, and Jack Yeats' painting of the swimming race, held in the Dublin Liffey, shows how an old dream of a divine river supports the contestants *in fact*. Like the Ganges, the city's river goddess is someone to be borne up by, and reborn from. Despite Liffey's recently acquired toxicity, the swimming race remains an annual event.

The hurdles of Atherne's ford lie in the river, and in *Finnegans Wake* it is the river herself who has the last word, as described by Campbell and Robinson. "She is the secret of the continuation of the jollification. Men, cities, empires, and whole systems bubble and burst in her river of time . . . All the contending parties . . . are mothered and cherished by her. Them she affirms and celebrates, as she slips between the river banks on her dream journey to the sea of renewal." Her unfinished sentence, which brings the book into the Bay, loops back to join immediately with the first word on the first page.

"But in that suspended tick of time which intervenes between her dissolution into the vast ocean and her reappearance as 'river-run,' a brave renewal has taken place. We know that she will be drawn up in dew and descend in rain upon the Wicklow Hills, and that the sun of a whole new day will run its course before she again leads us back to Howth Castle and Environs. A great deal will happen to everyone and everything during this day. And when the night comes again, bringing its release from sun logic . . . the timeless story of that slow combustion which ever consumes and sustains itself in the interior of the spinning atom, in the living world, and in the soul of man," will be retold.

LEFT *"And when night comes again, bringing its release from sun logic ..."* Joseph Campbell.

LEINSTER 3

original landings

Historically speaking, Labraid Loingsech and the Laigin originally represented Iron Age arrivals in the province where Dublin has since developed. At the same time, they echo much earlier landfalls, which are celebrated along the Leinster coast in myth and monument, as the following examples demonstrate.

LEFT *Glendalough, Co. Wicklow. In the sixth century, St. Kevin founded a monastery here. Remains of seven churches survive, together with an eleventh-century round tower, 112 feet (34 meters) high.*

THE DRIMNAGH FIRE MOUNTAIN, CO. DUBLIN

∽

A Neolithic monument (erected c. 2000 B.C.E.) possibly demonstrated how natural elements could be brought into controlled interaction over the body of the mythic founder of the province, the equivalent of Moen (Turfstack). Moen was an epithet of Labraid Loingsech, "The Speaker," here expressing his silence on entering his provincial ground.

At Drimnagh, the presumed solar-king was found in a stone cist on the Neolithic ground surface, together with a bowl decorated by an incised "secrets of plowing" pattern, in a four quarters design. Over his head, a swastika stone setting (a well-known solar emblem) was embedded in a stack of sods, which were then subject to an intense and even firing, so igniting an outer roof of stout alder-wood spears (perhaps representing pre-Gaelic "láigen") which shot their flames skyward.

This union of sun and earth was reflected in the belief, current till 1939, that the gold regalia of King John, a king from the east (Britain), lay under the mound, and shows how the original mythic event rolled through and beyond the confines of history.

Here at Drimnagh, location, structure, and iconography concur with ancient myth and recent folklore, to represent the province of Leinster as the fortunate province of dawn.

The coastal district of Leinster in which Drimnagh stands was known as Cuala, from the word *cualu* — "heap, mound, fagots," and sometimes used in the sense "phalanx of spears," and linked (by Keating) to a mythological invader of Ireland named Cuala. Thus the coast is named after the founder, and his initiatory mound, which *brought it into conscious existence*, since reality was founded on ritual behavior.

BELOW *Seaweed gathering. Since the fourth millennium B.C.E., seaweed has probably been used to fertilize Irish fields. Prior to that, Mesolithic wanderers fished and foraged along the shore.*

LADRA AT ARDAMINE,
CO. WEXFORD

A 20-foot (6-meter) high grass and bramble-covered mound, set on sea cliffs, is said to mark the spot where Ladra, "the first dead man who went under the soil of Ireland," was buried. He was the pilot and oarsman of the boat of Cesair, the founding goddess of Ireland, who sailed into Waterford Harbour with her fifty women, reaching shore between the future provinces of Leinster and Munster. On landing, Ladra took sixteen of her women "and was dissatisfied thereat . . . He died of excess of women, or it is the shaft of the oar that penetrated his buttock," according to *Lebor Gabála*.

This last droll circumstance is believed to be a medieval clerical insertion, a graffito that fails to conceal the underlying myth.

The name Ladra is related to the word *adna* meaning "aged," denoting the ultimate male ancestor of the Irish race, in a cosmogonic or foundation myth, predating the Speaker-Mariner Labraid Loingsech, and arising directly out of a primordial Flood. Yet both as mariners and introducers of new knowledge, the two have much in common, and Ladra is close to the word *adma* – "knowledgeable, skillful, dexterous."

Ladra and Cesair were brother and sister – son and daughter of Bith (Cosmos), the founding god of Ireland. "We seem here to be on the track of a myth of a divine brother–sister union," wrote Macalister, comparing it to the Greek Zeus–Hera coupling. In Ireland, he continues, "the original story knew of only one 'man,' Adna (Ladra), with one wife, Cesair, and a number of subordinate women."

These women were the ancestress-goddesses of Asiatic and European nations, who arrived with the divine couple in Ireland.

Constructed in this manner, the story enabled "the facts" of history and geography and of human settlements and migrations, to be associated with the creative love of two ultimate beings, whose incestuous relationship was a way of expressing the "one family" nature of the cosmos.

LEFT *Sugarloaf Mountain, Co. Wicklow, previously known as Cuala's Ear. The Irish* cluas, *"ear," also means "joy and gladness." Joyful First Fruits rituals were practiced on hilltops throughout Ireland until c. 1850, where local deities listened to the people's harvest prayers.*

RIGHT *Dancing at Glendalough, Co. Wicklow, 1930. Through the generations, Cesair's descendants have danced at the crossroads, to reinaugurate her sacred landscape, by love of life.*

ST. MAEDOC AND LADRA

The head of an early Christian cross is set into the north side of Ladra's mound at Ard Ladran (Ardamine) and is said to mark the spot where St. Maedoc of Ferns landed, after administering the last sacrament to St. David, patron saint of Wales, in 598 C.E. Here, on the Leinster shore, Maedoc built a church. He then converted the local ruler, Dima, to Christianity, and so represents another beginning.

Irish beginnings are often spun together by myth into a combined cord of hope, and in this case the incorporation of a cross into a pagan mound was matched in Maedoc's life. Like Ladra, he too was a child of Cosmos, conceived when his mother, Queen Eithne, saw the moon entering the mouth of her husband, while the king saw a star enter *her* mouth.

Thus Maedoc was generated when universal fire entered the lunar bowl and sailed toward the mind of human wonder. "My little fire," *mo Aed óc*, was what his nurses affectionately called the baby, hence Maedoc became his name. This "sunrise" title linked him to pre-Christian Leinster, where eventually he became bishop of Ferns, a town that lies 12 miles (19 kilometers) inland from Ard Ladran. Ferns was for a while the capital of the entire province.

Maedoc displayed many archaic attributes. After traveling from Wales on the back of a sea monster, he brought a sea-cow out of the ocean in order to draw a plow for three months. It returned to the sea after each day's work. He was also able to perform magic of a kind that was probably derived from the Neolithic, turning barley to gold, and back again, for the benefit of the poor.

CESAIR'S LANDING: WATERFORD HARBOUR

∽

Lebor Gabála recounts a creation myth involving the arrival in Waterford Harbour of the goddess Cesair. The word *cessair* means "carries, brings forth, draws out." The myth tells how, along with Bith, Fintan, and fifty women, Cesair landed at Bun Suainme, in Waterford Harbour. The name *Bun*, "thick end," and *suainme*, "cord, string, river confluence," denotes a hill over-looking the Waterford Harbour meeting of the "Three Sisters," alias the Suir, Nore, and Barrow rivers. These rivers have their sources around Árd Éireann, Ireland's central birth-mountain, in Co. Leix. Thus the "Three Sisters" may jointly be regarded as the fresh-water umbilical cord, linking the founding mother on the shore to her "land-self" and child-Ériu.

The fifty women who sailed to Ireland with Cesair are the divine mothers of other nations (Aithne of the Athenians, Inde of the Indians), bringing with them "world culture" in the first mythic boat known to have reached Ireland.

As a matter of archeological fact, Mesolithic hunter-gatherers arrived in Ireland c. 7000 B.C.E. to fish and forage. Large quantities of Mesolithic and Neolithic tools have been found along the Waterford Harbour shores. Myth and worked flint come together.

The integration of holy word and thing is also seen in the *lam-dia* or portable idol mentioned by *Lebor Gabála* as the divine inspiration of Cesair's voyage. Before setting out, Cesair had advised her followers: "Take unto yourself an idol . . . worship it . . .," and this is the counsel that their idol gave them: "make a voyage and embark upon the sea."

CONNACHT

battle of east and west

The province of Connacht is partly defined by comparison with Leinster. The stereotypes proclaim that Leinster is fertile and Connacht barren. Leinster's sunshine is contrasted with Connacht's cloud and heavy rain, her riches with Connacht's poverty, her urban success with the small and often failing townships of the West. Leinster stands for the triumph of newcomers, whereas Connacht is traditionally the last refuge of the defeated. The wisdom of Connacht, like that of King Lear, comes partly with the loss of power. This most westerly province of all Europe gains and offers insight *in extremis*.

The Irish word for west is *Iar*, which also means "the end, every extremity, everything last, after, backwards, blank, and dusky" – in short, the opposite qualities of east. *Iar* spreads into *iarsma*, "after-effects, remainder, remnant," *iartharach*, "furthermost," and *iartestimin*, "conclusion of a period." Western time and space combine in *iartaige*, "unhappy consequence."

Connacht in its entirety was *Iar*, and is still regarded as the most remote part of Ireland. "In the eighteenth century, the few travelers who crossed the Shannon had the sensation of entering another world," according to J. G. Simms. Several writers cautioned against taking the risk and spread rumors of a savage population on the west coast. Strangers who probed Connemara, like Thomas Molyneux in 1709, found no roads, and no bridges. Not until the nineteenth century did a Scottish engineer, Nimmo, construct a route to Clifden, while West Mayo remained isolated. This situation is reflected in the word *conn*, which conveys associations of traditional wisdom, hard of access.

With some misgivings, therefore, the traveler journeys to the west, carrying the burden of myth in the telltale haversack of language; the place of the west in the Irish tongue, *and* the act of traveling westward, were alike loaded with peril.

✛ THE LUCKY STONE ✛

The ancient high road to the west, Slighe Mhór, began at Áth Cliath, on the ridge "whereupon the High Street is sett," say the Annals of Clonmacnoise. Dublin's High Street is the start of the road. Before setting off, many travelers visited St. Audeon's church (built by the Normans in 1190, over a much earlier chapel dedicated to St. Columba). There, in the dark porch, still stands "The Lucky Stone," which "was daily kissed and embraced by numbers who believed in its reputed powers of conferring health and prosperity." This 3-foot (1-meter)-high eighth-century Christian gravestone was set up outside the church by the first Mayor of Dublin in 1309 beside a horsetrough. (Stolen in 1826, it was returned to St. Audeon's forty years later.) The cross arms, stretching equally north, south, east, and west within the engraved banks and ditches of its outer ring, unite the Christian symbol with the four provinces in the body of a grayish-black igneous rock, flecked with mica, like permanent stars, emerging upon the sun's final extinction, from the earth's molten underworld.

BELOW *The Lucky Stone, in the porch of St. Audeon's church in Dublin; 3 feet (1 meter) tall. This wheel-headed medieval stone cross conferred good luck on travelers who touched it.*

RIGHT *The Great Road,
Slighe Mhór (also called
Eiscir Riada, The Great
Riding), ran east–west
from Áth Cliath,
Dublin, to Galway Bay.
It bisects Ireland.*

The medieval "Blessing the Road Before a Journey" beseeches: "May this road be smooth, may it be a journey of profit in my hands. Holy Christ against demons, against weapons, against slaughters. May Jesus and the Father, may the Holy Ghost sanctify us! May mysterious God that is not hidden in darkness, may the bright King save us! May the cross of Christ's body and Mary guard us on the road! May it not be unlucky for us! May it be prosperous, expeditious."

An't Sligh Mhór ran from the Áth Cliath ford, along Dublin's High Street, through Corn Market and Thomas Street West, and out across the Central Plain. Having negotiated the Shannon, it finally reached Áth Cliath Medraige on the Connacht coast of Galway Bay.

Throughout this distance of approximately 110 miles (176 kilometers) ran the story of the god Blad or Blod. He had been nurtured under the Atlantic "by a daring king over Medraige, and over Herot [a territory in South Connacht]. Blod then fared in his ship from the *bottom* of pure-cold Galway from Áth Cliath [Medraige] in wide Herot, to Áth Cliath in Cuala [Dublin]." "Thence he came by many a turn to Point of

Nár" (Howth). Having completed this west to east journey, including the last few miles to Howth, Blod settled on the middle mountain of Ireland, Sheve Bladma, now called Slieve Bloom, halfway between the two fords. From there he balanced his submarine origin in the far west against the sunlit Howth headland in the east. Thus the stage was set for the battle of the sun gods, Finn in the east and Goll from the west, along the line of Slighe Mhór.

The Great Road partly owed its greatness to their struggle. Every traverse of the route was derived from the original event, with "ordinary" journeys following the divine prototype as far as possible.

EISCIR RIADA

An alternative name for Slighe Mhór was the Riding Ridge, or Eiscir Riada. From the Lucky Stone horse-trough at St. Audeon's church, the Riding (both as verb and noun) followed a series of natural gravel ridges or *eskers* aligned more or less east–west.

Because the gravel ridges are so numerous, and documentary evidence so slender, uncertainty exists concerning the exact route of the Riada, west of Lucan. C. O. Lochlainn's research of 1938 suggested two possibilities lying up to 6 miles (10 kilometers) apart, with the more southerly route passing across the Bog of Allen via Celbridge, Taghadoe, Monasteroris, Rhode, Croghan, and Kiltober, toward Durrow Abbey, Ballycumber, Togher, and Ballaghurt to reach the Shannon River at Clonmacnoise.

The Book of Leinster states that Clonard was on the route, so favoring the more northerly alternative, following the line of the present N_4 highway to the Shannon ford at Athlone.

Either way represented a god's route, real as a walker's blisters and aligned between sunrise and sunset. Medieval poets sang the Great Road's praises:

The line that divides Erin in two

was Escir Riada (it was no lie)

whose name held in bright renown

was the Great Road, greater than any tilled plain.

A road, the poet makes perfectly clear, was the sum of its events:

In this wise were discovered

the roads, the ancient mearings

as I found their high origin

their traditional rights, their local legends.

Some accounts put the western end of The Great Road at White Horse Hill near Clarinbridge, Co. Galway (*Cnoc an ghervain bhain*). Its Gaelic name means hill of the white steed and can be regarded as another version of a solar deity, repeatedly galloping into the equinoetial sunset hill, having completed the journey from Áth Cliath in the east.

The Hurdle Ford of Medraige lay just west of Clarinbridge, on a peninsula poking into Galway Bay, in Ballynacourty parish. The ford was built of whitethorn and brambles, against the men of Munster, and seems as much a barrier as a crossing. It was

✛ THE LEINSTER ESKERS ✛

As recently as the 1890s, geologists believed the eskers of Leinster to have been left behind by the Biblical Flood. Today they are regarded as the result of the melting of Ireland's last ice sheet, prior to 15,000 B.C.E. Eskers represent the gravel-choked ice caves made by the melt-water streams as they wound their way from beneath an ice-sheet retreating westward, according to J. Whittow.

Across Leinster these steep-sided ridges rise and fall in height in what is called a "beaded" manner, up to 328 feet (100 meters) high, in a "succession of mounds indicative of the normal recession of an ice-sheet terminating in standing water. Each 'bead' is really a partly formed delta, laid down at or near the mouth of a sub-glacial stream, and each represents the summer deposit when melt-waters were plentiful, while the less prominent part of the esker between the beads marks the winter phase." The repeated history of a struggle between sun and ice, and of summer and winter forces, is thus written into the prehuman land forms. Riders and walkers rise and fall to the same rhythm.

BELOW *"On Through Silent Lands." Oil painting by J. B. Yeats, 1951, Ulster Museum. Often starting from the mundane, the modern artist approaches and articulates myths-in-waiting. He shambles toward a rickety footbridge across a river. On the far side an iceberg drifts into view, as a version of the deep-frozen sacred.*

ABOVE *White Horse Hill, Clarinbridge in Co. Galway. At Galway Bay, the Great Riding comes to an end. From East to West, the solar horse-gods, Labraid and Finn, have won the entire island.*

constructed by The Seven Maines — in other words The Seven Days of the Week. They were said to be the sons of Connacht's chief goddess, Medb. Thanks to her and them, space and time were woven together at Medraige, so enabling the western province to enjoy a share of the words *medraige* — "merriment," and *meadhradh* — "mirth and song." From start to finish, the Eiscir Riada appears as a work of the gods.

The discovery of Slighe Mhór, The Great Road, as the east–west axis of Ireland immediately created northern and southern halves of the country as variant on the four provinces theme. The halves of Mug (south of the road) and of Conn (to the north) have featured in historical reality and got their present names from Conn of the Hundred Battles, 123–147 C.E., and his Munster rival.

FINN'S WAY

At Cnucha in Phoenix Park, overlooking Áth Cliath, there was a conflict between the solar powers of east and west, with Connacht gaining the victory. The demigod of the west, Aed (whose name means "fire"), attacked Luchet (*Luchair*, "bright") and killed him there, but not before Luchet had blinded Aed in one eye, so giving him the name Goll ("one eyed"). Goll then slew Cumall, the father of Finn, the eastern sun hero, and carried off his spoils and his head, hence there was an hereditary feud between Finn and the sons of Morna, along the line of the Great Road.

By far the strongest directional drive connected with the Eiscir Riada comes from the east–west shadows thrown by Finn the rising sun god, intent on avenging his father by killing Goll. In warrior-Celtic Ireland, the interplay of natural forces was viewed as war. That was the myth that the gods and their human tribes enacted. Similarly, Connacht men invading Leinster had Goll on their side, but as a tenth-century Leinster order of engagement says, "They must not be suffered to depart alive."

Sometimes the conflict is conducted with sadistic glee, as when Finn's women tie the aged western hero Garaid to their house-wall by his beard and hair while he is asleep, to prevent him from interfering with them. On awaking with a jerk, Garaid tears off his hair, scalp, and flesh. In revenge he "cuts nine stout fagots of ash and kindles fire in the house from floor to ceiling, setting the house in a great blaze; that old man had no mercy." The women plead to be let out in vain. Finn sees the smoke arising from Drumcree (between Mullingar and Kells, in Co. Westmeath) and gallops to the rescue, but on his arrival there is nothing left "but the stump of each stake in the earth, and black and charred fragments of the Fianna's 'winsome wives,' and his own beautiful dapple-cheeked Aitbe." Seeing this, Finn loses all his strength.

When fierce Garaid saw the women burned, he let fly a peal of laughter over them, to be heard among the Fianna throughout Erin. (His name comes from the word *gairid* – "laughs"). "Pleasant it is to me to find you thus, O women," said Garaid, "that you may learn for good not to mock at a miserable old man."

The everlasting war of the east–west road was no joke, yet it was often enjoyable, as for example, when moving west on a bright early morning in late September with the Fianna. Then, for mile after mile along the Eiscir Riada one can sense Finn's encouragingly warm hand on the back of the neck. Pausing at noon, the shadow topiary, trimmed sharp from the base of every tree, is swiveled northward. On either side of the ridge, stretching to the horizon, lie the sullen colors of the bog, dark brown where exposed by peat cutting and elsewhere an olive green, occasionally hazed over with heather in bloom. Cloud shadows maneuver like a phantom navy across this ocean; they are Goll's fleet, firing their showers, and passing on, through volleys of Leinster sunbeams.

The route to the Shannon is also riddled with the spear and arrow holes of the historical annalists, drawing attention to real armies, advancing and retreating along the route, whose ritual "hostings" were an important means whereby the contests of the gods were brought to life in mortal combat. In this sense medieval Irish history consists of successive reports on the repeated celebration of a pagan mass, where Finn and Goll, or their fathers, took turns playing the sacrificed deity. For the battalions of Leinster and Connacht war was a religious obligation.

The Men of Leinster are urged in the early tenth-century March Roll to

take to their never-failing weapons . . . ready for every attack, for a battle-rout against united Connacht. Let them march to the battle-rout without grumbling, let them all rise up for the fight to defend the warlike province which their father left them.

BELOW *The South Cross at Clonmacnoise, Co. Offaly, 10 feet (3 meters) tall, eleventh century. It employs the wheel of the sun's rotation, and stands at the crossroads of Ireland, where the Eiscir Riada fords the Shannon River.*

THE SHANNON FRONTIER

The boundary between Leinster and Connacht was and is defined by Ireland's greatest river, the Shannon. Where it could be forded in the summer, many interprovincial battles took place.

The weapons dredged from the Shannon fords in recent times contribute to the archeological evidence for religion-as-war. In 1844, at the Keelogue ford, for example, the engineer Griffith found "150 elfstones (stone arrowheads), 10 swords and brass spear-heads, 8 small brass spear-heads, 2 iron swords, 8 small iron spear heads, 10 pieces of teeth, 3 iron battle axes, 10 brass battle axes, 41 sundry broken spearheads, ornaments of scabbards, druids' rings, etc." He reported that "weapons dropped in mortal strife between the men of Leinster and the Connacht men, disputing the passage of the river," belonged to "distinct and no doubt very distant periods." At the bottom of a foot of silt overlaying the esker riverbed gravel were "stone

weapons of a very remote age" including "a great number of stone hatchets" overlaid by Bronze Age and Iron Age material remnants of battles fought on the same spot, spanning thousands of years.

As Griffiths was quick to remark, the struggle reached into his own lifetime, in that the British government had erected two defensive towers on the east bank to repel Napoleon, presumed to be leading fresh waves of Connacht raiders. Conversely, the medieval annalists record that in 985 C.E. "King Moyleseachlin with an army went into Connaught, and from thence brought many captives and rich boottyes."

Corresponding conflicts in Nature were also on the annalists' minds. They report hailstones as big as crabs, and how, in 688 C.E., "it rained blood in Leinster, and butter was turned into the color of blood, and how a wolf was seen and heared to speak with a human voice."

In 734 "there was a Dragon both huge and ugly to behold this Harvest seen, and a great Thunder heard after him in the firmament." This snake with wings,

escaping St. Patrick's attentions, could be regarded as a smaller version of the Eiscir ridge itself.

The dragon of 734 was both an historical singularity *and* an occupant of a cave in the depths of myth. There also, the gravelly ice-sheet meltwater trembled, in geomorphological fact, under a groaning ice-roof, as the esker was slowly born.

Finn's opponent in the Shannon wars was the giant Goll. Goll had ranged all over Leinster to the east coast. At Cnucha, he had killed Finn's father in battle, ensured Finn's emnity, and started another cycle in the east–west conflict.

Then having lost his comrade-in-arms, Suca Greatnose, Goll decided to retire into South Connacht, to the west bank of the Shannon. There "ten hundred handsome shield-bearers of the house of the grandmother of keen Goll gathered around him on the hillock of the rowan tree, to defend their province against the advancing Finn." (Both the hillock and the rowan tree are emblematic of a divine ancestress.)

Goll set his captains Feorann and Modha to guard adjacent fords while he protected a third.

Athlone, Shannonbridge, Banagher, and Keelogue were probably the adjacent fords concerned. These fords have been standard crossings throughout the human occupation of Ireland.

"Goll watched against Fionn (Finn) seventeen days without sleep" before sinking into an exhausted slumber. "Pleasant Goll . . . handsome of body," lay there, while Fionn led up six battalions, representing not only Leinster, but all the powers of the eastern world, including those of Britain and France – all directed against Europe's most westerly province.

Then "at close of night upon his couch, when men and woods were in one hue, Fionn of bright aspect awoke." Like the sun that he was, he climbed into the early morning, reached the ford, heard Goll snoring, crossed the river, and finding his enemy in a heavy sleep "unsheathed the hard sword above the son of mane-red Morna. Goll awoke and raised his spear." There the pair can be left for a while, like low-relief figures in a marble frieze, while Goll's origins are examined more closely.

THE ORIGINS OF GOLL

"One has only to go upon the track of Fenian folklore among the Connacht peasantry of today," wrote E. MacNeill in 1908, "to find that Goll is the foremost hero of every tale."

He is sometimes described as a giant of the Fir Bolg, the mythical Men of the Bag, a subject race, who according to Irish legend, were made to carry soil in

LEFT *Goll, folk-hero of Connacht. He is the one-eyed sunset god of the West, who opposed Finn at the Shannon.*

bags from fertile valleys to the tops of rocky hills for the benefit of their oppressors' farms in ancient Greece. By converting their bags into leather coracles, they escaped and sailed to Ireland, where they were again defeated, this time by the Tuatha Dé Danann at the first battle of Moytura, thought to have taken place at Cong in Co. Galway. After their victory the Tuatha permitted the Fir Bolg to remain in Connacht.

During the seventeenth century many of the inhabitants of Connacht traced their ancestry back to the legendary Fir Bolg. Goll, their paragon of valor, has one eye in the earth bag because he was of the underworld. The other, visible to mortals as the westering sun, gave him his alternative name, *Aed*, "Fire," and helps to explain why he is described as Red-Maned. Myth's

even-handedness establishes that Goll lost his first eye at the Battle of Cnucha, at the sunrise end of the Great Road. The fate of the second hung on the outcome of a Connacht fight.

Keeping at least one eye on (and in) the bag where the secrets of soil's power to generate life were stored, Goll could be said to be visiting a god of the underworld named Conn, the Conn with whom the people of the province of Connacht, as "descendants of Conn," identified.

Conn also means "head," suggesting a link with the Celtic cult of the severed human head, as the repository of inspired knowledge.

There is clearly some overlapping of function between Goll and Conn, though as a duo they

broadly correspond to the demigod and god layers of reality, so carrying the descending sun into the deepest recesses of the imagination. This is not to forget that some commentators call Goll himself "a sun deity who was also Lord of the Underworld."

G. Dumézil's research enables us to see Goll's battles as an essential death-dealing element that helped to keep the believing community alive and to place the Irish accounts in an Indo-European tradition. Once again, Ireland presented a near-universal scenario in terms peculiar to itself and showed how the specialized art of war was interwoven with the administration of the sacred, and the cultivation of fecundity, to give a true account of a violent natural order, and of the harmony within its conflicts.

THE WAR GODDESSES

One of Finn's captains, MacLuighdech, called his war-horse Badb, and so flew to battle on the wings of the hooded crow. This aggressive carrion-eater, 17 inches (43 cm) long, is known in Ireland as the hooded Royston, or scarecrow, and as a manifestation of the war goddess, Badb. Her gray back and belly divides a black head and tail, giving the bird a *caille*, or hooded appearance. Her loud "Kraa-Kraa" voice, labored flight, and menacing hop-hopping along the ground, and her attendance over unburied corpses of every kind, helped to establish her reputation. The word *badb* conveyed the "rage, fury, and violence" of the goddess. Not so many years ago, even sturdy men

would abandon projects for the day if they heard her call, wrote W. M. Hennessy, since the sound prophesied slaughter or misfortune:

The red-mouth Badb will cry around the house.

For bodies it will be solicitous.

Pale Badbs shall shriek.

Badbs will be over the breasts of men . . .

says the battle story, *Bruiden Da Choca*. (The "house" stood on the Eiscir Riada, at Breenmore Hill, 8 miles (13 kilometers) east of the Shannon a hilltop fort with extensive views into Connacht.)

In Ireland, Badb merged with her sister Mórrígu (Great Queen), and both could take on the features of a human hag as described in the *Battle of Magh-Rath*:

Over his head is shrieking

A lean hag quickly hopping

Over the points of their weapons and shields

She is the gray-haired Mórrígu.

Dusk's gray cloud-feathers, and the black gloss of midnight, were awaiting Goll's sunset army, as it retreated into the arms of the terrible mother. Badb is an Irish version of Kali (the Hindu "terrible goddess"). Her other sister, Nemain, destroyed her victims by driving them mad.

The war goddesses may be said to embody the horrors of the eating and being eaten to which all life is committed, and which finds mythic expression in the life and death of the sacrificed god-hero.

THE CONNACHT CAMPAIGN

On the west bank of the Shannon, Goll fought a losing battle on the side of the dying day and sinking year. Through him, Connacht myths are able to speak of the clash of elemental forces in superhuman terms.

This is what MacNeill calls "the oldest form of folklore nature myth, where the mysterious forces of

nature are deified, and the phenomena they produce appear as the wars and quarrels . . . of the gods, – the struggles between light and dark, summer and winter, fair weather and storm."

Consequently, the folktales of Connacht, though they may seem absurd in detail, are rational in their overall effect, in that they succeed in integrating human hopes and defeats into a much bigger drama. In this way they differ from a modern rationalism, which is so rational in detail, yet unreasonable to the point of madness in its broader consequences. They were involved with war *in* Nature, as distinct from war *on* Nature. For all our skill in measuring, we are now frequently surprised by these "unforeseen side-effects," whereas in antiquity there *were* no side-effects at all, since everything was presumed to be interconnected. Goll stands at the hub of a narrative of defeat touching every aspect of life. Therefore the societies that told his story were unlikely to be ambushed by unknown forces.

Finn did not kill the sleeping Goll on the Shannon riverbank, but sheathed his sword. Here, as on several other occasions, a companionship amounting almost to identity took over. As different aspects of a single solar reality, they had even fought side by side at the Battle of the Sheaves.

Nevertheless, in Connacht Goll *did* retreat before Finn, and though offering fierce resistance, behaved as if he knew he must lose.

Yet when Finn and his men are ensnared by the three Hags of Winter in front of the caves of Keshcorran, Co. Sligo, it is Goll that comes to the rescue. Winter-in-Connacht was Goll's natural territory. Finn had seen

…three phantom sprites come out of the side of the [Keshcorran] hill. Devilish was the guise of the

women. They spell-bound my companions. Three black unsightly mouths, six white eyes never closing, three red bristling heads of hair, six twisting legs under them, three warlike swords, three shields with their three spears — it was not an easy task to gaze on the women or their gear.

Rough gray iron of wizardry they had mounted on poles, giddiness and faint sickness came over Finn and the Fian at the sight of them.

They reduced Finn to "a withered quaking ancient," and left seven battalions of Fian in the same plight "around the door of the bone-strewn Ceis . . . bound and cast into a house underground."

One of the hags was named Camog (meaning a small bag, which suggests that she was related to Goll, being a goddess of the Fir Bolg or Bag Men). Cuilleann (Holly) and Iornach (Spindle, or Skein of yarn) were her companions. This trinity of Neolithic Winter deities tied up the invaders with cobwebs. Goll, in

LEFT *Hurling match, Ireland, capturing one split second, on the seventh day of August, 1998. In myth, a moment can become an endless struggle, as between Finn and Goll. They play out their east to west, Leinster v. Connacht, sunrise v. sunset war or sport.*

turn, bound up Iornach, "fast in fetters," and forced her to return Finn and his men to their proper shapes. Then "right speedily," Goll burned the hags' abode. "I left black ashes that house at the foot of the Ceis" When Iornach escaped and challenged Finn in single combat, Goll intervened again, and "by clean force I cut her head off with my blue blade."

Finn, once freed, ruthlessly turned on and killed Goll's grandson, Fedha son of Cainche, whose name means "songbird" (an act that might represent the silencing or migration of fledgling songbirds at summer's end). "Without him I am lonely," said Goll, who then abandoned all hope of any friendship with Finn, and resumed the fight against his armies, but by rescuing Finn from the clutches of the Hags of Winter, Goll had sealed his own death sentence at Finn's hands. Goll was a selfless hero.

WAR AND SPORTS IN CONNACHT

From the remotest times, the sports field has been the battleground of mythic truths. In modern Leinster–Connacht relations the stylized Neolithic pattern has reemerged, having cast off the brutality of actual interprovincial warfare, so much a feature of Irish life from the Iron Age onward, which perhaps still imparts intensity to sporting contests between east and west.

For example, in C.E. 1990, "*Magnificent McGrath fails to save unlucky Sarsfields,*" declares the *Connacht Tribune*, describing how a Connacht team lost to a Leinster team, for a place in the All-Ireland hurling club semifinal. "The match was played in front of a fanatical Ballinasloe crowd of 4,000, and at an extraordinary pace in difficult underfoot conditions." The hero was not Goll, but McGrath.

His display will live long in the memory . . . it was as near perfection as made no difference. His inspiring leadership deserved a better fate.

McGrath's exhibition of hurling was undoubtedly one of the best ever seen on a Galway GAA field. He seized on to his responsibilities with an authority and vengefulness which was quite extraordinary in its

intensity. But oh, how that commitment was so gracefully complemented with the more subtle skills of the game. McGrath's superb handling, lithe turns, darting runs and unerring accuracy were all condensed into one moment of second-half hurling magic in the 48th minute when he emerged from thickets of ash near the left sideline to stroke over a magnificent point from 60 yards.

Not till the dying minutes did the Leinster side finally deliver the fatal blows to a side almost unable to stomach defeat. Final Score: Sarsfield 0–12, Ballyhale Shamrocks 2–8.

A mythology that ignored war would soon be overwhelmed by the forces it had failed to recognize. The wisdom of Goll and Connacht concern the ability to engage in war and absorb war's impact to the benefit of the country as a whole. Ultimately, the Connacht myth brings the mortally wounded hero to that womb of the goddess available to every inhabited island – the depths of the sea.

This denouement follows the plot of the setting sun, as it rolls, fat and bloody, down Connacht's huge cliffs toward oceanic infinity. The Connacht road leads eventually to the rainlashed, ocean-whittled, and wind-scoured austerities of Connemara and the Nephin Beg mountains.

Driven across the province, Goll finally perched on a bare crag on the cliffs of Iar, or west Connacht, with the ocean as his only future. "Wide is the sea around us, and I on the narrow crag: hunger for food is betraying me, and thirst is overmatching me . . . still more it takes the beauty from my cheek to have to drink bitter strong brine." Connacht has always been the land of brave losers, especially in its remote and mountainous west.

From his last toehold on the cliffs, Goll claims to have killed thirty hundred of the enemy, including Dubh Lughaidh – "Black Want." He had been refused help at Emain Macha in Ulster, and at Tara in Meath, because those kings had been too frightened of Finn's revenge. Then (a bitter blow) the royal palace of Rathcroghan in his own province had shut him out for the same reason. Only his wife and the piles of men he had slain remained with him. After thirty full days

without food or sleep, he cried out, in despair: "I was the deed-vaunting champion: I have a waist of bone. I was golden-weaponed Iollan [expert]. Tonight I am Goll the unsightly."

He recalled that "from Hallowtide till May I supported the entire Fianna," and "the chase of Corann of the hillocks was held by us without refraining." (Corran means "hook, or pruning hook," which suggests that Goll's struggles included a role in driving the momentum of the farming year before him.)

Rather than he should starve to death, his wife advises him "to eat of those bodies at thy side, [and] drink of the milk of my breasts." He refuses, but asks his "clear one of rosy cheeks, to prepare to depart the morn before my slaying." He speaks to her as if she is the sky, whose pink beauty, he knows, will soon fade once he, the light of her life, has dropped into the ocean. Preparing himself for that reversed birth, he asks her to take away his tunic.

Considering her own fate she cries out: "O Goll . . . alas for those whose friends are few, which way shall I take?" With the stoicism that holds the natural order together, he replies: "Seek the camp of Fionn of the Fianna; wed there, gentle one of red lips, some good man worthy of thee." She is to go to his enemies and accept the new sun of the east into her vast spaces, so to enjoy the dawn of another cycle.

Goll's destiny was to slither down the rocks through lank seaweed, and to drop into the western ocean. *Acallamh na Senórach* says that he died after he had retreated "to Carrac Guill in the west," which was presumably an ocean-girt rock-stack off the Connacht coast. There he was beheaded by Dubh Dithre's son, Mac Smaile (*Dubh* – "black," *dithre* – "feeble, spent, exhausted"). This was the same Mac Smaile who had reaped with the Fianna at the Battle of the Sheaves. *Smál* means "embers or ashes." Thus was Goll, light of the western fire, the setting sun, smothered, till his blackened head rolled powerless beneath the waves of midnight. In a sense he died by his own hand, since ash is the product of fire, just as the word *golighe*, or "setting of the sun," carried his name and his remaining eye out of sight, in a dignified exit.

CROAGH PATRICK

After his death, Goll may have gone to the phantom Island of Brâzil, believed to lie off the southwest coast of Connacht. It was named after Bres, the son of Ériu, fathered by the Fomorian sea god, Elatha. "Bresil" was a magic realm, neither sea nor land, yet both. Brazil, South America, was named after it.

Whether or not Goll was resurrected in an offshore Otherworld, Connacht mythology, like that of every province, sought a suitable place on the mainland to reenact its own rebirth. Connacht's nativity occurred annually at the start of harvest at a conical mountain, tipped with white quartz. It is called The Reek, or Croagh Patrick, and anciently Cruachán Aigle, perhaps from *aige* – "act of celebrating or holding festivals." It stands 2,500 feet (762 meters) high, overlooking the Atlantic and Clew Bay, Co. Mayo – the salty bag from which came the Fir Bolg farmers, mythic ancestors of the entire Connacht population.

From the mountain top one can see hundreds of islands in the Bay. Traditionally there are said to be three hundred and sixty-six, enough for a year and a day. They were known as *Insule Fortunate*, "The Fortunate Islands," on maps and in Irish as Insi Modh, from *modh*, "a measure," of time, or of grain, and may have been regarded as the progeny of the mountain.

OPPOSITE *The Atlantic cliffs of Connacht. Here Goll, starving and defeated, sank with the setting sun into the oceanic abyss. Or did he reach the magic island of Brâzil, said to lie just off the west coast, and after which Brazil in South America is named?*

✥ LUGHNASA BIRTH ✥

Every year at Lughnasa, people came to witness the mother goddess give birth, though until the mid-nineteenth century only women were permitted to climb the steep 830-feet (250-meter)-high scree slope that led up to the summit of the mountain top. The Rev. James Page reported: "None but those that are barren go there, and the abominable practices that are committed there ought to make human nature in its most degraded state blush."

ABOVE *Statue of St. Patrick with Croagh Patrick beyond. Of the 60,000 people who climb the 2,510-foot (765-meter) summit on August 1st, some go barefoot.*

PREVIOUS PAGES *Clew Bay, Co. Mayo, with the Croagh Patrick pilgrimage mountain beyond. At each step and from every angle, an exquisitely volatile beauty comes to meet the traveler. The sacredness takes over, as a matter of fact.*

Folklore describes the struggle between the attempts of St. Patrick to overthrow both the harvest god and the ancient mother goddess of The Reek, which has now been converted into the holiest mountain in Christian Ireland. On the first Sunday in August, 60,000 people annually ascend the peak to honor the saint. However, in the Irish manner, they often come in a mood of "double coding," rather than to celebrate a total Christian victory.

St. Patrick's struggle against the goddess of the mountain reached a climax when she confronted him as a great bird, Corra, and as a monster serpent, alias "The Devil's Mother." He allegedly drove her from the mountain. She escaped to Lough Derg, Co. Donegal, where the saint encountered her again at his "Purgatory Lake" (Part One).

Yet as Thackeray discovered in 1840, her spirit lived on at Croagh Patrick. After the business on the mountain came the dancing and lovemaking at its foot. Fifty tents were set around "a plain of the most brilliant green grass," where they sold "great coarse damp-looking bannocks of bread . . . a collection of pigs' feet . . . huge biscuits, and doubtful-looking ginger beer. There were also cauldrons containing water for 'tay,' with other pots full of pale legs of mutton . . . The road home was pleasant; everybody was wet through, but everybody was happy."

THE SHANNON AXIS

The mythic structure of Ireland was an amplification of symmetries discerned in Nature. Thus the chief north–south axis of the country, based on Ireland's longest river, the Shannon, was believed to terminate in an outpouring of supernatural wisdom comparable to the Eiscir Riada's Brâzil.

The *Dindshenchas* describes how the river known to humanity, personified as a maiden, goes in search of this undersea spring of sacred knowledge, for lack of which her reality is incomplete. "The maiden right active, Sinann, radiant, ever-generous, bright streaming Sinann, yellow-haired Sinann of the Tuatha Dé Danann, yearned for, and sought after, the secrets of magic wisdom." She had acquired all other accomplishments, but lacking that form of knowledge, she traveled "to a spring not sluggish, under the pleasant sea in the domain of Connle or Condla to gaze upon it." This spring of Connla lay in an Otherworld, under the poet's music-haunted hazel tree.

Connla's well, loud was its sound

beneath the blue skirted ocean;

Six streams unequal in fame

rise from it, the seventh the Sinann.

There Shannon literally found herself, in the fountain-head of wisdom.

Sagacity was disseminated from the well when the ripe hazel nuts, on falling into the water, were swallowed by sacred salmon, who carried the "ideas" upstream. Alternatively, the milk from the nuts was converted into the air bubbles seen to rise along the Shannon's course. These were the *bolg fis*, "bubbles of knowledge," or *bolg imbais*, of "inspiration." The priority given to the hazel nut in Neolithic ritual deposits proves the antiquity of its supernatural associations.

The Shannon as known to modern geography rises "in an upland basin walled by the precipitous gritstone scarps of the Leitrim plateau," in northernmost Connacht. The *Dindshenchas* explains how it migrated there from Connla's Well:

The well fled back [to the land], (clear fame

through the murmur of its musical lore!)

before [i.e. ahead of] Sinann, who visited it

in the north, and reached the chilly river.

Like a salmon, the source sped upstream to the Shannon Pot, its earthly source.

From Connla's Well to Shannon Pot is a long 198-mile (320-kilometer) journey between worlds, and between different ways of knowing. Thanks to Sinann, the wandering river goddess, the Two became One along Ireland's north–south water-spine. She gave her life to achieve their integration.

Shannon Pot is a steep-sided, clayey, oval hole that is twenty-two paces long by fifteen wide, set in a melancholy landscape of boulder-strewn, rushy pastures, and close to a ruined farm, 6 miles (9 kilometers) northeast of Dowra. This underground river-exit, coming from a hidden watercourse in the concealed limestone, is sometimes as placid as a mirror, and yet after heavy rains, boils and bubbles like an overheated cauldron. To that spot "the comely lady" Sinann came and was drowned. She merged with her own water, having no life outside it.

Every province wanted a share of the Shannon's merit and sent their poets to "Contentions of the Bards" to compete in verse for her hand. Following a fifteenth-century contest at Killaloe the judge, himself a poet, awarded the river to Ulster, the only province through which the Shannon does not run. Yet the Ulster–Shannon link is emphasized again by Geraldus, in his twelfth-century account: "A branch [of the river] divides *the furthest districts of Ulster* from Connaught, and after various windings falls into the Northern Ocean . . . Thus flowing from sea to sea, it separates the fourth and western part of the island [Connacht] from the three others."

This imagined northern outlet persists in Irish folklore to this day among people living around Shannon Pot. They believe that an underground stream connects it to the Claddach River, which can be seen emerging at the Marble Arch cave system in Ulster. From there the water flows into Lough Erne, in order to enter "the Northern Ocean" at Ballyshannon on Donegal Bay. This "extended" river was thought to play a part in the agrarian cycle, and in farms an old belief is still recalled, that chaff thrown into the water at the Marble Arch cave will reemerge at Shannon Pot.

BELOW *Supplicants walk around the Lecht Bennian station, on Croagh Patrick. They repeat set prayers seven times, in honor of St. Patrick's altar-boy. Then, with a dab of the hand, they transfer some of the cairn's power to themselves.*

PART FOUR

CONNACHT 2

Erne weddings

Traditionally regarded as the province of wisdom, through its myths Connacht articulates the principal east–west and north–south mythic axes of Ireland into its own boundaries. It thus gives structure to complex issues.

In a sense, all the myths of Ireland are concerned with boundaries, for at the frontier, what is divided is also brought together, face to face. Near provincial borders dangers and opportunities arise of every kind. There, supernatural and natural changes can be expected, requiring dramatic exposition and regulation by the storyteller's art. Hence the significance of the Falls of Assaroe at Ballyshannon on the Erne River, close to the Connacht border with Ulster. *Ess Ruaid*, their Irish name, means "Red Cataract." The mythical Northern Shannon and the real Erne River here jointly enter the ocean.

In contrast to Eiscir Riada, an area that tends to emphasize martial encounters, at Ess Ruaid and along the Erne it is mainly the opposite sexes who confront each other, especially during *gam* (November), the month of weddings.

Ess Ruaid previously held the fate of the nation suspended in its glassy roar, though now it has been obliterated by changes in water level, following the building of a hydroelectric station.

Sometimes referred to as The Salmon Leap, The Falls drew together sunset, fire, water, humanity, fish, and vegetable life forms. In the seventeenth century M. O'Clery reported: "The Irish people . . . speak of the salmon of the Red Cataract, and say that when the sun goes to the west, and shines on the Red Cataract, the water turns reddish, which seems to arise from a red weed growing on the rock inside the waterfall."

Pre-Christian sanctity attracted Christian attention, and the twelfth-century Assaroe Abbey was built immediately above a natural cave that contained two bullauns of triangular shape, sitting side by side on an altarlike ledge of rock. At least six centuries earlier, St. Patrick had desired to "set up at Ess Ruaid . . . in the place where are *Disert* and *Lecc Patraic* [his cell and bed]," but a local leader, Coirbre, resisted the saint and ordered two of his men to drive Patrick away.

"Not good is what you do," said Patrick. "If a dwelling were permitted me here, my city with its Ess-Ruaid through it would be a second Rome of Latium with its Tiber, and thy children would be [my] successors therein." The saint then cursed the north, or Ulster, side of the river belonging to Coirbre with barrenness of fish. Then on *Sith Aeda*, the tomb of the drowned pagan king of the falls, Patrick prophesied the birth of St. Columcille.

OPPOSITE *Ess Ruaid, the Falls of Assaroe. The River Erne at Ballyshannon, Co. Donegal. The falls, now obliterated by a hydro-dam, were named after the god or king, Ruad, "Red." Goll swam here as a one-eyed salmon.*

BELOW *Falls of Assaroe, Ballyshannon. Two thousand salmon a day were caught at this "lofty, loudroaring … seamonsterful cataract," according to early medieval accounts.*

ABOVE *Achill Island, Co. Mayo, faces the Atlantic surf. From such places, mythic voyagers sailed into the ocean and had strange other-worldly adventures on fabulous islands of the imagination.*

To pagan and Christian alike, in medieval times "the Falls of Assaroe" were used proverbially to denote eternity and everlastingness. At that time they were employed to run the turbines of a supernatural cycle, discharging as myth. The technicians were the gods and demigod heroes who labored and often gave their lives to connect humanity to the cosmic power grid that they embodied.

The deliberate obliteration of the Falls of Assaroe prompts the question: has convenient access to light and heat rendered human imagination obsolete over wide areas where it was formerly active? Perhaps the consumer has been inoculated against a mythic engagement with Nature, now that sources are systematically converted into resources.

AED

The *genius loci* of Ess Ruaid was Aed, a word meaning "fire." He was the fire prince (or king) of Royal Ess Ruaid. As Aed Ruad (Fire Red), son of Badurn, king of Ireland, he was drowned there while gazing at his image and swimming the rapid. His gravemound, Síd Aedá, is on the rapids' brink, and "his body was born into the elfmound there." (This tumulus, on the north bank hilltop, was obliterated by the construction of a fort in 1798, designed to repel Napoleon. An Episcopal church now occupies the site.)

Aed is described as "rich with a good father's wealth," and as Argatmár's grandson. (*Argat*, "silver," gave him a lunar pedigree on his mother's side.)

Another story recorded in the Middle Ages says that a soldier came to him, a match for a hundred men, and was persuaded to stay for one year in return for a hundred men's wages. When the year was over, Aed refused to pay. Enraged, up rose the hireling, "fiercely holding his tall spear-shafts," and "roused his sureties" against Aed, who was bathing in the rapids. "Though thou set the sea against me," said the comely high-king of Erin, "though shalt never get from me aught but the same as any soldier." The king "broke upon the soldier the stars visible and invisible," an enigmatic phrase that expands the scope of the story to include an Otherworld firmament.

But the soldier would not be intimidated, and "incited sea, wind, sun, ether, and firmament" against the king, to avenge Aed's betrayal of the elemental powers on which his reign depended. Aed had flouted the rules of fair exchange and was therefore drawn back to extinction.

The anonymous spear-carrying soldier whose *láigen* (spear) may indicate that the forces of Leinster had been driven to the western ocean, lured Aed by means of the "sun's sultriness" "to enter the rapids and bathe . . ." "till Aed was drowned therein, by a miracle of sea and mighty wind. Hence Ess Ruaid, [or] Aed Ruaid's Rapid is said." Justice was done by solar fire on royal fire.

The Assaroe stories continue to describe a fire god's annual death in an archaic nature religion, at the hands of a virile rival from the east, Finn or his surrogate. Nor was it an *absolute* death, but rather a re-arrangement of form comparable to the return to the solar furnace of a flaring prominence. *Aed* (fire), and *goll* (one-eyed sun) were interchangeable names, and when the sun dropped below the Atlantic horizon beyond Donegal Bay, its "death" was presumed to be only an aquatic metamorphosis, enabling Goll to turn into a mythical salmon, who swam back to the Falls as Goll Essa Ruaide!

GOLL AS SALMON

So The Great Silver (Argatmor) makes his inspired leap from the Otherworld depths, back into the river systems known to humankind. This legendary fish unites Goll and Aed at the Falls and links both of them to the Connla Well salmon, at the mythical southern end of the Shannon system.

> That is a well at which are the hazels and inspirations[?] of wisdom . . . the hazels of the science of poetry, and in the same hour their fruit, and their blossom and their foliage break forth, and these fall on the well in the same shower, which raises on the water a royal surge of purple. Then the salmon chew the fruit, and the juice of the nuts is apparent on their purple bellies. And seven streams of wisdom spring forth and turn there again.

At Connla, so at Ess Ruaid, the spots on the salmon's sides, its natural markings, were interpreted as a sign of supernatural origins, coming from within.

The Goll-Salmon, leaping up the Falls on its annual spawning journey, epitomized the divine

BELOW *In the lakes about Ballyshannon, the oceanic deities mingled with those coming from Queen Medb's síd at Rathcrogan, Co. Roscommon.*

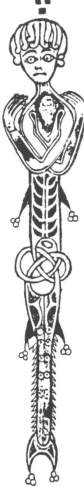

economy at work, just as the supernatural may be regarded as a countercurrent sustained within the ordinary flow of natural forces.

On the riverbank, who but Finn should be seen, roasting a salmon? According to Connacht and Donegal folktales, he was cooking it over a fire for a one-eyed giant, but burned his thumb when touching a heat blister that had risen on the side of the fish. Then, sucking his injured thumb to cool it, Finn found that all knowledge was revealed to him, including how to set about killing the giant. The giant was probably Goll in terrestrial form and another form of a legendary, one-eyed fish, "Goll below the waves."

Egyptian mythology tells us how the god Horus lost an eye and gave it to the dead Osiris to eat, the latter thereby being equipped with a soul. "From Ireland and from Egypt we seem to be listening to faraway echoes of one and the same primitive story, of sunrise and sunset. The tearing out of the eye appears to be connected with the creation or re-creation of sun or of moon."

LADY RUAD

Another Ess Ruaid story concerns an Otherworld female named Ruad. That at least "was her name in her first husband's time," a statement that alerts us to the possibility that she was a goddess, choosing a new husband annually, at Samain. Her lovers had included Aed-Srónmár, "Fire-Bignose," to whom she had given "great love." This reference sets a Halloween tone of an eternal maiden seeking a virile mate, as at Rannach Crom Dubh. Her *ruad* is the virgin's blood, ready to be spilled in the river. *Ruad* means "dark red," the color of "bloodstains," and, O'Rahilly asserts, is one of the names of the god Dagda, of whom Lady Ruad was probably the partner.

Lady Ruad arrived alone in the estuary, below the Falls. She had traveled in a bronze boat, with a tin sail. The boat belonged to Abcán, the dwarf poet of the Tuatha Dé Danann, and the sail could be the white lunar sickle of a maiden desiring fulfillment. The preferred metals are pre-Iron Age.

She had come from the northern ocean, "with Ireland on the larboard side" leaving behind the pure sagacity that can be found in the sea, her inheritance. "When she went with Gaeth (*gaeth*, "the Sea"), son of Gaes Glan (*gaes*, "intelligence," *glan*, "pure"), her previous dwelling is described as *Mag Maen*, "The Great Plain of Dumbness.""

Once again, it is clear that myth involves an arousal to speech, or song.

After the silence of the western deep, Lady Ruad yearned to hear voices again. Therefore "the Tapered-fingered came on a path of happy love," and, as a goddess of love, "That fair and modest maiden happened upon the famous bay below the Falls, . . . and she asked in no uncertain wise that the river should be her freehold, [saying] 'This is the brightest inver [estuary] in Erin.'"

"Then Aed saw her from the seat he occupied, but he knew not who the girl might be, and she knew not what land she was in." Across the estuary, "from a burden of sea-maids," she heard the mermaids'

melody. "Then she fell asleep at the music, among the streams of the eddying bays, tumbled over the bow of her boat, and was drowned, [and therefore] never reached the hero her love." Or, "she leapt overboard, not mastered by a spell, but by the doleful music of the fairy mounds. So from her comes the name Ess Ruaid with its greatness." (As a language word, *ess* means waterfall, boat, *and* death.)

One can interpret her death as Christian alteration of an oral tradition, with the new cult of virginity replacing a pagan love match. Yet if Lady Ruad is salt water, her "drowning" becomes a lying-in-wait for the inevitable fall of her lover (the cataract) into her arms, in a union audible and visible to all.

From the long reaches of Upper and Lower Lough Erne, the sluggish Erne River creeps in silence till, falling through space, it roars into the receptive body of the ocean, personified by Lady Ruad. Myth tends to grow at places where the hidden voice is heard and where stored energies are unleashed in divine encounter. That Aed was of a sacred pantheon is

ABOVE *Bronze
sword-hilt, from the
River Erne at
Ballyshannon, Co.
Donegal, c.100 B.C.E.
It may have represented
the sacrificial hero, Aed,
or Diarmaid.*

confirmed by an alternative title of the Falls — Ess
Duind, named after Donn, god of the underworld, son of Duban (from *duban*, "aroused
up"), son of Bile, from *bile*, "tree." This family
tree brings the Ess Ruaid events into alignment
with the *axis mundi*, thereby "centering" the island at
the start of a new year, and at the place of the festivities.

The desire of the goddess, and the arousal of the
god, provided the underlying theme. The arrival of the
craft under the Falls signified the *hieros gamos*, or
divine wedding; consequently the cataract ran red.

A fragment from the Yellow Book of Lecan makes
it plain that the Dagda, greatest of all the Irish gods,
wished to identify with Aed at his marriage. Therefore
the Dagda says: "I *am* Aed Abaid of Ess Ruaid, that is
the Good God of wizardry of the Tuatha Dé Danann."
Lady Ruad, we may take it, was his bride, and their
union brought land and sea together.

DIARMAID AT ESS RUAID

At the end of every year, toward the Falls of Assaroe
galloped Diarmaid, consort of Gráinne. He came
mounted backward on the boar to which he clung;
their destinies were tied together in a death ride.
"When the beast reached Ess Ruaid it gave three swift
leaps across the Fall, hither and thither, [but] it could
not put Diarmaid off." Nevertheless, these jumps
signaled Diarmaid's end.

Diarmaid's year and a day with Gráinne was
nearly over. He had suspected that her attention was
already turning elsewhere and had taunted her about
her feelings for "the youth in the green garb" — the
hidden prospect of spring, waiting to push him aside.
Co. Roscommon folklore rumors that Gráinne was
having an affair with a giant named Cuithach (*cuithach*,
"hurtful, destructive").

When he was first threatened by the boar in
North Sligo, Diarmaid had struck at it with his sword
Fearless, but the weapon broke in two; a sign of
weakening sexual potency.

Then the hero, still on the boar's back, was galloped to a mound on top of Ben Bulben overlooking

RIGHT *Ben Bulben, Co.
Sligo. Here Diarmaid
was killed by the magic
boar, on whose back he
had earlier leapt the
Falls of Assaroe.
Diarmaid was the
lover of Gráinne at
Lough Gur, and
throughout Ireland.*

the Sligo coast, there to be thrown off and gored by the beast, till the hero's bowels and entrails "lay about him." Yet Diarmaid summoned up the strength to pierce the boar through the navel, and killed it.

Finn (who had been hunting Diarmaid all year, ever since he had run off with Gráinne from Tara in Leinster), then came up to gloat. "I like to see you so," said Finn, "and I regret that all the women of Ireland are not looking at you now, for your beauty is turned to ugliness and your good form to deformity." Diarmaid's fabulous spear, *Ga Buidhe an Lamhaigh*, which combined martial, solar, and phallic virtues, was useless to him. Prior to the battle with the boar, Gráinne had advised him to put it aside and to take instead *Ga Dearg Duinn*, the "red, ruddy, or blood-colored spear," better suited to his imminent death; but he had not done so, preferring to keep faith with the gold weapon of happier days, such as those he had spent with her around Lough Gur. But in Co. Sligo, the boom of Ess Ruaid spoke of Gráinne changing her partner, and so he died.

PARTHOLÓN AND INIS SAMER

Two hundred yards downstream from the site of the Assaroe Falls lies a small, fish-shaped island. Now called Fish Island, its Celtic name was Inis Samer, the Isle of the lapdog Samer. There lived Partholón, the mythic "king" who, in *Lebor Gabála*, led the settlement of the country. He set up house within sound of the Falls with his wife Delgnat and his servant Tobar.

Macalister identifies Partholón with Bith (Cosmos). Bith's cairn was erected on the Ulster-Connacht boundary at Slieve Beagh, 42 miles (68 kilometers) from Inis Samer. The name "Partholón" is thought to be a version of Bartholomew, and both forms may be the outcome of a Christian scribe's attempt to insert the name of the only apostle for whom claims of noble blood have ever been made, into a pagan cycle.

"His story, like Bith's, is connected with the creation or re-creation of the sun or of the moon, with their death at setting and rebirth at rising, involving ritual combat. He combines these echoes with the

RIGHT Inis Samer (Summer Isle), Ballyshannon, where Delgnat, Partholón's wife, made love to Tobar. In revenge, Partholón killed her dog, Samer. This Samain, or Summer's End, myth describes an old god being ousted by next year's youth.

function of a vegetation god who must die under the strokes of the winter-daemon." Queen Delgnat's eventual desertion of Partholón in favor of a younger mate is the standard mythic way of expressing the ruthlessness of the seasonal drama.

As the ultimate river of Harvest Home, the Erne was, in Partholón's estimation, "the most fruitful which he had found in Ireland." From his house in midstream, he then "went a-hunting and a-fishing" and he left his wife and his henchman Tobar to guard the island. The woman bade the henchman pair with her. He refused. The woman called him a coward. At last, he consented "because the woman was reviling him. From that indecency and folly, which those two wrought, the name clave to the creek, *Da Econd* [of the two fools]." Thereafter thirst seized them and they

drank of the measures [vessels], and tubes of Partholón, [who] came to the house at the end of the

day and perceived the taste of Tobar's mouth and that of Delgnat upon the tube and so became aware of the misdeed; great wrath seized him, and so he killed his wife's lapdog, which was called Saimer, whence Saimer's Island has its name . . . so this was the first jealousy and the first lust in Erin. Thereafter the servant escaped, fleeing at random, and was eaten by dogs and birds.

Beneath the tone of monastic misogyny that has colored the written account, a pre-Christian structure survives, as does the Arcadian mood of the accompanying verse, in speaking of the lovemaking isle:

The place where it was done,

after its fashioning certainly —

great is its sweetness that was there that day

in the land of Inis Saimera.

The gold tubes used by the lovers are matched by the wheatstraws employed in Welsh oath-swearing rites, while the cup or bowl has been acknowledged as the vessel of the feminine by most cultures. The name of the male lover, Tobar, attached itself to the vessel, for as a language word, *toba* can mean "drinking vessel." *Tobach*, "the act of reaping," produced the necessary straws. That the initiative is taken by Delgnat "is entirely in keeping with the archaic pattern."

The queen is not cowed by Partholón's protests, but answers, in Keating's rendering: "Do you think that it is possible that woman and honey be near one another, new milk and a cat . . . or a man and a woman in private without their meddling with each other?"

Master, fair one, Partholón!

when longing for a pairing comes, it is not easy to subdue it.

See thy speckle-colored cattle-herds

in their tight bond they have desire!

See thy sheep of fair garb

that tarry not for a pairing master!

Foaming milk of thy horned cow, be it not trusted to a kitten.

✠ HORNS OF GOOD BORG ✠

Overlooking Lower Lough Erne, a stone circle erected c. 2000 B.C.E. on the Co. Tyrone shore at Kiltierney still displays the horns of Good Borg in the "recumbent" (skull) and two uprights that form a group on the west-northwest side of the eight-stone ring. Facing her father's stonehorns across the circle is "Erne" herself, represented by the carved bullaun stone, deliberately hollowed to collect water, which, until very recently, was used in matters of female fecundity.

An Iron-Age bronze brooch, excavated from a nearby cairn, shows the open vulva together with coiled serpents in a different form. Both the stone and metal images have antecedents traceable to the Paleolithic.

ABOVE *Grianan Ailech, Co. Donegal. This stone dun marked the north end of Partholón's four-fold division of Ireland, between his four sons.*

Macalister regards her verse as "primarily a fertility spell," and the king's slaying of the dog as a surrogate offering for himself.

Frazer has collected numerous instances of comparable substitutions. The sacrifice enabled Partholón to live out thirty years of occupation as a culture hero, introducing the arts of cattle-rearing, building, cooking, brewing, dueling, and guesting – offering hospitality. He was also credited with clearing four plains and creating numerous loughs and rivers. Then he divided the country among his four sons, using the Eiscir Riada as the east–west boundary, intersected by a north–south frontier, running from Ailech Neit (the hill near Derry, on which stands the imposing fortress of Grianan Ailigh overlooking Lough Foyle), to Ard Nemid, an isle in Cork Harbour, Munster.

To recreate the four quarters was a feature of many divine plans – a desire passed from god to god, and the joint effort of deadly rivals. Thus we learn of Partholón and Delgnat's attempt at the grand design, that "Ita was their hireling, or Toba was his other name." *Tobar* means "source, spring, well"; *Ita*, "corn" (*Ith*). Partholón's rival was therefore himself, when young. "Ith, like Tobar, is a sort of rebirth of Partholón." But Tobar never ascends the throne. Instead he disappears *into* Nature via the digestive tracts of wild beasts.

As for Partholón, a folk practice reported from Co. Waterford shows that his spirit as an end-of-harvest god continued to stalk the fields of Ireland into the nineteenth century:

> The Day of Parthanan comes a short time before the end of Harvest, and everybody tries to have his crops mown before then, because on that day Parthanan is said to go round threshing every grain from corn still standing. To deny him these pickings, men would hastily roll over and flatten the unmown remainder of their crop.

PARTHOLÓN AND NEMED

In Ireland there was a strong "family resemblance" between the sons of supposedly different mythic invaders. Nor were such similarities regarded with dismay, for in the age of myth, "originality" involved the incorporation of origins, just as the sapwood of a tree incorporates in heartwood the secret of its strength. Consequently, The Four Sons of Nemed, described in *Lebor Gabála*, are remarkably similar in their names to the "four sons of Partholón." Ultimately, they were all children of Bith and the birth-giving goddess Cesair.

Commentators detect an overlap verging on synonymity between Partholonians, Nemedians, and Fir Bolg, as recapitulations of a common agrarian mythic cycle. Read together they make muddled "history," but are valuable pointers to a "very ancient stratum of tradition . . . highly suggestive of primitive myth."

SAMER'S END AND LOUGH ERNE

The Erne River in which the island of Inis Samer lies was previously known as the Samer or Samhair River. This archaic title deepens further the involvement of Lady Ruad and Aed (along with Delgnat, Tobar, Partholón, and Saimer the dog), in versions of a summer's end drama, which stretched upstream to incorporate Lough Erne.

Lough Erne "first showed its troubled waters . . . on a radiant evening in harvest," when "the noble Erne [who was] chief among the maidens in Rathcrúachan [the *sid* of Medb, fairy queen of Connacht], fled with a troop of women to the plain where now Lough Erne lies." They had been frightened by the emergence from the Caves of Crúachan of the "grisly shape and rough brawling voice of the giant Olca Ái." One version of the story says that although Olca Ái's purpose was "to contend against Armargen the Black-haired," Olca incidentally "shook his beard . . . and gnashed his teeth" at the boys and girls of the country, "[so that] they went mad, and ran toward Ess Ruaid."

Meanwhile, the queen-goddess Medb had given the potent symbols of her divine sexuality, her "comb, and casket unsurpassed," to Erne, "chieftainess of the girls of Crúachan," and they were in the maiden's possession when she was drowned with her party, under the waters of the new lough, "the blameless vast noble lough Erne," with its "pure light portion," which even the Christian god exalts, says the poet.

The effectiveness of the casket given by Medb to Erne depended upon a male response, which may be visible today in the notable concentration of stone effigies sited on islands in Lower Lough Erne. The row of eight statues situated on White Island are thought to have been carved before 900 C.E. and include a broadly smiling female, naked except for a very short cloak. She sits in a knees-apart manner, reminiscent of a sheela-na-gig, and has sometimes been classed as such. Her lack of breasts indicates a

LEFT *Gold casket with solar symbols, 2¹/4 inches (6 centimeters) diameter, c. 800 B.C.E., this miniature enclosed* grianon, *"sunhouse," may have been worn internally by the goddess' human representative.*

RIGHT *Boa Island "Janus" sculpture, Lough Erne, 29^1/$_2$ inches (75 centimeters) tall, fifth century* C.E. *Back to back, the rival gods of consecutive years demonstrate the reversibility of Time itself, since Samain, November 1st, was both the end and the start of a year. Past and Future are tied to an eternal NOW.*

prematernal state and was probably the sculptor's way of distinguishing between a maiden and a mother. Next to her (now set in a twelfth-century chapel wall) is a heavier female who is depicted carrying a box or perhaps a casket – even *the* casket of Medb; this second figure has the same rounded cheeks as her partner, and the hint of a smile. She may represent the maternal aspect of the libidinous maiden. Both have a pedigree traceable to the Old Stone Age in mainland Europe.

On nearby Lusty More Island a 4-foot (1.2-meter)-high megalith, carved as a woman, is "grasping something in each hand," as she opens in sexual readiness.

At the west end of Boa Island is a pillar statue of seventh-century date, 28 inches (70 cm) high, generally regarded as depicting two gods, back to back, with crossed arms. The cases of Diarmaid and his rival, the youth in the green garb, and of Partholón with his servant Tobar, supply the narrative theme of a male pair whose destinies are entwined, as the goddess abandons one male consort for another at Samer's end. One head of his "Janus" image wears a forked beard. Both have arms crossed, and share a broad belt, and "hair," braided in a "corn dolly" manner.

At Crúachain, the sacred capital of Connacht, the emergence of the underworld libido was shown and felt in the bulllike figures of Olca Aí and his partner and rival, Armargen the Black-haired (*Olca* meaning "he who wrongs a saint," with *aí* meaning "poetic inspiration"). These powers are comparable to the Lios bull at Lough Gur. It was at Samain that Medb gathered the forces of Ireland and set out from Crúachain to seek the Brown Bull of Cualgne in Ulster to match against her own Whitehorn. The maiden Erne's paternity further strengthens the bull link, since her father, the loud-shouting Borg-Ban, was also known as Good Borg the Bellowing (see page 171), which has a very bovine ring.

Whether called Erne or by some other name, the emergence at Samain of the New Year maiden from Queen Medb's *síd* is a recurring feature of Irish myth, and lived on in the traditional behavior of young women at Samain. The following oral account by a Co. Donegal woman is of her mother's mid-nineteenth-century experiences.

Hers was the last generation of young girls in the district to spend the summer herding on the mountain pastures before returning a few days before Samain to the company of the young men in the lowland farms. At that festival she "came out" from the mountain cave, following the archaic behavior track: "The girls were delighted to be coming home after such a long stay in the hills, and they had a very merry time for a week after their return. Their people and the neighbors made them very welcome and it is they who were in good health and heart on their return – strong, healthy, ruddy, full of blood, with not a care in the world except to have a fine time."

BELOW *Farm, Ballyconeely, Co. Galway, At Samain, young women returned with their herds from the mountain pastures, to celebrations in family homesteads.*

PART FOUR

CONNACHT 3
flood, fish, word

The indulgence of appetites on the human level was patterned on the presumed behavior of the gods. Gluttony and sexual desire meet in the Dagda and his young mistress, the daughter of Indech. In Connacht they feasted on each other and on the fruits of earth and ocean; however, she was a Fomorian princess and so, like Lady Ruad, represented the power of her Oceanic father.

WINTER FLOOD

The orgiastic flood of Samain quickly took on the threatening quality of wintry inundation, engulfing whole territories, and giving another twist to the Lough Erne story: "Once the land under the Lough was the territory of a tribe called the Ernai who were drowned there when the Lough was created, and thereafter the lake burst *throughout the land of Erin*, and this is truer," says the Edinburgh *Dindshenchas*, where the lough is presented as the model for a national submergence.

At the onset of winter, fierce gales and a drop in evaporation with falling temperatures, together with increased tides, were to be expected, as medieval "Winter" poems record: "The sea is running high . . . the voice of the barnacle goose sounds frequently . . . wild waves run . . . each least lake grown full; a full lake each puny pond." "Ireland's fish wander the more," says the poet of "Winter Cold." "Each fine furrow is a river, and a full pool is every ford. The size of a great sea is every angry lake . . . each lashing lake — a sea strong."

The *Dindshenchas* carries the idea of national inundation to the primordial time of Bith, father of Cesair, and the first "man" ever to settle in the country. Fleeing here, forty days before Noah's Flood, his hope of escaping the world inundation were disappointed.

The waters "overtook him on Sliab Betha [Slieve Beagh], and he was for a whole year beneath the waves, and then the sea gave him up again, and he was found dead on the mountain." That mountain overlooks the Erne Valley, and Bith's experience may be regarded as the prototype for Aed's submergence in the arms of the inrushing sea goddess. In terms of Bith's role in the Ulster–Connacht dialogue, some ancient sources call his mountain "one of the hills of Connacht, Sliab-Betha ever fresh." In both provinces, repeated floodings brought the old gods to life again in storytelling, as in physical fact.

OPPOSITE *Prior to the introduction of modern drainage, large parts of Ireland were subject to winter floods. Samain floods were associated with sexual arousal and secretions of the Fomorian sea divinities. The Irish* fo-mair *means "under sea." In the fall, their rainclouds drenched Ireland.*

LEFT *The one-legged Sciapods of Eurasian fable reappear in Connacht as Fomorian sea-gods, leaving one leg in the abyss of the sub-conscious (or prenatal) state. Fomorians are our hidden selves.*

The Gaelic word *turboch* denotes lands that become winter lakes, and what the traveler Lithgow wrote in 1619 is applicable to the modern winter landscape, despite many drainage projects:

And this I dare avow, there are more rivers, lakes, brooks, strands, quagmires, bogs, and marshes in this country, than in all Christendom besides; for travelling there in winter, all my dayly solace was sinke downe comfort, whiles boggy-plunging deepes kissing my horse belly, over-mired saddle, body and all; and often or ever set a-swimming in great danger, both I and my guides of our lives; that for cloudy and fountayne-bred perils, I was never before reduced to such a floting laborinth . . . in five moneths space, I quite spoyled six horses, and myself as tyred as the worst of them.

BELOW *Peat bog, Connemara. Waterlogged Ireland preserves mosses and grasses from 5,000 summers as peat or "turf." This vegetable "memory bank" incorporates the fossil tree-stumps of Neolithic forest felling.*

The sense of an entire country swamped was confirmed for him by finding that even *within* houses "in foule weather scarcely can they find a drye part, whereupon to repose their cloud-baptized heads." The ancient Irish word for winter was *Gaimrad*, from *Gam*, marriage; for in winter the elements of earth and water were conspicuously intertwined.

Annual floods were assimilated on the mythological level; for example, when two horses, belonging to Macha, daughter of Aed of Ess Ruaid, are released from her *síd*, "A stream broke forth after them, and there was much foam on that stream, and the foam spread over the land exceedingly."

The *Dindshenchas* of the Plain of Louth states: "The sea covered it [this plain] thirty years after the flood, hence it is called 'darkness of the sea,' or 'it is under the sea's roof.' Or there was a magic sea over it, and an octopus therein, having a property of suction. It would suck in a man in armor till he lay at the bottom of its treasure bag. The Dagda came with his 'mace of wrath' in his hand, and plunged it down upon the octopus chanting these words: 'Turn thy hollow head! Turn thy ravening body! Turn thy resorbent forehead! Avaunt! Begone!' Then the magic sea retired with the octopus."

In the myth cycle, the annual saturation of Ireland brought the entire country through the flood of coition, leading nine months later to the harvest birth event. The Samain affair, typified by Delgnat and Tobar, is the origin of the next amniotic sea, a gestation with which every part of the country identified, and so shared in the accumulation of "prenatal waters." They spread around Lough Erne, and along the Shannonside meadows, filtering across the Midland Plain, singing the quiet music of the resaturated bogs, while roaring in great fury down every mountain gulley.

Ireland does not claim to have *invented* the link between topographical flooding and feminine secretions. Rather, in the prehistoric world, hydrographic changes were often related to aspects of human reproduction. For example, in a story from ancient Persia, known to Herodotus, the mother of Kyros had a dream many months prior to his birth. Falling asleep in a sanctuary while tending goats, she dreamed "that so much water passed away from her in giving birth that it became a large stream, inundating all Asia, as far as the sea." The belief, widespread in Europe, that conception took place by immersion in water, also served to unite the month of human marriages, Gam, with the regularly observed flooding of the Irish landscape at the start of the winter. Then the whole island "died" with the passing of the old year and was conceived again in water, prior to its eventual rebirth during the following summer.

THE FOMORIANS

Perambulations from Connacht take us into the formless northwestern ocean, where, in the uncertainties beyond sunset, wave after wave of mythic rivals are seen to lose their grip on Ireland.

Through the agency of the migrating divine salmon, and of other gods, Connacht myth also surges northward, to the farthest reaches of Ulster, thereby completing a sunwise national cycle. So, the mythic monster is seen to swallow its own tail (and tale).

In Ireland, the supernatural beings most closely identified with inundations were the Fomorians. Folk etymology interprets their name as *Fo*, "under," with *muir*, "sea." Living mainly in the ocean, or on offshore islands, the Fomorians were regarded as coeval with the world itself. From their base on Tory Island, beyond the extreme northwest tip of Donegal, they regularly invaded the mainland.

They were often portrayed as one-legged, one-armed giants, or in the words of *Lebor Gabála*, "men with single noble legs, and with single full hands," a condition midway between man and sea-serpent.

They represented the human admission that beyond the walls of organized beings and specific consciousnesses lay a sea of mutations. Fomorians laid claim to the solid land of Erin, knowing that without their contribution it would soon atrophy into a rigid state. They were particularly active at the onset of winter, when the crack between the ending of one year and the start of the next was wide enough for the

forces of chaos to slip through, to alarm the population with a flood of darkness from the northwest, and to remind the individual of black forces concealed within the psyche.

At that season the Fomorians are reported to have claimed their annual tithes from the Irish at Mag Cetne, on The Plains of Tribute, which lay on the south side of the Ess Ruaid Falls, stretching toward the Drowes River along the coastal plain of north Sligo, and referred to in the Annals of Connacht as Mag Cetne of the Fomore. "The extent of that tribute," wrote Keating, "was two thirds of the children, and of the corn, and of the milch kine of the men of Ireland, to be offered to them [the Fomorians] every year on the eve of Samhain."

Low-lying coasts were particularly vulnerable to attack by the Fomorians. The *Dindshenchas* for Mag Muireisce in Co. Sligo, "that was visited by the strong rushing wave," speaks of a tumult of life-forms that was spewed directly from a sea monster, in an anarchic manner. Other accounts recall that there was "a warm flood, an inundation of dead fish," and a time when "the sea belched forth with thousands of children throughout Erin's four lands" (provinces).

ABOVE *Tory Island, beyond the northwest tip of Co. Donegal, was regarded as a Fomorian base. From there, on Samain eve they demanded two-thirds of the children, milch-cows, and grain of Ireland.*

THE NEMEDIANS

The mythical Nemedians were unwilling to pay Fomorian tithes. Instead they attacked Tory Island to destroy the "enemy" tower. The Fomorians then brought up reinforcements from Africa. During the ensuing battle, according to Keating, neither side noticed the sea "coming up under them, with a gigantic wave . . . filling up every side around them, and all but one boatload of Nemedians were drowned."

This last boatload sailed away, watched by the Fomorians who returned to their native watery depths from where, for hundreds of years, they nursed an Ireland cleansed of human inhabitants back to health.

Each new group of mythical invaders was confronted by the Fomorians. Neither men nor gods could escape the dialectic. Of the Danann's battle with the Fomorians, Gray says that "it stands at the center of Irish mythology." It is the stuff of eternity. Today the place of the battle, Moytirra, Co. Sligo, is a scattered community of small farms on a thin-soiled limestone plateau, overlooking Lough Arrow in Co. Sligo, where huge blocks of limestone rest as the ice-sheet left them, scattered across the terrain. The 16-foot (5-meter)-high Eglone stone, an erratic of magnesium limestone, stands erect. Others, like mortally wounded soldiers, lie around in the rushy pastures together with the remains of Megalithic court tombs, dating from the early third millennium B.C.E., in a timeless landscape. Nor is the battle forgotten by the present inhabitants, who are proud to occupy land of such significance.

The Dagda's tactic at the Second Battle was to deny water to the Fomorians, the element that they loved the best.

And the Dagda asked the cup-bearer what power he wielded. He answered that he would bring the twelve chief loughs of Ireland into the presence of the Fomoire, and they would not find water in them, however thirsty they were. [Lough Derg, Luimnig, Corrib, Ree, Mask, Strangford Lough, Belfast Lough, Neagh, Foyle, Gara, Loughrea, and Márlock were named.] They would then proceed to the twelve chief rivers of Ireland — the Bush, Boyne, Bann,

LEFT *Mam Ean, Co.
Galway, 1842. Print by
by W. H. Bartlett. Here
the descendants of
Connacht's mythic Fir
Bolg do the rounds of
holy cave, spring, and
lough, in the time-
honored earth worship.
The Fir Bolg were allied
to the oceanic Fomorian
deities, and were togeth-
er defeated by the
Tuatha Dé Danann at
Cong, Co. Galway. This
was the first so-called
battle of Moytirra.*

Blackwater, Lee, Shannon, Moy, Sligo, Erne, Finn, Liffey, and Suir — and they would all be hidden from the Fomoire. Druids promised three showers of fire upon the Fomoire, and to lock their urine into their bodies, and into the bodies of their horses. The Dagda said, "The power which you boast, I will wield it all myself." "You are the Dagda ['the Good God'] said everyone . . ."

At the end of the battle the Fomorians returned to the sea. However, several of the protagonists, Bres and Lugh for example, had parents coming from *both* camps. The purpose of the battle was to illuminate "the principles fundamental to the ordering and maintenance of human society," including "the contractual and magical aspects of sovereignty," writes Gray.

TUAN

After Partholón's tribe was wiped out by plague, the work of reconstruction fell on the sole survivor, his brother's son, Tuan. *Tuan* means "wholeness." How could he live up to his name and father a new and healthier human race?

Irish mythology implies that the recovery of good order involves the sacrifice of human separateness from the rest of the living world. Thus for nine hundred years Tuan lost his human form, "And these are the shapes he was: a hundred years he had in the form of a man, three hundred years in the form of a wild ox over waste places, two hundred years in the form of a wild stallion, three hundred years in the form of a solitary bird, a hundred years in the form of a salmon." In that shape a fisher took him to the queen of Lord Red-neck, the Ulster King. The queen desired the salmon to mate with her. "So he was urged of her, and of her Tuan was conceived at last."

When a goddess and shape-shifting man come together, a new human race may be initiated. Thus Tuan-the-fish fathered Tuan the first human child, in the *síd* of Grianan Ailech near Londonderry, the northern marker of Partholón's division of Ireland. Fishy Tuan reclaimed the female womb as a symbolic universal ocean. The human-child born from that deep

could then arrive in the land-world with the knowledge of submarine wholeness. A new human order could then arise, having a purified bloodstream modeled on the salmon's habitat. His river connected earth to sea, Fomorians to sky deities, and fish with people. Renewed hope flows from the story.

LEFT *Tuan as a fish. After plague had wiped out Partholón's divine tribe, Tuan, the sole survivor, was obliged to take on various animal guises, so experiencing the unity of all life forms.*

✠ FISH, TONGUE, AND MYTHIC WORD ✠

The annual migration of the salmon through Atlantic Irish waters from west to north provides a natural context for the linkage of Ess Ruaid and Grianan Ailech salmon myths. They collaborate in order to make the sound of a new utterance, and a renewed cycle. Hence, it is the queen of the far north who touches the salmon with her tongue.

In many Indo-European languages, the final part of several words meaning "tongue" also serve as terms for "fish." This fish-tongue amalgam can be assigned to a very early date, with "tongue" being derived from "fish." (In Achill Island, Co. Mayo, the sole-fish is called *teanga cait*, literally "tongue chaff.")

These coincidences may arise from the mythic need for verbal conception, whereby a tongue, sounding in the bowl of the mouth, is involved in every divine birth, since the story must be told before any parturition can be seen as sacred. A deity is born when word of mouth and delivery from the womb are twinned together.

OVERLEAF *Achill Island, Co. Mayo. In many languages, the word for "tongue" derives from "fish." As a salmon, Tuan swam around Ireland into a queen's mouth, and told his secret. Via her womb, she then bore him back to human form. At root, mythic word and deed make a recreation love-affair.*

MIDE

the center stone

The Irish word for province, *cóiced*, also means a fifth; yet the ancient and continuing division of the island into the *four* provinces of Ulster, Munster, Leinster, and Connacht seems to leave no room for a fifth part. The discrepancy has sometimes been explained by recalling how, at certain historical periods, Munster was subdivided into two, thereby turning the four provinces into five. Yet many scholars think that the elusive fifth stands for something more fundamental.

The likelihood is that ever since the Stone Age (and despite numerous boundary changes in detail), Ireland has been subdivided into four provinces, held together by a mystical fifth, territorially elusive, yet vital to the cohesion of the whole sacred array.

The fifth province was called Mide. The four-plus-one pattern, of which Mide formed the center, could be seen as the outcome of Ireland's compact shape. Malin Head in the far north lies 248 miles (400 kilometers from the south coast of Munster, compared with a maximum island width of 210 miles (340 kilometers). This makes a quadrilateral division around a shared center point a convenient arrangement.

But since the mythic view of reality declares that efficiency is the outcome of magical accord between the seen and the unseen, there is more to Mide than just simple geometry.

In Mide, people could encounter the gods on the most sacred ground. Like a good idea, its space was small yet extendable. As a national "head and brain," it coordinated intelligences from the other provinces.

Human spatial awareness has always been profoundly affected by the cardinal directions of the human body, to the furthest horizons of terrestrial and spiritual possibilities. Ancient god-filled space normally displayed the symmetries of the worshiper's

frame, just as the envisaged gods often took anthropomorphic form. The left-right balance (Ulster–Munster), of human eyes, ears, nostrils, nipples, testes, arms, legs, and sets of fingers and toes, disposed evenly on either side of a central axis, is bisected at right angles by the equally physical reality of back (Connacht) and sunrise-facing front (Leinster). From Mide, the qualities specific to the mythic space of each of the surrounding four provinces were differentiated and coordinated into a divine island metabolism.

G. Dumézil confirms that "the natural concept of four cardinal points and a center is found widely on every continent," and forms the basis of numerous cosmologies. The Indian *Rig Veda* speaks of the five directions as North, South, East, West, and "Here." In ancient Ireland, Mide was "Here" to everyone. It was held in common.

Mide, the notional center of Ireland, was conceived as a point where an umbilical cord attached the country to the womb of the gods, who endlessly created and sustained its existence from above and below. Yet Mide was a real place, namely the Hill of Uisnech or Uisneach, now in Co. Westmeath. It was also identified with the large boulder called Aill na Mireann, standing on Uisnech's southwest slope, *and* with the various archeological sites visible on the hill.

LEFT *Aill na Mireann, the "Stone of Divisions," Uisnech, Co. Westmeath, 15 1/2 inches (4.75 meters) high. Through the different faces of this natural limestone bolder, Ireland's four provinces are said to combine. Set in a saucer-shaped, ring-banked hollow, the stone is also regarded as Mide, the mystical fifth province and a sacred reality, underlying the other four. Iris* mide *means "middle, center, and neck."*

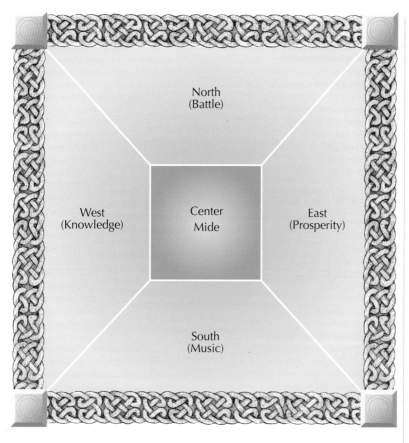

North
(Battle)

West
(Knowledge)

Center
Mide

East
(Prosperity)

South
(Music)

ABOVE *The five provinces of Ireland. Each was by tradition ascribed a particular aptitude: "Knowledge – West, Battle – North, Prosperity – East, Music – South," combining as "Royalty at the Center."*

The extensive view of the Irish midlands gained from Uisnech may also be regarded as integral to Mide, but not in the sense of the political annexation that King Tuathal Techmar attempted (and for a while sustained) in the second century C.E. Nor should mythic Mide be confused with the modern counties of Meath or of Westmeath.

Seen from Mide, the energies of the four provinces could be woven by enlightened observation into a web of radial and concentric "place-events." From Mide, the array of distant hills and mountains, and the solar and lunar risings or settings that coincided with their summits, were the stuff of a god-given mandala. This served to reveal Sacred Ireland in its entirety, and set it within the orb of a divine universe, rendered synonymous with the eyeball of the human worshiper.

The Irish word *mide* means "neck," and the fifth province may be regarded as the means of joining head to body, idea to thing, and body to soul. Mide was almost nothing, yet it was everything. It was the making of a divine island, called by the name of a living

goddess, Ériu. In her name every province had a place. She was their collective origin and product, the comprehensive landlady, who built, owned, named, and lived in the island-home.

THE STONE OF DIVISIONS (AILL NA MIREANN)

The entire fifth province of Mide can be condensed into Aill na Mireann, the Stone of Divisions. This fissured and fragmenting limestone boulder stands on the southwest slopes of Uisnech Hill 98 feet (30 meters) below the summit, where it was deposited during the last Ice Age as a glacial erratic, before the first human beings arrived in Ireland. Its gray mass, measuring nearly 16 feet (5 meters) high, traditionally symbolized Ireland, united in its divisions.

The Yellow Book of Lecan describes how the god Fintan, son of Ocean, returned to Aill na Mireann: "It is long since I drank a drink of the Deluge over the navel of Uisnech," says the god, implying that the Flood of prenatal waters were also centered over Ireland's "mother" stone. Fintan's task was to reestablish the Stone at the core of national life, after Tara had threatened to disrupt the pattern.

He was asked: "O Fintan, how has our island been divided?" He replied, "Knowledge in the West, Battle in the North, Prosperity in the East, Music in the South, Royalty at the Center." At Aill na Mireann, the attribute of the provincial directions combined into a synthesis, where "royalty" was the display of the divine on earth.

"The points of the great provinces run toward Uisnech, they have divided yonder stone through into five," explained Fintan, "And he assigned a ridge of it to every province in Ireland."

The stone's central role continued to be acknowledged in the present century, when, in the struggle for Irish independence from British rule, a hole was sunk into the top to receive a flag-pole around which political meetings were held.

The ancient ring bank, measuring 26 feet (8 meters) in diameter, which surrounds the stone and sets it in

LEFT *Bronze figure with a cloisonné enameled body. Cut from an early medieval Irish bowl, it was found in a Viking grave at Milkebostad, Norway.* Mide *can mean "neck." The god Mide is up to his neck in a five-province array.*

187

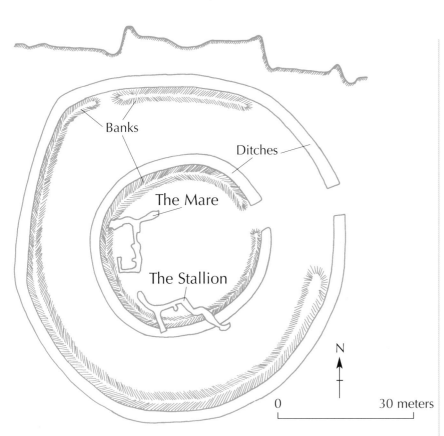

Banks

Ditches

The Mare

The Stallion

N

0   30 meters

ABOVE *Stable of the horse deities, Uisnech, Site 17, fifth century C.E. This 262-foot (80-meter) diameter wheel-shaped enclosure conceals two elaborate sets of tunnels, which can be read as monumental subterranean images of the divine mare, pursued by the stallion-god Dagda, who lived here. (The Iron Age "hill figure" of the horse-goddess Epona, carved at Uffington, England, gallops in the same way.)*

RIGHT *Uisnech Hill, Co. Westmeath. From here Dagda and the horse-deities rode out, to pull the sun-chariot around Ireland.*

horse god Eochaid Ollathair had a house on Uisnech, "with Ireland stretching equally far from it on every side, to south and north, to east and west." Eochaid's name is derived from the word *Éach*, "a horse," and *O'llathair* means "father of all." This horse god of the central hill was synonymous with the Dagda, the chief of the Dananns, "who used to work wonders for the people and control the weather and crops."

The prehistoric Uisnech stables of the Dagda as horse god may have been found by Macalister in 1929, at site 17, situated on the north flank of the hill, facing the same god's Ulster house at Grianan Ailech. In outward form, site 17 displays an outer circular rampart and ditch, 255 feet (78 meters) in diameter, with a raised inner hub, also surrounded by a bank, and with an internal ditch. Both rings have an entrance aligned to the north–east.

a saucer-shaped hollow, confirms that it was the center of attention. Great hunks of the limestone rock have now split, and wedged themselves into a heap against the southeast side. The weathering on these pieces shows that the collapse probably happened prior to the first human arrivals.

Irish myth suggests that the subdivision of Ireland from Aill na Mireann was reenacted by successive waves of settlers who wished to claim divine sanction for their invasion. Thus Giraldus wrote of the "Five Sons of Dela" (*alias* the Fir Bolg), that on "coming to Ireland from Greece . . . their bounds met at a stone . . . called *Umbilicus Hiberniae*, the navel of Ireland, because it stands in the middle of the country."

THE UISNECH HORSE TEMPLE

At the still center of Ireland, one would expect the fastest forms of the sun deities to take a rest. Therefore at Uisnech the solar horses were stabled. According to the *Wooing of Étáin* manuscript, the

Beneath the paved floor of the inner ring lie two sets of tunnels or *souterrains*. The southern souterrain was possibly designed to resemble and *be* the Dagda as galloping stallion. He addresses his partner, the northern *souterrán*, shaped like a mare.

For Iron Age communities, the assumed integration of spiritual and physical life was brought to reality partly by means of gigantic images of the living gods. That was the tradition inherited from the Neolithic community, an orthodoxy that remained unchallenged until the arrival of Christianity. In subsequent oral belief these buildings continued to be called giants and giantesses, reflecting their construction as supernatural beings.

When laid out on this scale, the hidden gods could be seen *and* entered; idea, icon, and physical experience were combined.

✛ ST. PATRICK AT UISNECH ✛

In the fifth century C.E. Uisnech was visited by St. Patrick, according to Tirechán, who claimed that the saint "remained beside Petra Coithrigi at Uisneach, intending to establish a church. He was opposed in this ambition by the two sons of Niall, Fiachu and Endae. Patrick began to curse them, but no sooner had he said 'A curse…', than his follower Senchall interjected '…be on the stones of Uisneach.' 'Be it so,' said Patrick, and ever since the curse fell, the stones of Uisneach have not been of any use, even as washing stones," that is, stones suitable for heating washing water. The limestone of Uisnech is notably fissured and prone to fracture.

✤ UISNECH AND STONEHENGE ✤

Exchanges between Uisnech and Britain took another form in the medieval belief, reported by Geoffrey of Monmouth, that Stonehenge came from Uisnech. He wrote: "They are mystical stones, and of a medicinal virtue. The giants of old brought them from the farthest coast of Africa and placed them in Ireland, while they inhabited that country. Their design in this was to make baths in them, when they should be taken with any illness. For their method was to wash the stones and put their sick into the water which infallibly cured them . . . There is not a stone there which has not some healing virtue."

Uthor Pendragon was sent to Ireland at the head of fifteen thousand men, in order to bring the stones to Britain. Having defeated the Irish king, Gillomanius, the British advanced on Uisnech, and came to The Giants' Dance, the sight of which filled them with joy and admiration. However, the men were unable to shift the megaliths till Merlin personally "placed in order the engines that were necessary, and took down the stones with incredible facility."

ERIU AND THE SONS OF MÍL

Lebor Gabála describes how Ériu returned to Mide in order to negotiate with the invading Sons of Míl. Equally, *their* prospects of settlement depended on reaching an accommodation with her. Standing at the center of her island-self, she held the title deeds of legitimacy, sealed by the continuity that she could confer on newcomers. Consequently, the Sons of Míl (usually identified with the gods of the Celts, invading after 500 B.C.E.) "had a colloquy" with Ériu at Uisnech. She said: "Long have soothsayers had knowledge of your coming. Yours shall be this island forever; and to the east of the world there shall not be a better island. No race shall be there more numerous than yours." "Good is that," said Amorgen, their poet; "good is the prophecy." "No right were it to thank her," said Eber Donn, eldest of the Sons of Míl, "thank *our* gods, and our *own* might." "To thee 'tis equal," said Ériu; "thou shalt have no profit of this island, nor shall thy progeny." Then, turning to the others, she asked: "A gift to me ye Sons of Míl, and ye children of Breogan, that my name shall be on this island." "It shall be its principal name," said Amorgen, who was content to accept it as the established key to the island's sanctity, and the seed-bed of his hopes.

On the political level, it was customary for the claimant to the high throne of Ireland to "marry" Ériu at a ceremonial *banais rígi*, or "wedding feast of kingship."

Though militarily defeated, Ériu ensured that Eire remained hers. Hers was the mind and body within which kings and gods, including Lugh and Jehovah, came to life. It had been so since the start of human experience in Ireland, according to Macalister, who equates her name with Cesair, the "bringer forth" of the land, which was symbolized by the primary hill of

earthe, and her blew vaynes trayling through every part of her like ryvoletts. She hath one master vayne called the Shannon.

She hath three other vaynes called the sisters, the Seuer, the Noyer & the Barrow, wch rysing at one spring, trayle through her middle partes, and ioync together in theyr going out. Her bones are of polished marble, the grey marble, the blacke, the redd, and the speckled, so fayre for building that their houses shew like colledges, and being polished, is most rarely embelished. Her breasts are round hillockes of milk-yeelding grasse, and that so fertile, that they contend with the vallyes. And betwixt her leggs (for Ireland is full of havens), she hath an open harbor, but not much frequented.

Prior to the mechanization of thought in seventeenth-century England, those who had come for conquest sooner or later entered into the body of Ériu's sacred word, name, and land, and in doing so, played out the role of the male gods. Like Geároid Iarla, they consummated the mythological marriage anew, sharing her bed, her food, and the grave of her out-stretched form.

As traditionally understood, Ériu was an active not a static deity. Her name means "the regular trav-eler," according to O'Rahilly, who points out that although she was primarily the deity of Ireland's

Uisnech, and by the complementary birth-mountain, Árd Éireann, on Slieve Bloom.

The contract collapsed only when the invading powers ceased to believe in the land's divinity and came to regard Ériu as no more than an allegorical figure ripe for economic exploitation. This reduction is anticipated (and not without some affection) in the writings of Luke Gernon, a seventeenth-century English officer in Ireland. He wrote:

> *It was my chance once to see a map of Europe . . . described in the lineaments of a naked woman [and] in such a forme will I represent our Ireland.*
>
> *This Nymph of Ireland, is at all poynts like a young wenche that hath the greene sickness for want of occupying. She is very fayre of visage, and hath a smooth skinn of tender grasse. Indeed she is somewhat freckled (as the Irish are) some partes darker than other. Her flesh is of a softe and delicat mould of*

BELOW *St. Patrick's Well, Uisnech. The saint came to Uisnech to dispute with pagans.*

New Grange tomb engraving, Co. Meath, c. 2,400 B.C.E. *It may represent the triple goddess — Ériu-Fódla-Banba. Ériu was the whole island, Fódla its divisions, Banba its hidden parts.*

plains, mountains, rivers, and springs, her scope went beyond that to include the sun. Her nominated husband was Mac Greine, meaning "son of Sun," and he was the grandson of the Dagda, and she herself often bore the epithet "*ain*," as in "*Ériu ain*," and "*i nErind ain*," wherein she effected a merger with the goddess Áine of Munster, and therefore brought a power to the Beltaine festival at Uisnech. There she also acted as foster mother to Mide, whose job it was to distribute the sacred fire, derived from the sun.

ÉRIU – FÓDLA – BANBA

Ériu was one name of a triple goddess. Her "sisters," Banba and Fódla, being synonymous with her, were therefore alternative names for Ireland.

In Ériu's colloquy at Uisnech, her sister-goddess Fódla or Fotla is sometimes named in place of Ériu, as participating in the bargaining with the Sons of Míl.

As a word, *fotla* (*fodhla*), "explaining, revealing, and division," is related to *fodlach*, "a division, a part," and to *fothla*, "withdrawing, deducting, and abducting."

Ériu and Fódla are complementary. Ériu is the "whole" and Fódla is the "parts." They are both necessary to an understanding of Ireland, and both are required at Aill na Mireann, where the whole and the parts appear together.

Similarly, in marrying a male version of the sun god, Ériu (as the whole island) chose the grandson of the Dagda, Mac Greine, the whole sun, *grian*. By way of contrast, Fódla was wedded to Mac Cecht, (*checht* meaning "plowshare"), to suit her distinctive cutting and dividing role.

At Aill na Mireann, Fódla-Ériu combined to reveal their interdependence. (Without subdivision there can be no characters, and thus no action. Without the whole, there is no shape to the play.) Hand-in-hand the divine sisters lay these inescapable truths on the stone, which reflects both their name-words in its outward appearance; the rock is divided, yet whole.

Another aspect of the collaboration between the two, as described in *Lebor Gabála*, is that when one is at Uisnech the other appears on Slieve Mish, a mountain near Tralee in Co. Kerry, and vice versa. Since *mis* means "a month," and its related *mistae*, "menstrual flow," an Uisnech-Slieve Mish axis may be said to illustrate the fusion of Space with Time. The world of Ériu-Fódla was, it appears, a space–time continuum, where interchangeable terms operated.

Additional weight is lent to this possibility by Fódla's appearance at a third place (in another version of the same text), namely at Slieve Éblinne, also called Felim, in Co. Limerick. Since this mountain was (and is) one of a group of twelve clustered around, and so including the Mother Mountain, Mauher Slieve, a division of the year into twelve months may have been the intended reference.

While Ériu and Fódla were concerned with the establishment and subdivision of Ireland's surface, the third member of the trinity, Banba, appears to have had responsibility for the country's vertical axis. Banba married a sun god named Mac Cuill ("son of Holly"), which suggests a honeymoon spent in the midwinter underworld.

MIDE FIRE AND DRUIDS' TONGUES

According to the *Dindshenchas*, Mide, foster son of Ériu, was the first to light a fire in Erin. It was "a mystic fire." "Hard by Uisneach he kindled it" reported Keating. From his foster mother's central hearth, for "seven years good was it ablaze . . . it was a sure truce, so that he shed the fierceness of the fire for a time over the four quarters of Erin . . . and from that fire were kindled every chief fire and every chief hearth in Ireland."

LEFT *Fair Day at Castlewellan, Co. Down, c. 1910, with Banba, the divine Sow. Revered in central Europe since the fifth millennium B.C.E., in Irish myth her ground-rooting tendencies made her a celebrated goddess of the vertical axis from the underworld.*

RIGHT *From Uisnech, hills and mountains in twenty counties can be identified. Beacons lit on their summits, answering Mide fire, could unite the provinces in a two-way ring of observances. A further outer array of hilltop fires is intervisible between Ring One and all coasts.*

Sun and ritual bonfire were regarded as different manifestations of the divine eye. Beltaine (May 1st) fires, traditionally lit in pairs, showed the deity to have both eyes on the start of summer.

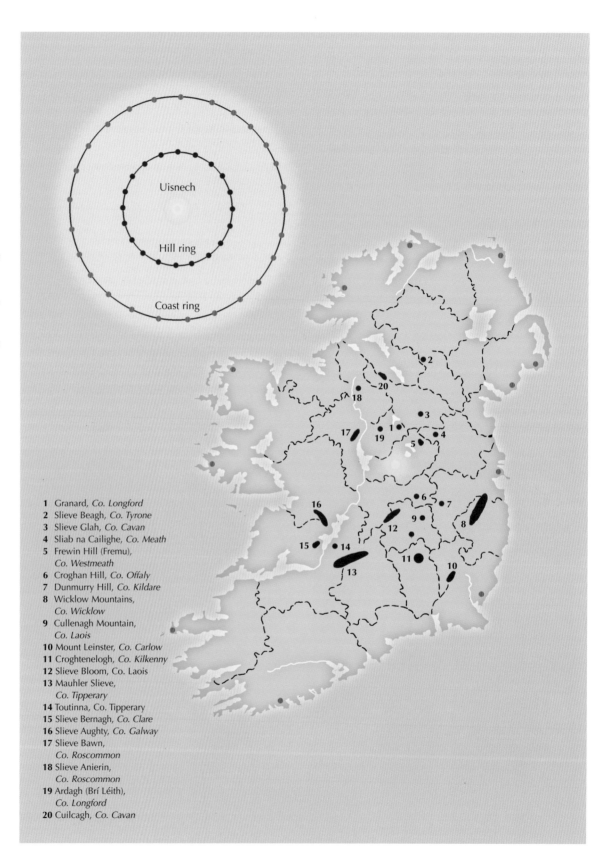

1 Granard, *Co. Longford*
2 Slieve Beagh, *Co. Tyrone*
3 Slieve Glah, *Co. Cavan*
4 Sliab na Cailighe, *Co. Meath*
5 Frewin Hill (Fremu),
   Co. Westmeath
6 Croghan Hill, *Co. Offaly*
7 Dunmurry Hill, *Co. Kildare*
8 Wicklow Mountains,
   Co. Wicklow
9 Cullenagh Mountain,
   Co. Laois
10 Mount Leinster, *Co. Carlow*
11 Croghtenelogh, *Co. Kilkenny*
12 Slieve Bloom, *Co. Laois*
13 Mauhler Slieve,
   Co. Tipperary
14 Toutinna, *Co. Tipperary*
15 Slieve Bernagh, *Co. Clare*
16 Slieve Aughty, *Co. Galway*
17 Slieve Bawn,
   Co. Roscommon
18 Slieve Anierin,
   Co. Roscommon
19 Ardagh (Brí Léith),
   Co. Longford
20 Cuilcagh, *Co. Cavan*

In return for the sun-goddess-derived hearth-fire, without which domestic life would have been impossible, Mide and his successors asked for the tithe of flour and pork. Mide the god was concerned with the art of sharing and the harmony that flows from its practice, as a matter of mythic truth.

But in the Iron Age, the Irish druids suddenly refused to pay the Uisnech pig tax, protesting that "the smoke of Uisnech has brought an ill mood to our mind, . . . Hateful to us is the fire that hath been kindled in the land." "Then Mide the untiring assembled the Druids of Erin into one house, and cut out their tongues (a harsh presage) . . . and buried them under the earth of Uisnech in mighty Mide, and sat him down over the tongues, he, the chief seer and chief poet."

As a metaphor, Mide's action implied that poets who oppose or are indifferent to the exchange of gifts between worlds are no poets and had better fall silent. The purpose of language, as heard at Uisnech, was to articulate a sense of cohesion.

UISNECH HILL AND THE FIRE-EYE

Seen from any direction or distance the Hill of Uisnech fails to dominate. It stands discreetly tucked in among undulating countryside. The summit rises 593 feet (181 meters) above sea level, but is less than 260 feet (80 meters) above the nearby valley road from Athlone to Mullingar. Nor is the Hill's form memorably compact. Lobes run north, south, and west, while three or four swellings compete with the "real" hilltop for preeminence. Uisnech is grass-colored, with a glint of gray limestone showing through here and there. Black and white bullocks romp about.

Yet looking *from* Uisnech, another kind of view can be had. In every direction, hills and mountains animate a horizon where foreground greens are dyed in easy stages to make oceanic blues. These hint at seas lying beyond the topographic panorama, and in a complete encirclement. At Uisnech we sail in the good ship Ériu. Sixty years ago Macalister wrote: "It would be difficult to match in Ireland the range of prospect from the top. The view embraces the whole central plain, and the rim of hills which enclose it on all sides. Landmarks in no less than twenty counties are to be identified from the summit."

Yet in trying to reconstruct Uisnech as a center of pre-Christian Irish gravity, Eliade's warning that sacred space should not be confused with the simple space of "realistic" human observation should be remembered. "In mythical geography, sacred space is *the* essentially real space, and in the archaic world the sacred is the only indubitable reality." Therefore the question remains, what was the view from Uisnech worth in sacred terms?

Ancient Mide was encircled by peaks and hills that contributed varying elements (and in differing degrees) toward a complete web of sacred relationships. The ring of "real" views was passed, via sight to insight, in a symbol-making process activated by ritual, and thereby turned into myth. In this way, the landscape became an authentic version of a divine life story, and Ériu breathed again.

At night, the process was probably assisted by beacon fires, lit in response to an Uisnech hearth. As Macalister observed, "beacon-fires lit upon its summit could be seen over a quarter of Ireland, and in most directions the hills upon the horizons could relay the message of the beacon as far as the sea coast. The claim of Uisneach to be the center of Ireland is thus quite justifiable, even though it may not be mathematically accurate."

Consequently, by employing only two concentric beacon rings around the central Uisnech fire point, the entire country could be encompassed within a single intelligence, in a great "fire-eye," glittering simultaneously on many a muddy estuary and pebbled shore, from sea to sea. Such a nationwide double ring of bonfires would have been a coordinated work of community art on a colossal scale. Each widely scattered group may be assumed to have assembled on their regional mountain to contribute a fire to the overall pattern, thus knowing, and being known by Ériu, the idea of Ireland. Eye symbols engraved in the fourth millennium B.C.E. show the presence of the "eye goddess" in Ireland.

ABOVE *The Lia Fáil — Stone of Destiny — said to roar when kings stood upon the Hill of Tara. Iron Age warriors rejected Uisnech and set up an alternative national center at Tara, 40 miles (64 kilometers) further east.*

✠ THE FIRE-EYE ✠

Confirmation of the ancient fire-eye pattern comes from John Toland, an Irish-speaking scholar, born in the Inishowen peninsula, who, in 1740, recalled chains of fire-beacon sites, "which being every one . . . in sight of some other, could not but afford a glorious show over a whole nation." He states that at each site a pair of fires was lit (perhaps complementing the paired human eyes), "one on the carn," or heap of stones, "another on the ground," together evoking the rising sun. These "prodigious" fires were lit on May Eve, for the Beltaine festival. He adds: "I remember one of those Carns on Fawn-hill . . . known by no other name but that of Bealteine, and facing another such Carn on the top of Inch-hill."

BELTAINE AND THE UISNECH FIRE TEMPLE

Keating, the seventeenth-century Gaelic historian, lends Uisnech weight to these bonfire reports by clearly specifying Beltaine as the time of the annual *oenach* or gathering at Uisnech: "It was at Bealltine that this fair took place, at which it was their custom to exchange with one another their goods, their wares and their valuables. They also used to offer sacrifices to the chief god they adored, who was called Beil, and it was their wont to light *two* fires in honor of Beil in every district in Ireland, and to drive a weakling of each species of cattle that were in the district between the two fires as a preservative to shield them from all the diseases during that year."

"Beil" has long since been dismissed as his invention, but the twin fires, confirmed by folk practice, though losing their Uisnech-coordinated shape, flickered on in every village of the nation, and "the more ignorant Irish still drive their cattle through these fires, as an effectual means of preserving them from future accidents," wrote E. Ledwich in 1804. In Limerick City, May Eve is still called Bonfire Night.

Macalister's 1927 excavation of a hilltop sanctuary, "the most important enclosure upon the summit of Uisnech, at the head of an ancient roadway," revealed a substantial layer of ash across the southern arc of a prehistoric ring ditch, which "must either have been a relic of a perpetual fire, or else (and more probably) of a great bonfire lit at frequent intervals."

This is strongly suggestive of a sanctuary site. Carcasses of animals had been burned on the site, and vast quantities of their bones were scattered about promiscuously. He interpreted these conflagrations and feasts as the Beltaine fires of Keating's seventeenth-century report, and as the national hearth mentioned in the *Dindshenchas* — "the tangible traces of the great sacred flame, which made so deep an impression upon folk memory."

This near-circular sanctuary, 180 feet (55 meters) in diameter, was defined by a ditch 47 inches (120 cm) deep and 39 inches (100 cm) broad at the base, making a simple ring that nevertheless may have acted as the pupil to the eye of the *greater* fire ring, visible all around the horizon, linking distant mountain to mountain, just as Aill na Mireann symbolically incorporated all the rock of Ireland into its relatively small body. The sanctuary ditch was probably dug in the Neolithic, and certainly before the Iron Age. Filled with a brown soil (mixed along its western circumference with layers of "black" vegetation), the ditch may also have stood for the marriage ring of Ireland's agricultural hopes to the divinities of fire. These gods may have been represented further as effigies, set in the massive post holes that, in pairs, addressed the ring's easterly sunrise entrance.

As the May Eve twilight dropped into true blackness, we may suppose that the bonfire lit at Uisnech, and believed to be supernatural, initiated the farflung circles of fire. Through them the goddess reoccupied and *saw* her whole land, and by the embers, promised to return next day with an entire summer's sunshine.

Old Irish *súil* means "eye" *and* "sun." So, in a word, the gap between human subject and divine object disappears as a light-beam enters the eyeball. *Súil*, the divine intelligence, integrates with the eyes on earth of bird and beast and humankind and thereby enters the brain and heart. This is typical of mythic perception, where phenomena become distinct and separate only to reunite in a god-given word. No wonder that the

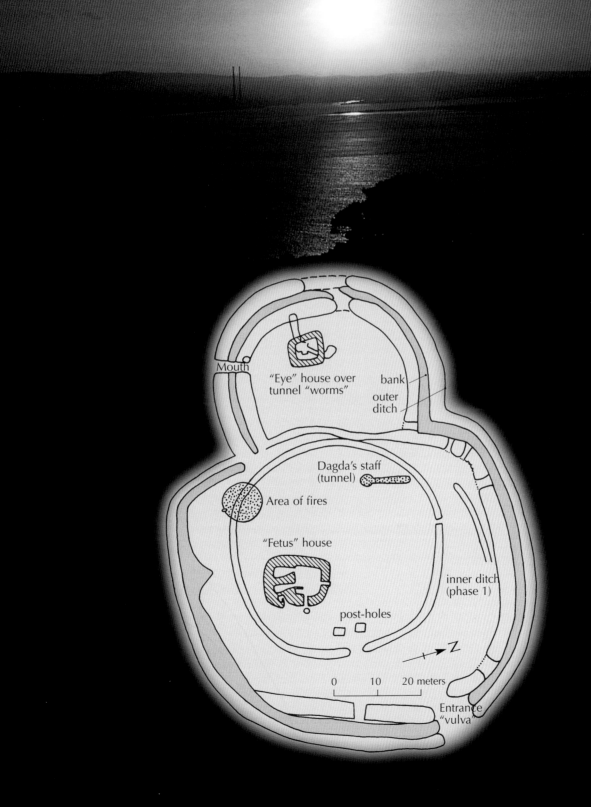

Mouth

"Eye" house over
tunnel "worms"

bank

outer
ditch

Dagda's staff
(tunnel)

Area of fires

"Fetus" house

inner ditch
(phase 1)

post-holes

N

0   10   20 meters

Entrance
"vulva"

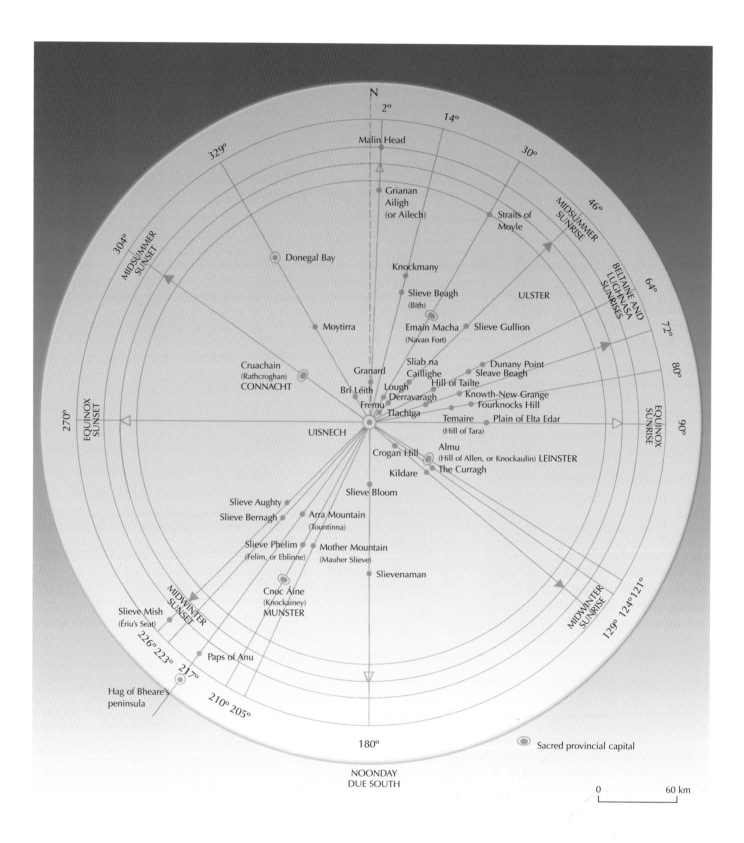

N

2°

14°

329°

30°

Malin Head

304°

MIDSUMMER SUNSET

Grianan
Ailigh
(or Ailech)

Straits of
Moyle

46°

MIDSUMMER SUNRISE

Donegal Bay

Knockmany

Slieve Beagh
(Bith)

ULSTER

BELTAINE AND
LUGHNASA
SUNRISES

64°

Moytirra

Emain Macha
(Navan Fort)

Slieve Gullion

72°

Cruachain
(Rathcroghan)
CONNACHT

Granard

Sliab na
Caillighe

Dunany Point
Sleave Beagh

80°

270°

EQUINOX SUNSET

Brí Léith

Fremu

Lough
Derravaragh

Hill of Tailte

Knowth-New Grange

Fourknocks Hill

Tlachtga

Temaire
(Hill of Tara)

Plain of Elta Edar

90°

EQUINOX SUNRISE

UISNECH

Crogan Hill

Almu
(Hill of Allen, or Knockaulin) LEINSTER

Kildare

The Curragh

Slieve Bloom

Slieve Aughty

Arra Mountain
(Tountinna)

Slieve Bernagh

Slieve Phelim
(Felim, or Eblinne)

Mother Mountain
(Mauher Slieve)

Slievenaman

129° 124°121°

MIDWINTER SUNRISE

MIDWINTER SUNSET

Cnoc Áine
(Knockainey)
MUNSTER

Slieve Mish
(Ériu's Seat)

226°223°

217°

Paps of Anu

Hag of Bheare's
peninsula

210° 205°

180°

Sacred provincial capital

NOONDAY
DUE SOUTH

0   60 km

population stumbled up mountains through darkness to have this good fortune visibly confirmed. There they heard the crackle of yellow furze turning momentarily orange as it leaped above the winter world of gray and black ash, to usher in the first dawn of the summer half. (The *Vita Tripartita* expressly states that on Beltaine Eve every domestic hearth-fire in Ireland was quenched. This imposed darkness further served to focus attention on Uisnech, from where, it was hoped, the sacred gift would rise again, later that night.)

The divinity of the fire-eye was confirmed in the ninth century C.E. by Cormac, who stated that *aed*, "fire," and *dea*, "goddess," were two faces of the same word, which he links to the Roman Vesta, goddess of fire. The etymology is fanciful, says Murphy, but adds: "It may well be that in the Old Irish period it *was* usual to associate *aed*, 'fire,' with a god." What emerges is an integration of the elemental fire and the divine eye, as demonstrated in the Uisnech-centered national fire ring – a single leaping presence, appearing variously as flame, sun, and as the sparkle behind the concentric rings of the human pupil. Fintan, Uisnech's advocate, was one-eyed, and one meaning of Old Irish *aed* is "eye" – the connection being "the pupil," which is "the fire of the eye," and cognate with Latin *aedes*, so validating Cormac's classical allusions.

Whitley Stokes found the primary sun deity, Áine, located *within* the name of the Beltaine festival, preceded by *belt*, "white." He wrote: "The root of Beltaine, as I divide it, is perhaps the same as that of Lithuanian 'white,' *baltas*, plus *aine*." *Belt* could refer to the white lunar eye, so making a balanced title, where the May Eve moon preceded the arrival of the sun syllable. This reflects Beltaine ritual, which emphasized the transition from night *to* day. The word of the principal Uisnech festival, Beltaine, may bring the eyes of night and day together.

Hills, suns, and bonfires combined with the worshiping community to make seeing a divine contact – a means of beholding and being observed by the godhead, in shared regard. Uisnech-centered Ireland still offers a way of finding the holy in the visible, an art sometimes believed lost to the Western world. A Mide walk undermines the enthronement of dualism.

LEFT *Twelfth-century chancel window at Rahan, Co. Offaly. The solar chevrons familiar from prehistoric Irish gold disks here face east, toward the sunrise, around a four-plus-one central pattern.*

✠ THE SUN CIRCLE, ✠ ERIU'S WEB

Throughout prehistoric Britain and Ireland, it was by noting the positions on the horizon where sun and moon rose and set that people orientated themselves, and attempted to achieve a harmonious relationship with a divine cosmos. In Ireland, that task was primarily organized from Uisnech. Particular attention was paid to the solstices, equinoxes, and the midpoints between them – the quarterdays, which served as the thresholds of the farming year.

What was done at Uisnech did not, of course, obviate the need to carry out comparable rites at the local level. So, nineteenth-century farmers in Co. Kilkenny, accompanied by servants and domestics, walked the boundaries of their land after Beltaine sunset, carrying the implements of husbandry and seed grains, stopping at intervals to address the four quarters from east, sunwise, to north.

At Uisnech all these parochial efforts, and the achievements of major sacred sites in each of the four surrounding provinces, were integrated into one grand design. Seen from Uisnech, the gods did their rounds of the country in a fair distribution of divine favors.

OPPOSITE *Ériu's Eye: a year of regard. Ériu's eyes were like flashing sunbeams, say the medieval Cóir Anmann. Significant solar sunrise and sunset alignments link sacred sites in the four provinces to the fifth: Uisnech.*

PART FIVE

MIDE 2
Ériu's eye: national observations

Solsticial sunrises and sunsets and quarterdays, as seen from Uisnech, relate to an array of mountain peaks, hilltops, and striking water features. Significant solar sunrise alignments link sacred sites in the four provinces to the fifth, Uisnech. An Uisnech-based sunwise rotation through these correlations will now be attempted, encompassing the whole island.

Alignments of the sites from Uisnech are stated in degrees from true North. Their distance from Uisnech as the crow flies is given in kilometers. An asterisk is used to indicate intervisibility between neighboring sites on the same alignment. A double asterisk denotes intervisibility with Uisnech.

2°E: GRANARD, CO. LONGFORD. GRIANAN AILIGH (OR AILECH) AND MALIN HEAD, CO. DONEGAL
◌◌

(I) GRANARD, AND THE ASH OF UISNECH [32 KM]**

Craeb Usnig, the mythic Ash Tree of Uisnech, was the central tree of all Ireland. It crashed northwards in the time of the sons of Aed Slane, c. 600 C.E. The date corresponds with the destruction of the pagan cosmic scheme by St. Patrick and his followers. In falling, the tip of the tree reached Granard (another Grian-derived name), in Co. Longford. "The Ash of populous Usnech . . . due northward [it] fell, as far as Granard," showing that Craeb Using was no ordinary tree, but a national *axis mundi*, acting as a cosmic spindle or centre pole. Then it swung like a compass needle into northern darkness, when seen by the light of a Christian god's agent.

The pedigree of the tree is given by Fintan. He claimed to have planted it as a berry, and set four

other berries at distances of scores of miles around it, in a reiteration of the one-plus-four pattern, echoed by the Roman augur.

(II) GRIANAN AILIGH [170 KM]

Beyond Granard, on the same alignment stands the major sacred hilltop site of North Ulster, Grianan Ailigh. Three concentric ring banks enclose a massive stone "cashel," whose wall is five paces thick at the base, and can be entered only through one east-facing door, barely three feet wide.

The hill is cited in *Lebor Gabála* as the northern marker of Partholón's four-fold division of Ireland.

ABOVE *Grianan Ailigh, Co. Donegal. This cashel was home to the Dagda. It was also the* grianan, *or house of hibernation, for Gráine, the sun goddess, and the super-natural maiden Ailech.*

LEFT *Sliab na Caillighe Co. Meath, Cairn T, 3200 B.C.E. The head chamber of this hag-shaped tomb displays a megalith carved with sun, zig-zag "water," and beef carcass symbols.*

The Dagda is said to have lived there, along with the solar husbands of Ériu, Fódla, and Banba. The word *grianan*, "sunhouse," derives from *grian*, "sun," and Grian, the sun goddess. Grianan Ailech may be regarded as her midnight and midwinter hiding-place.

The theme of incarceration is developed further in the *Dindshenchas* stories of Aed ("fire"), son of the Dagda, who was buried there, and Ailech-the-white, a divine maiden who had a house built around her on

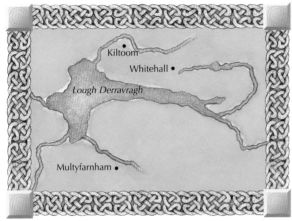

the same site. Made of "red yew" (a *síd* wood), it was overlaid with pure unwrought silver, gold, and bronze, and decked inside with bright gems, so that "alike were day and night in the midst of it."

The Grianan thus stood for a state of equilibrium, prior to seasonal and diurnal fluctuation.

But Grianan Ailigh was also the home of that most active god, the Dagda, who was "good at everything," and the master of crafts, including agriculture and warfare. His feats emanated from a Uisnech-Grianan Ailigh base-line. Having a house at both places, he was Ruad Rofhessa, Lord of Perfect Knowledge, and Eochaid Ollathair, Father of All. This comprehensiveness was the hidden foundation of his energetic performance in the world.

(III) MALIN HEAD [211 KM]

"The development of the mythical feeling for space always starts from the opposition of day and night, light and darkness," writes E. Cassier, and from Uisnech the search for darkness runs on toward Malin Head, Ireland's most northerly point, lying on the same northern line. The headland is still referred to on local roadsigns as Banba's Crown; Banba was the version of Ériu most closely associated with the underworld. Malin Head is a toothy crown of dark rock, licked white in places by far-flung ocean spray. Fierce gales frequently rage here.

14°E: SLIEVE BEAGH, CO. FERMANAGH. KNOCKMANY, CO. TYRONE

(I) SLIEVE BEAGH [97 KM]**

Slieve Beagh is the legendary burial place of the mythic founding father, Bith or Cosmos. Viewed from Uisnech, Bith's mountain-grave aligns with the famous Neolithic chambered cairn at Knockmany, 11 kilometers farther north.

(II) KNOCKMANY [108 KM]*

This ruined monument stands on top of a steep-sided conical hill, and its megaliths are incised in the passage grave style of c. 3000 B.C.E. One face shows Áine-the-hag, cloaked, and bent with age, yet busily generating the phenomenal world. While Bith, as ultimate god-head, dreams up the reality of all-inclusiveness, on the same Uisnech axis Áine, goddess of specific actions, stirs the re-creation mound, to empower the eruption of separate forms. He inhales everything, and holds a long pause.

30°E: LOUGH DERRAVARAGH. EMAIN MACHA. STRAITS OF MOYLE

(I) LOUGH DERRAVARAGH [23 KM]

From Uisnech this line clips the wings of the swan-shaped Lough Derravaragh. The lake, measuring 10 kilometers from tail to open beak, was regarded as sacred in oral tradition and illustrates the opportunistic nature of the Irish mythic process. Because the Lough Derravaragh was swan-shaped, it attracted swan stories.

OPPOSITE *Malin Head, called Banba's Crown, Co. Donegal; the northern tip of Ireland. There Manannan mac Lir, sea god, lay with the land goddess. At nearby Main Well Fair, on August 15th (Feast of the Ascension of the Blessed Virgin Mary), men and women "frisked and played in the water all stark naked."*

LEFT *Lough Derravaragh, Co. Westmeath; a swan-shaped lake, which attracted the legend of the swan-children of Lir.*

RIGHT *Emain Macha (Navan Fort), Co. Armagh, was the sacred and political capital of pre-Christian Ulster. In myth, the enclosure was drawn by the horse-goddess Macha, using her brooch pin.*

At Lough Derravaragh, the four children of Lir (father of the sea god, Manannán) were turned into white swans by his jealous second wife and condemned to spend three hundred years there, and three hundred on the Straits of Moyle between Ireland and Scotland. After that, "when the woman of the South is mated with a man of the North, the enchantment is to have an end." Since three of the swan children were boys, there is a suggestion of male swan gods, migrating from the far north (as swans in fact do, every year) to a point close to the umbilicus and the Eiscir Riada in order to wed with the southern half of the country. The line of this narrative combines accurate bird-watching with a desire for a north–south sacred marriage, at a swan-shaped inland water.

(II) EMAIN MACHA [110 KM]

According to *The Fate of The Children of Lir*, it was "to the Hill of the White Field in Armagh" that the swans flew at the end of their sufferings, to visit their father Lir, who lived there. This "White Field" may possibly be Emain Macha, the ancient capital and chief sacred site of Ulster. Measured along the same 30° line, Emain Macha is exactly midway between Lough Derravaragh and Garron Point, the Irish shore of the Straits of Moyle, or North Channel, separating Ireland from Scotland, where the *same* swans were forced to spend another three hundred years.

Another tale says that *emuin* means "twins," and that the goddess Macha, though heavily pregnant, was forced to race against the king of Ulster's chariot team, across the arena named after her. She won, but the effort caused her to give birth to a son and daughter "at the end of the field."

This may reflect the Neolithic goddess delivered in bondage to warlike newcomers. Brought back under duress to a royal enclosure once sacred to her, she nevertheless outclassed them in fecundity and speed. Then she transferred her labor pains onto the assembled warriors, and so reaffirmed the priority of natural processes over an addiction to warfare.

A visit to Emain Macha is enough to confirm that her birth-giving aspect was retained. The swelling natural hill, enclosed by the banks, and culminating in

the earthen mound, 19 feet (6 meters) high and 148 feet (45 meters) across, continues to evoke the theme of pregnancy. The north could not survive without it.

EMAIN MACHA AND CNOC ÁINE

All the provinces, including Ulster and Munster, were believed to join at Aill na Mireann. Now it should be added that if the line from North Strait via Emain Macha to the Uisnech omphalos is projected southward into Munster (210° E of N), it passes over Fódla's seat on Slieve Phelim, and then bisects the summit of Cnoc Áine, which, with the nearby Lough Gur, forms the principal sacred metropolis of Munster. This straight line joins the capitals of Áine and Macha, and locks their respective provinces across the Uisnech center stone. Straight as a sunbeam, or a shaft of moonlight, the axis depicts the inescapable rivalry between dark and light, sacrifice and birth.

By their incorporation into the line, Fódla and Ériu (representing islandwide interests) ensured that the lively tension between north and south was kept within manageable bounds, for the good of the parts and the preservation of the whole. This mythic achievement formed the basis of a political unity, surviving hundreds of wars. The Ériu–Fódla balance was maintained until the mass settlement of Ulster by the British caused the myth to be rejected in the northern province, with well-known consequences.

48°E: SLIAB NA CAILLIGHE, CO. MEATH [40 KM].**

SLIEVE GULLION, CO. ARMAGH [101 KM]*

By undertaking a slow rotation at Uisnech, the hold of the central hill on the surrounding country seems gradually to accumulate, and the sharp outline of Sliab na Caillighe (the Mountain of the Hag) comes into view. This ridge of three summits, known locally in 1828 as "The Witches Hops," is the site of the famous Loughcrew "Cemetery." In every sense this is an outstanding group of fourth-millennium passage graves, profusely decorated with engraved designs of the same era. The central summit is crowned with the biggest "tomb," Cairn T. Cairn T was known in the locality (and in archeological literature) as the tomb of Ollamh Fódla. The Book of Four Masters says that he was "the first law-giver of Ireland," and arbitrarily assigns his death to 1277 B.C.E. *Ollamh* means the highest rank of poet, and Fódla is none other than Ériu's sister, the goddess of divisions, here seen applying her power to the division of time as well as space, within Nature's law. Seen from Uisnech, Cairn T aligns with midsummer sunrise. If this line is extended a further 65 kilometers it runs straight into

the hollow body of the Cailleach at the hag-shaped chambers of the south cairn on Slieve Gullion, Co. Armagh, where Finn was swallowed up and turned into an old man.

From Uisnech the paired monumental hags of Leinster and Ulster burst into flames together on midsummer morning. Though Slieve Gullion is not visible

and known as The Hag's Chair, offers the necessary two-way view to Uisnech and Slieve Gullion.

The critical sunrise was probably encouraged by the lighting of Midsummer Eve bonfires at all three locations — a seasonal ceremony that persists to this day in some districts.

The white quartz pebbles that originally surrounded and perhaps covered Cairn T suggest a concern with light, which is borne out by the many solar-eye designs, engraved within the goddess-shaped interior of the monument. Ollamh, the chief poet of Fódla, lived and died inside the goddess whom he served, for the "tomb" described her living essence. Her legs are the entrance passage, the central chamber her body, off which lead two arms and a head. The "head" chamber displays a fine array of "sun-eyes." Fieldwork by Mullen and his team has proved that the rising sun at the March and September equinoxes also featured in the original range of concerns, being the average of the midwinter and midsummer extremes.

Equinoctial sunrises still illuminate and bring to life the two most elaborately engraved "sun-eyes" in the Cairn T "head."

✤ THE CAILLEAGH ✤

Pondering on the folk beliefs current around Loughcrew and Slieve Gullion in the 1830s, O'Donovan concluded that the Co. Meath hag "is the [same] very old lady whose shade still haunts the lake and carn of Slieve Gullion," adding that at Sliab na Caillighe she was called Evlin by the people, "for whom she was and is still a living presence ... [This] famous hag of - antiquity, Cailleagh Bheartha (Vera), came from the north to perform a magical feat in this neighborhood, by which she would obtain great power if she succeeded. She dropped her apronful of stones on Sliab na Caillighe." (The apron is the divine womb, translated into the language of dress.) O'Donovan noted the belief that the same Cailleagh had turned Finn (the youthful sun god) into an old man on Slieve Gullion. After midsummer, old age was his fate.

BELOW *Midsummer to midwinter sunbeam line.*

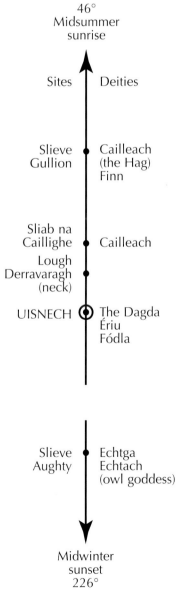

46°
Midsummer
sunrise

Sites | Deities

Slieve Gullion — Cailleach (the Hag) Finn

Sliab na Caillighe — Cailleach

Lough Derravaragh (neck)

UISNECH — The Dagda Ériu Fódla

Slieve Aughty — Echtga Echtach (owl goddess)

Midwinter
sunset
226°

from the national center stone, the message and the spectacle could be passed on from Sliab na Caillighe, which *is* intervisible with the Co. Armagh mountain. Here is another instance of sacred communication along the Uisnech radial spokes, suggested by Macalister. A mighty throne-shaped limestone boulder, set into the periphery of Cairn T as part of its original furnishings

⊠

64°E: HILL OF TAILTE, SLEAVE BEAGH, CO. MEATH. DUNANY POINT, CO. LOUTH

(I) HILL OF TAILTE [56 KM]*

From Uisnech this is the line of sunrise at the May (Beltaine) and August (Lughnasa) quarterdays. Down this line Ériu could look to the place of her death at Tailte, or Teltown, its Anglicized form. Teltown was renowned as the greatest start-of-harvest *oenach*. There the goddess of the corn, Tailtiu, symbolically gave her life under the sickle, having first cleared the forest to create the fields.

After her death, St. Patrick said, "Victorious was the proud law of Nature; though it was not made in obedience to God, the Lord was magnifying it."

The most prominent earthwork is the circular platform, 367 feet (112 meters) diameter, and 18 feet (5 meters) high, formerly surrounded by an outer ring.

BELOW *Tlachtga, Hill of Ward, Co. Meath, has four massive concentric ring banks. From here, Samain, November 1st, sunset occurs over Uisnech.*

(II) SLEAVE BEAGH [71 KM]*

The same axis incorporates Sleave Beagh — another hill named after Bith. Prehistoric ring banks and tumuli decorate the 745-foot (227-meter) summit of this ridge. From there the sightline runs on, across Mount Oriel, to Dunany Point, on the coast.

72°E: TLACHTGA (HILL OF WARD), KNOWTH-NEW GRANGE, CO. MEATH

(I) TLACHTGA [46 KM]**

This hill near Athboy, Co. Meath, rises to 380 feet (116 meters). Its importance was emphasized by a huge prehistoric ring fort, consisting of four concentric banks and ditches, surrounding a platform 26 feet (8 meters) wide crowning the hilltop. This format seems to echo the Uisnech design of center stone and four provinces.

The 72°–252° axis, joining the two sites, points to a late November sunset and to the Samain moon at the southern standstill of its nineteen-year cycle. At Tlachtga, sky–earth relations were observed and maintained by monumental and bonfire responses, which divided the year into winter and summer halves.

The ring fort at Tlachtga represents an Iron Age warrior superimposition on a Neolithic site, and it was from here that the fire of the Uisnech cycle was "stolen" by the new capital, set up 20 kilometers to the east at Tara. Samain, the perilous gap between years, represented a point of weakness in the Uisnech design. Here the incoming hierarchy struck. By simultaneously honoring and bending the Uisnech web, they used its ancient authority to suit their rival purposes, in an adroit manipulation of the mythic order.

Keating attributes this change to King Tuathal, who was the first to burn victims at Tlachtga as a signal that the Tara *Feis* or Festival might start. Tara and Tlachtga are intervisible.

Law-making and, in time, the writing of annals, were aspects of the Tara event, where each new king "married" the goddess of the land, yet where women were debarred from entering the banqueting hall. (The new masters maintained an ambivalent relationship to the feminine.)

ABOVE *Knowth Passage Grave, Co. Meath, c. 2450 B.C.E. Twin passages, opening due east and west, receive every equinoxial sunrise and sunset in March and September.*

(II) KNOWTH-NEW GRANGE [73 KM]

Extending the Medraige–Uisnech–Tlachtga line by 27 kilometers to the northeast, into old Ulster, we come to the great bend of the Boyne River, where stands the fourth-millennium monument called Knowth. Damaged in the Iron Age, the twin passages under its Neolithic mound open due east and west, to receive equinoctial sunrises and sunsets.

80°E: TEMAIR (HILL OF TARA). FOURKNOCKS HILL

(I) TARA [63 KM]**

"Like two kidneys in a beast" was how Fintan described the relationship between Uisnech and Tara. Intervisibility between the two sites may just be possible across the northern shoulder of the intervening hill at Killuoan. As the seat of the high king of Ireland

in the first millennium C.E., Tara's power was superimposed over the old egalitarian union that had been focused on Uisnech since the Stone Age. Nevertheless, the claim of every Tara king to rule over the provincial kings depended entirely on his marriage to the goddess of the island, Medb, at a place named after the goddess Tea, who had died at Tara and imbued the hill with its original sanctity. Thanks to Tlachtga and Tea (*te*, "hot, lustful, wanton"), Tara remains within the compass of the Uisnech design.

The megalith called Lia Fáil stands close to the center of the Tara monuments. *Fal* or *Fáil* was another term for Ireland. As a language word *fal* means "arm-bracelet." When this stone arm was combined with the gold ring made by the moving sun, the kingdom was reestablished by divine right. Hence the Lia Fáil is the Stone of Destiny, which roared when kings stood on it. Perhaps the sound combined the orgasm and labor pains of Tea with those of another recurring Tara "queen" – Medb. The Tara Medb, central to kingship rites, is probably an eastern version of Medb, a goddess of Connacht, whose sanctuary lies at Rathcroghan in Connacht, and almost the same distance as Tara from Uisnech.

(II) FOURKNOCKS [79 KM]*

Tara aligns between Uisnech in the west, and the notable Neolithic tomb at Fourknocks Hill, 17 kilometers farther east. There, in the large central chamber of the main temple, stands an image of the goddess, engraved with eyes, a nose composed of the lozenge motifs, familiar in many parts of the Neolithic world, and with a smile as broad as a cow's horns. The stone was instantly recognized by the workmen who excavated the site as anthropomorphic, and later accepted as such by the archeologist.

90° (DUE EAST, EQUINOX SUNRISE): THE PLAIN OF ELTA EDAR, CO. DUBLIN [90 KM]

According to the *Dindshenchas*, this coastal plain was the first to be settled in all Ireland. To it, Partholón returned to die. From the Uisnech navel stone, the founding act of agriculture aligns with sunrise at the equinoxes, and the average of all sunrises throughout the year. Howth Head (Benn Étair) is associated with the sun goddess Étar (wife of the divine plowman-king, Eochaid Airem). She overlooks the plain and the eastern end of the Eiscir Riada.

Eastern sunrise and the first arable land were thus aligned by the national Uisnech eye, so that Étar and her plowman could complete the necessary task.

LEFT *View from the Hill of Tara. The High King had to "marry" the goddess of Ireland upon the Hill of Tara, so continuing an aspect of the Uisnech plan.*

LEFT *The goddess Tea at Tara. Carved megalith in Tara churchyard. She gave her name to Tara. Irish té means "hot, wanton, lustful."*

121°E: ALMU (THE HILL OF ALLEN OR KNOCKAULIN), CO. KILDARE [55 KM]**

This 662-foot (202-meter)-high hill is completely surrounded by bog, to a degree that in nineteenth-century maps it is called The Isle of Allen.

Long after it was abandoned as the sacred seat of the Leinster kings in the eighth century C.E., "it continued to symbolize the ancient glories of the Leinster-man, taking its place in the national scene alongside Emain Macha and Rathcroghan," according to A. P. Smyth, the sacred capitals of Ulster and Connacht.

"Far-famed Alenn! delightful knowledge," sang the Old Irish *Hail Brigit* poet. What knowledge? Smyth insists that "the importance of the symbolism and ancient associations of these sites, as preserved in the *senchus*, or traditions, cannot be overestimated," and points out that eulogies to Almu continued to be written into the seventeenth century, despite the Norman and Tudor conquests.

Rising from water, Almu served as a creation mound, a world mountain – a new hope in the flood, close to the midwinter sunrise line from Uisnech.

As so often in the Uisnech pattern, Almu was a goddess, who continued to be acknowledged (having by then been reduced to the rank of a human female) into the Middle Ages. "Almu, beautiful was the woman . . . one of no common line . . . Almu the all white . . . she was fair of foot, the daughter of Beccán the bright-robed." "All white is the fort . . . as if it had received the lime of all Ériu . . . Almu the all-white." Here the white maiden, the white goddess of dawn, paints the walls of her home – a color complementary to the blood red hue of Rathcroghan in Connacht, the midsummer sunset house. This stood at 180° to the Almu–Kildare complex at the reversed end of an axis drawn through Uisnech to Rathcroghan, which was the western home of the goddess Medb.

The seesaw operated by a white and a red goddess around the Uisnech pivot is referred to in what K. Meyer calls "a very ancient poem": "Round Alenn, Cruachu fairest . . ." In a seventh-century poem "Round Alenn, [and] Cruachu" are again put together.

LEFT *The Hill of Allen, Co. Kildare, otherwise called Almu or Knockaulin, is the legendary birthplace of Finn McCool and seat of the Leinster kings. Since the Stone Age, it has served as Leinster's sanctuary, equivalent to Emain Macha (Ulster) and Rathcroghan (Connacht).*

ABOVE *Croghan Hill, Co. Offaly, beneath which Brigit is said to have made metal cauldrons and pots. Every year Finn sent one of his men from the Hill of Allen, to go under this hill.*

Recent excavation, 1969–75, has proved that, as with Emain Macha, the Neolithic community was established on the summit of Almu, where they dug a circular trench, more than 65 feet (20 meters) in diameter, and left pottery, stone arrowheads, and a disk bead in the ground. Continuing occupation through the Bronze Age led eventually to successive circular timber structures being built in the Iron Age over the Neolithic circle, implying continuity. The grandest was a double arena, with tiered seating, and a fenced approach, fanning open toward the east. This building has been interpreted as a ritual corral for animals. The "head and body" arenas, joined at the neck, also suggest the "fat lady" shape of the Mother Goddess-as-Architecture, known from Neolithic Irish passage graves, and later prehistoric sanctuaries both in Britain and Ireland. (In a mythic age, buildings modeled on the shapes of gods were thought to be the most effective.)

124°E: THE CURRAGH, CO. KILDARE [61 KM]

As a language word, *curragh* or *currac* means "a racecourse, a plain," and a "journeying or flowing, as of a horses mane, or human hair."

Comparable to the chariot track around Lough Gur, and Macha's course at Navan, The Curragh was where the Kildare goddess of the midwinter fire, and the Almu kings of Leinster came together with one of the fastest of earth's creatures, the horse. (Horseracing on the ground was an important ritual means of urging the solar chariot across the sky, for the two zones were interdependent.)

The Lives of Irish Saints sometimes describe Brigit in a chariot, coming from Heaven to Kildare, and her pre-Christian equine form perhaps lived on as the White Mare, or *láir bhan*, until recently paraded at midwinter, in the form of a hobby horse.

Horseracing at The Curragh continues to this day, as Ireland's premier — one might say *sacred* — horseracing venue.

Thus Leinster and Connacht are united through Uisnech via their sacred centers, as firmly as Ulster and Munster were held by Emain and Cnoc Áine, across the same Uisnech stone. Whoever "ruled" Almu in the political sense, tapped into this mythic resource. For example, Finn MacCool, born at Almu (with or without historical reality), was bound to assume the status of a rising sun god, since that role was a function of the site. Keating says that "the hill came to belong to him in the right of his mother." His "chair" is a small mount on the summit, on which a battlemented tower was erected in 1859.

129°E: MIDWINTER SUNRISE: CROGHAN HILL, CO. OFFALY. KILDARE (CILL DARA), CO. KILDARE

⁀

(I) CROGHAN HILL [25 KM]**

Seen from Uisnech, the midwinter sun rises over Croghan Hill, a cone-shaped peak, 760 feet (232 meters) high, 25 kilometers from Aill na Mireann. Tradition says that St. Brigit, the chief female saint of Ireland, was born close to Croghan, and took the veil on the hill. This conjunction of the midwinter sunrise, seen from Uisnech, and St. Brigit at Croghan Hill, replicates in the landscape what the New Grange entrance-box framed architecturally.

At midwinter all Uisnech eyes were turned in anxious hope toward Croghan Hill, and the magic underworld beneath it, known as Brí Ele. In early literature, Ele is represented as a maiden and a goddess of awe-inspiring beauty. Every year one of Finn's young men went out from the Hill of Allen (Almu), his stronghold in Co. Kildare, to meet her and was lost forever, in her *síd* beneath Croghan Hill. *Ele* means "prayer, praise, incantation and salve." In this spirit the youth gave his life in worship.

"Ele" was probably a twelfth-century pseudonym for Brigit in her underworld guise, and designed to allay Christian disquiet over the continuing worship of the pagan fire goddess, whose name is derived from "Brig," "the Great One."

(II) UISNECH, CROGHAN, CILL DARA, AND THE TRIPLE BRIGIT

The well-known tendency for the prehistoric goddess to manifest as a trinity has been explored in the Ériu–Fódla–Banba trio, and it can be shown that Brigit also spread herself in three equal parts down the Uisnech–Croghan–Kildare axis, following the line of the first midwinter sunbeam. She is the "fiery arrow" who joins her sanctuaries together.

Cormac explained her triple nature as that of three sisters, the first of whom was goddess of poetry, and daughter of the Dagda. Since *he* often lived at Uisnech, so did she.

She was the spark of thought, and the flaming word, when poet and listener cry out: "I see!" "Therefore this Brigit is a goddess whom poets worshiped for very great and famous was her superintendence." Viewed from Uisnech, the second being of the trinity, Brigit-as-Begoibne, or "woman of the smithery," was inferred to underlie the distant Croghan Hill, whose pointed summit coincided with the midwinter sunrise.

Croccan means "vessel, pot, or cauldron," and at Crochan Hill the smith-goddess made pots, including the sacred cauldrons from which the future was poured. "The future" included the Shannon River as known to humanity. The *Dindshenchas*, in one version, states that the river's source lay under Brí Ele on the Eiscir Riada, at a well called Linn Mna Feile, "the Pool of the Modest Woman." Thus the chief north–south

BELOW *Wishing Stone, St. Brigit's Cathedral, Kildare. Anyone threading an arm through this hole to the elbow may have a wish granted, since the individual is visibly united in mind and body with the divine St. Brigit.*

and east–west natural coordinates of Ireland were believed to flow from the same supernatural bowl at the start of each solar cycle, when the land was recreated by dawning sunlight.

As H. T. Knox observed, Crúachan Brí Ele "was not merely the name *of* the hill, but of something from which the hill took its name" – a magic vessel. Its supernatural crafting was considered to be the fundamental event, underlying, and in a sense *causing* the natural hill to arise. Brigit's pagan cauldron lived on as the Christian "grail," and St. Brigit is credited with "mending a wonderful vessel, one of the rare treasures of the king," which had been smashed.

(III) CILL DARA (KILDARE), THE CHURCH OF THE OAK GROVE [58 KM]

Visible from Uisnech down the midwinter sunrise axis, across the level Bog of Allen stand the Dunmurry Hills, and beyond them on the same line is St. Brigit's Cathedral of Kildare. There her cult took its Christian form on a prehistoric foundation. Outside the North Wall of the cathedral, the substantial footings of her cell, a Christian fire church, are preserved, where the "eternal flame," which survived until 1530, opens toward Uisnech.

If the Uisnech midwinter sunrise axis, 129°, is extended from Kildare a further 37 kilometers, it cuts into the southern flank of the tallest mountain in Leinster, Lugnaquillia, named after the sun god Lugh. Beyond lie the gold mines of the Wicklow Mountains, Ireland's chief source of gold, in use by 2000 B.C.E. Gold was the uncorruptible deity in the rock.

180°: SLIEVE BLOOM, CO. LAOIS. SLIEVENAMAN, CO. TIPPERARY

∽

(I) SLIEVE BLOOM [45 KM]**

The next important stations on the national sun cycle lie due south from Uisnech. Down the line of the noonday sun stand the Slieve Bloom Mountains. They, and the highest point of the range, Árd Éireann (the Height of Ireland), had great mythic importance.

Uisnech and Slieve Bloom enjoyed a seasonal and topographic partnership. Uisnech's chief festival was at Beltaine (the low hill of May Day), while Slieve Bloom was the World Mountain of Lughnasa, when the pregnant goddess gave birth.

Standing north and south of the Eiscir Riada at comparable distances from that equinoctial line, Uisnech and Árd Éireann, as a pair, jointly achieve a dynamic equilibrium within the annual process.

The grassy summit of Árd Éireann is called Crúachan, and there the national harvest bowl, fashioned in midwinter at Croghan Hill, was at last filled to the brim. Slieve Bloom remained an important place of Lughnasa pilgrimage till 1940.

LEFT *Along the midwinter sunrise line from Uisnech and Croghan Hill stands St. Brigit's Cathedral at Kildare, "the Church of the Oak Grove." There her cult continued the solar-fire theme. Until 1530 an "eternal flame," facing Uisnech, was maintained at Kildare.*

The ceremonies had more than local significance. As the name Árd Éireann implies, the mountain was *the* Height of Ireland and stood symbolically for the whole country. It was the culmination of a birth process drawn from sea to sea, and raised under the noonday sun, as seen from Uisnech.

Its cosmogonic role is further underlined by the Nore, Suir, and Barrow rivers, the Three Sisters at whose mouth Cesair, the founding goddess of Ireland, landed. All three rivers rise in the neighborhood of Slieve Bloom, so associating the mountain with a primary birth act, the bringing of Ireland into existence.

It was in the woods of Slieve Bloom that the sun god Finn grew up, safe from his father's enemies.

(II) SLIEVENAMAN [112 KM]*

Slievenaman's conical form (2,360 feet/719 meters) overlooks the most southerly of the three sisters, the Suir River, and carries the eye from Leinster into Munster.

You might expect beliefs to have accrued at this mountain, since it marks the climax of the daily solar arc viewed from Aill na Mireann. And, indeed, the divine events of Slievenaman represent a peak in the daily and annual drama.

The stories often revolve around Étaín, a sun goddess, whose beauty gave rise to the phrase "as fair as Étaín." Caught in a triangle of love, she was torn between Midir, the "elf-king" of the northwest, her husband, who lived under Ardagh Hill, Co. Longford,

in the *síd* of Brí Léith, and her *second* husband, Eochaid, the eastern horse king of Tara. This conflict, described in *Tochmarc Étaín* (The Wooing of Étaín), expresses her solar movements around and under the horizon. (A straight line between Brí Léith and Slievenaman passes directly over Árd Éireann, the highest point of Slieve Bloom.)

Étaín's arrival at Slievenaman (which means "mountain of the cunning feet"), followed her seizure by Midir from Eochaid's court at Tara. Although surrounded by his rival's armed retainers, Midir escaped with her. Holding his sunspears in his left hand, Midir threw his right arm around her, and the couple rose lightly into the air and disappeared through a roof-window in the palace. The last that the king and his warriors saw of them was as two white swans circling once, before they pointed their necks toward Slievenaman and vanished in the southern sky.

From the union of Midir and Étaín, their son Donn was born. Finn saw Donn under the mountain, presiding over a magic mansion, where 28 warriors were entertained by as many beautiful blonde virgins, one of whom sat on a crystal throne. It was as if the peak of the sun's path had cast dark Donn's bright antithesis deep into the rock. Taking after his father Midir, whose name means "Rays of Sun," Donn fills the underworld with a confident display of buried light – a fire unseen on the mortal plane. As a sun god, Finn had a seat (Seefin), on top of the mountain, which proves, says Keating, that he *really* existed. Until recently, young local women would race each other up the mountain, for the privilege of "marrying" him there.

205°E: MOTHER MOUNTAIN (MAUHER SLIEVE), CO. TIPPERARY [102 KM]**

The Mother Mountain is one of twelve mountains in a compact area known as The Twelve Mountains of Éblenn. The mountains are named after a goddess of that name from Brug na Bóinne, who eloped with a young lover, after deserting her husband, the king of Cashel. "That there was originally a Lughnasa assembly on Mother Mountain can hardly be doubted," says MacNeill.

Being the tallest of the group of twelve, Mauher Slieve may be regarded as the maternal aspect of the libidinous Éblenn, and it is visible from Uisnech by bonfire light.

210°E: SLIEVE PHELIM, CNOC ÁINE, CO. LIMERICK

(I) SLIEVE PHELIM [114 KM]*

It was on Slieve Phelim, alias Eblinne (1,575 feet/480 meters), that Fódla and Ériu, representing the parts and the whole of Ireland, took turns keeping watch.

O'Rahilly says that Eblinne was both a mountain and goddess name. She and it were synonymous. "The idea underlying the word *éblenn* is the radiation of heat and light, and the resultant feeling of pleasure and well-being, or of energy and passion."

(II) CNOC ÁINE [139 KM]

Cnoc Áine, and the associated Lough Gur monuments, have a secure place in the Uisnech design.

215°–217°E: ARRA, CO. TIPPERARY. PAPS OF ANU, CO. KERRY. BHEARE PENINSULA, CO. CORK

∽

(I) ARRA MOUNTAIN (TOUNTINNA) [90 KM]**

This mountain (1,475 feet/460 meters) was the home of Fintan the White, restorer of Uisnech, who arrived in the first boat with Cesair. Arra, where he survived the Flood, is Ireland's Ararat. It rises at the meeting of Leinster and Munster, with a fine view across Lough Dergdere and the Shannon into South Connacht. The remains of Megalithic tombs, now called the Graves of the Leinstermen, stand below the summit.

(II) PAPS OF ANU [214 KM]

Across the cast flank of the Arra Mountain and 124 kilometers distant, an Uisnech-to-Paps-of-Anu alignment carries a beam of national intelligence from the center to the most remarkable topographic symbols of maternity. Fintan's flood mountain therefore enjoyed the remote protection of these combined influences and may have been selected on that basis.

(III) BHEARE PENINSULA [261 KM]

The same alignment ends on the Bheare Peninsula. There Áine-as-Hag, the Caillighe Bheare, reputedly had her home. On the surface of Ireland there is, after all, no escape from the cycle of life and death, nor from the sea that both nourishes and inundates.

226°E: SLIEVE AUGHTY MOUNTAINS, CO. GALWAY [82 KM]**

This range is 1,175 feet (358 meters) high and is the line of midwinter sunset, seen from Uisnech. As with Ériu in her flesh-tearing guise, so here, the owl goddess tears into the remains of the year with beak and claw. On the same midwinter sunset line, 124 kilometers beyond the summit of Slieve Aughty, lies Slieve Mish, Co. Kerry, which, *Lebor Gabála* says, was Ériu's seat in the far southwest. There, with Banba, she presided over the death and rebirth of the year.

304°E: CRÚACHAIN (RATHCROGHAN), CO. ROSCOMMON [61 KM]

Just as the midwinter sunrise, seen from Uisnech, led to a special sanctity being ascribed to the Almu–Curragh–Kildare landscape in the southeast, so sacred value was attributed to the midsummer sunset in the northwest. The Uisnech balance was maintained by recognizing such complementary opposites.

By following the sunwise story of Midir and Étaín, via Slievenaman, we are eventually led to the spot where, in the Uisnech design, they touched ground on the evening of the summer solstice. Étaín and her retinue embodied this annual event – the most northerly sunset of the year, when they entered a *síd*, called Síd Sinche, in Co. Roscommon, identified with a souterrain also called the Cave of the Cats.

This cave, which aligns with midsummer sunset on the Uisnech web, became the supernatural focus around which the sacred capital of Connacht developed. No fewer than sixty-eight pre-Norman monuments "which appear to be mainly ritual in character," are bunched together around the *síd*. These are from every period, including the fourth millennium B.C.E.

Étaín is said to have traveled to Crúachain from Slievenaman (the apex of the sun's course), in the company of her maid, Crochen Croderg. Crochen was the setting sun personified. Her first name is based on

223°E: SLIEVE BERNAGH, CO. CLARE [97 KM]**

Aibhinn, the fairy queen of West Munster, sister of Áine, lived on this mountain, west of Lough Dergderc, and is still spoken of in the district. Her *síd* was at a crag called Craganeevul, near a well called Tobereevul. Aibhill, alias Aibhinn, meaning "the lovely one," was said to be the queen of twenty-five Co. Clare banshees. She featured prominently in eighteenth- and nineteenth-century Irish verse of the region and was seen washing clothes in a stream prior to a disaster. She foretold the death of the king-hero, Brian Boru. She is ultimately an appellation of the sun goddess and, as a language word, describes "cattle in heat."

croch, "saffron or cream," and her second, Croderg, means "blood red." Given in full, her name describes how the sun changes from yellow to red as it sets — the very transformation that she embodies. The Bodleian account states that her eyebrows, eyelashes, and entire head were red. Keating calls her "Redskin."

Crochen admired the radiant *síd* to which Étaín and Midir had led her. "Then said strong Crochen, 'What fine house is this where we have halted? O Midir of the splendid feasts, is this thy spacious dwelling?'" Midir explained that his own home lay "nearer to the sunrise," but as a reward for her journey, he gave Crochen the sunset *síd*, and renamed it Crúachain after her. Then Midir and Étaín, concerned to start the next solar cycle, passed northward, leaving Crochen behind at Crúachain. In due course, she gave birth there to Medb, goddess-queen of Connacht.

Oweynagat, The Cave of the Cats, is Crochen's *síd*, 2,297 feet (700 meters) south-southwest of the great mound of Rath Crúachain. The cave is a modified natural limestone fissure, 426 feet (130 meters long), and probably refers to the cats, who, in northwest European myth, drew the solar chariot across the sky.

✤ OWENYNAGAT CAVE ✤

In 1779, the Oweynagat Cave was known as "The Hellmouth Door of Ireland," challenging St. Patrick's Purgatory for the title, except that here, instead of Christian associations there was a belief that a woman, clinging to the tail of an unruly calf, had been led through the cave, down an underground tunnel, and had reemerged, 29 kilometers to the north at the Caves of Keshcorran, the haunt of the Winter hags. Beranger teased his guides about this, and with their help searched the Cat's Cave for a possible lower exit, "but the solid rock was everywhere; and there was neither door nor window nor crevice where the woman and her calf could pass." Not to be denied, "the country people said that the Devil had stopped up the tunnel." And it could be argued that a Devil-ridden Christianity had indeed blocked the worship of the great cycle that spun between midsummer eve and Keshcorran.

Cats' eyes, blazing in the dark, confirm their daytime mythic duties. The involvement of cats in solar orbitings may also explain Aill na Mireann's other name, The Cat Stone, since folk names are rarely arbitrary.

Rath Crúachain, the principal monument in the complex, consists of a natural mound, artificially scarped in antiquity into a near-circular shape, 295 feet (90 meters) diameter, with a domed surface, and a crowning "nipple." The "nipple" was a 6.5-foot (2-meter)-high mound on the summit, surrounded by a circular "aureole," in the form of a bank and ditch, 32 feet (10 meters) across. This summit feature was clearly visible in a nineteenth-century survey, and in Beranger's drawing of 1779, though only faint traces of it now remain. Here the kings of Connacht were inaugurated, by marriage to Crochen's daughter, Medb. The word *Medb* is cognate with English, *mead*,

For the island vessel to ring true, it had to be rotated throughout the year from season to season, and from sid to sid, on either side of Croghan Hill, Co. Offaly, where Brigit-the-Smith worked on it so hard.

329°E: BRÍ LEITH (ARDAGH HILL), CO. LONGFORD [22 KM]

After leaving Crochan Crodberg behind at Rathcrogan, Midir and Etain continued their great circuit northwestward beyond the point of midsummer sunset, as witnessed from Uisnech. Seen from Uisnech, Brí Léith (650 feet/198 meters), the síd of Midir and Étaín, is only 31° from true North, where, at Irish latitudes, no setting sun has ever reached. Yet what was invisible as a surface phenomenon shone brightly in the imagination. In mythic consciousness, withdrawal from one plane of reality implied re-emergence on another. Consequently the sun goddess Étaín, alter ego of Áine, is described "on the fair green of Brí Léith" as a "woman with a bright comb of silver adorned with gold, washing in a silver basin, wherein were four golden birds, and little bright gems of purple carbuncle in the rim of the basin." She wore a cloak with "silvery fringes and a brooch of fairest gold… On her head were two golden yellow tresses, in each of which was a plait of four locks, with a bead at the tip of each lock. That hair seemed to them like the flower of the iris in summer, or like red gold after burnishing." Étaín was the epitome of inaccessible glory and was coveted by the mythic horse-king of the east, Eochaid.

46°E: FREMU (FREWIN HILL), CO. WESTMEATH [13 KM]

Radio masts point skyward from Frewin Hill's 560-foot (171-meter)-high twin summits and what makes it special is its weight of myth. Here Eochaid Airem, horse king of the east, dared to settle close to the east–west frontier, 14 miles (22 kilometers) from Brí Léith, Midir's stronghold. The hill has been identified as Dun

the intoxicating drink fermented from the honey of flowers, including elderflowers, and associated with the English fairy queen, Mab.

In Irish, Medb's name means "The Intoxicating One," and Connacht was called "The Fifth of the Intoxicating One." Her liquor gave access to a hidden maternal domain, symbolized in her own mother's *crochen* or drinking cup.

Medb of Connacht was regarded as sister to, or "the same as" Queen Medb of Tara, whom the high king of all Ireland had to marry before he could assume the title. Tara and Rathcroghan lie 64 and 61 kilometers respectively from Aill na Mireann. Joining east and west together, Medb appeared in both places, to offer her cup to the king, just as Étaín had served wine at Tara to her eastern husband, Eochaid, prior to arriving at Rathcroghan with Midir.

Fremu, the fort of Eochaid-as-Culture Hero and innovator.

Fremu is derived from the word *frem* – literally "a root," and "to implant." Figuratively it means "a source, origin, or rootstock," and is related to *Fremamail* – "radical, primary." In Irish myth Fremu Hill, or Dun Fremu, marks a departure from the wilderness in favor of farming. Considering the effect of plowing as a form of cutting, it comes as no surprise to learn that Fremu was considered "a judgment seat of Fótla." The islandwide goddess of divisions and furrows appeared to give her approval to the new work.

The zone around the north side of the hill is where Midir and Eochaid came to their final battle, where Midir stood for the repository of elemental powers, and Eochaid was the innovative god, deviser of machinery and agricultural techniques. Support for Eochaid came from the Fir Bolg, whose task in Irish agrarian myth was to help prepare the soil. The *Dindshenchas* described how, having first visited Tara, Eochaid's palace in the east, two Fir Bolg brothers arrived in Westmeath and gave their names to Loughs Owel and Ennell, which lie close to Fremu, and began to marl the land.

They were "giants." The first, *Ainind,* means "mighty," while Uair his brother was described as "a boy of huge stature." At Lough Owel, named after him, he was permitted to break a taboo that said he should drink only cold water from the sea, suggesting that the lough might be regarded as an interior ocean – the amniotic sea. As a language word *uair* means "coldness" and "an hour," the twenty-fourth part

of a day. So, the subdivision of space, by plowing and marling, had an effect on time, changing it into a succession of task-laden periods – a definite cultural advance, for better or worse.

On midsummer morning, who should rise at Fremu, which stands on the Uisnech-Sliab Caillighe alignment, but Midir, Étaín and her handmaiden Croghen Croderg, according to the *Dindshenchas,* and to watchers of that annual dawn. They are on there way to Rathcroghan, making the longest sky-ride of the year. In rising thus at Fremu, Midir, the god of unqualified Nature, can be seen to have already infiltrated Eochaid's stronghold of culture, implying that nature and culture cannot be kept apart.

Both Fremu and Brí Léith lay in the ancient district of Tethba, which, considering its location around the north side of Uisnech, is derived from surprisingly hot ingredients: *teth,* meaning "warm, hot, scalding, ardent, sultry," and *tethin,* "of the sun," and "like a fiery blaze." Tethba was also the secret name of Étaín's daughter, fathered by Eochaid; Tethba the girl, and Tethba the district resolve the enmity between Midir and Eochaid. Her name may derive from *tet,* "a rope or cord." She ties one midsummer sunrise alignment to the next, and her birth-string leads straight to the omphalus on the Uisnech Hill.

There is no gap, and no rest between the annual cycles. Tethba's young legs are there already to take up the running.

MIDE 3

Uisnech and consciousness

After completing the Grand Circuit, returning to the starting point at Aill na Mireann is to revisit the eye of a ceaseless event-storm. The Ireland of the five provinces was an immensely busy place. One of the functions of the center stone was to anchor all this activity into a sense and a point of repose, without denying the need for action. This paradox was resolved through the god, Mide, who was synonymous with the center stone, and the central province that bore his name.

Mide, the master of ceremonies at Uisnech, combined in his ancestry the complementary qualities of wakefulness and somnolence. He was son of Brath, and *brath* means "act of reconnoitering, of revealing, a revelation, a sign." Yet this Brath was in turn son of Deaith, and *deaith* is "idleness, inactivity, and indolence."

The Beltaine bonfires were lit only once a year, but may burn on, as buried memories, long after their flames falter and conscious thought of them has died away. Sigmund Freud writes of "the importance of *optical memory* [by which] it is possible for thought-processes to become conscious, through a reversion to visual residues, and in many people this seems to be a favorite method. Thinking in pictures [he adds] is unquestionably older than thinking in words."

It follows that the Uisnech myth may originally have been seen before it was heard. Equally, another ring of bonfires might be the best means to recall lost Uisnech words, glowing like peat, with the energy of completed summer songs.

Freud continues: "A mental element, for instance an idea, is not as a rule permanently conscious. On the contrary, a state of consciousness is characteristically very transitory and often lies latent, or unconscious." He then distinguishes between the *latent* capacity for recall, which he calls a task of the *preconscious*, and the churnings of chaos and raw appetites in the *unconscious*, or *id*. In terms of Irish myth, the id might be characterized as the realm of the Fomorians.

Irish myth shows that the boundaries between psychic realms are neither impermeable, nor static. Over thousands of years, much transference has taken place between what, in prehistoric times, was known at a conscious or preconscious level, to the level of the modern id, and there, the Uisnech eye lives on.

> In the id, which is capable of being inherited, are stored up vestiges of the existences of countless former egos [including those that looked out from Uisnech in antiquity]. The experiences undergone by the ego seem at first to be lost to posterity, but when they have been repeated often enough and with sufficient intensity in the successive individuals of many generations, they transform themselves, so to say, into experiences of the id, the impress of which is preserved by inheritance, and when the ego forms its super-ego out of the id, it may perhaps only "be reviving images of egos that have passed away, and be securing for them a resurrection."

In this way, the fire of prehistoric Uisnech rekindles in the depths of our being, and the lure of the archaic takes on a strength verging on the irrational; for that is where, in our makeup, it is usually lodged, till permitted to rise from the depths.

LEFT *The House of the Ancestors, Poolnabrone Chamber, Co. Clare, third millennium B.C.E. Ireland's and Uisnech's traditions were sustained by the combination of divine and ancestral spirits, offering their accumulated wisdom to each mortal generation in turn.*

CONLE AT UISNECH

The story of Conle at Uisnech is the tale of Everyone. He was the son of Conn of the Hundred Battles, high king of Ireland in the second century C.E., and Conle's adventures are known from eighth-century manuscripts.

One day Conle the Red was beside his father on the hill of Uisnech. He saw a woman in wonderful attire approach him. Conle said: "Where do you come from, woman?" "I come," said the woman, "from the Land of the Living, a place where there is neither death, nor sin, nor transgression. We enjoy lasting feasts without preparing them and pleasant company without strife. We live in great peace. From that we are known as the People of Peace."

"With whom do you speak, boy?" said Conn to his son, for none saw the woman save Conle alone. The woman answered:

"He speaks to a beautiful young woman of noble race whom neither death threatens nor old age. I love Conle the Red, I call him to the Plain of Delight, where reigns a king victorious and immortal, a king without weeping or sorrow in his land since he became king.

"Come with me, Conle the Red of the jeweled neck, red as flame, your hair is yellow over the bright noble face of your royal form. If you come with me, your beauty will not lose its youth or its fairness forever."

Conn consulted with his druid Corán, who

sang against the woman's voice so that Conle did not see the woman after that, . . . [but] she threw an apple to Conle. Conle was for a month without food, without drink. He cared not to eat any food but his apple, and his apple did not diminish for what he used to eat of it, but was still whole. A longing then came on Conle for the woman he had seen.

A month from that day Conle was beside his father in the plain of Archommin and he saw the same woman approach him, and she said to him: "There above sits Conle among lifeless mortals waiting for a gloomy death. Living immortals invite you. You are a hero for the people of Tethra." Then Conle says, "It is not easy for me, for I love my people, but a longing for the woman has come upon me." The woman answered then and said this: "You have a longing greater than all

other desires to go from them over the sea, so that we may come in my ship of glass to the dwelling of Boadach [boadach, "preeminent"] . . . though it is far away, we shall reach it before night. It is the country which delights the mind of anyone who goes there. There are no people there save only women and girls." When the maiden had finished speaking Conle sprang away from them so that he was in the ship of glass, or crystal coracle. The pair rowed then over the sea away from Ireland and they were not seen since....

LEFT *Conle's Embarkation. (Launching a currach, Co. Donegal, c. 1900). Prince Conle and the Apple Woman prepare to depart for her Otherworld, The Land of the Living. In Ireland, every mundane act can carry traces of sacred story.*

Perhaps they traveled to that well of wisdom called Connle, the mythic source of the Shannon, in the western ocean. Connle may have been named after Conle of Mide, in an attempt to reestablish the link between Ireland's longest river, the flood of prenatal waters, and Ériu's principal omphalos, Aill na Mireann.

The voyage involves no split between spirit and matter, and no division into good and evil. Instead, as so often in Irish tradition, the mysterious female offers a fusion of materiality with the ineffable. Beyond the sunset and beyond the visible, her ship carries this achievement into the realm of pure and timeless bliss.

But who *was* she? MacCana argues that "she can hardly be dissociated from those goddesses such as Áine and Aoibheall, whose fairy dwellings constituted familiar landmarks in the Irish landscape." The apple-woman's journey extended the rings of Ériu's bonfires, in the Uisnech array, till they merged with an ocean of stars, securing in that union the prospect of eternity.

That is how far the Uisnech eye can see.

HOME

domesticated deities

The gods whom poets celebrated, priests worshiped, and kings obeyed, depended for their popularity upon frequent entry into the homes of the people. In the ordinary house, divine adventures were rediscovered in the corresponding family events of birth, marriage, and death. The real-life dramas of human existence, when considered in their vivid contrasts and reiterated patterns, were absorbed into the tales of the heroes and gods, as told and retold around the domestic hearth.

This conjunction of supernatural and natural affairs was further reinforced by family ceremonies, repeated in an annual cycle. Domestic rites ensured that humanity's share in the divine drama was not left to chance or to poet-priests, but belonged to all. By house rites, the quality of eternity was touched at regular intervals and formalized into a reliable framework. A collective inner tranquillity thus survived the impact of physical hardship and remorseless change.

It is no coincidence that Brigit, the deity most obviously identified with the sacred flame, has lasted the longest in popular esteem. No god has leaped the pale between pagan and Christian worlds more successfully than she. For millennia she linked the human hearth to the Uisnech wheel, bringing its grandeur into the home, and Brigit-on-the-hearth remained the focus of worship long after the Uisnech design had been lost. Her fire was the central feature of every house and constituted one end of a flaming axis reaching to the chamber of pure imagination. She put the family in direct touch with ultimate mysteries. "Brigit, excellent woman, a flame, golden, delightful. May she, the sun-dazzling, splendid, guide us to the eternal Kingdom," sang St. Broccan in the seventh century.

Christian history tells that St. Brigit was a woman born in a druid's house at Tocharmaine in 453 C.E. Yet she invested her humanity with divine qualities, for her name continued to mean "the Great or Sublime One," from the root *brig*, "power, strength, vigor, force, efficiency, substance, essence, and meaning."

At sunrise on the first day of spring, her birthday, February 1st the quarterday, a column of fire rose from her infant head, and neighbors saw the house aflame from earth to heaven; but when they entered to rescue her there was no fire. This brief supernatural flame joined cradle to sun and night to day.

LEFT Reconstructed Iron Age homestead, Craggaunowen, Co. Clare.

BELOW Home. Sunlight, lamplight, and firelight combine with warmth and shelter as gifts from the household deities. The house demonstrates in miniature the Uisnech array.

RIGHT *"Harnen the oaten farls." A Co. Antrim kitchen, c.1900. Open hearth and griddle; with wool-winding frame, left.*

It was told how a druid watching the stars in the middle of the night saw a fiery column arising out of the house where she was residing, at Loch Mask. She reached up to the unfathomable heights of space from smoke-filled ordinariness; she was a great traveler.

Brigit's head-fires also served to associate Home with Temple. For example in Ardagh "a fiery column flamed out of her head up to the ridge of the church," while her own religious house at Kildare revolved around a fire, which was kept alight continuously. Equally she enabled people to see flames coursing through their farm tools, so bringing those worn sticks into the sacred realm:

> *Brigid went into a house and brought out a harrow [a wooden rake]. She held it up over her head and every one of the pins gave out a flame like a candle. All the people turned back to look at the shining harrow that was such a great wonder.*

Human clothing was created under the comprehensive circle of her cloak, for she had laid it, "wet on the rays of the sun, and they held it up the same as hooks." The human family's garments could share the virtue of her cloak, providing the right rituals were observed.

Dozens of stories concerning Brigit's miraculous doings point toward the numinous opportunities playing around the home, and to the need for householders to offer hospitality to the goddess-saint, so that her benefits might accrue. The well-known Irish instinct for hospitality may be traced to the expectation of entertaining the divine.

The Celts inherited a series of morning devotions centered on the hearth, called Blessing of the Kindling. "The Kindling of the fire is a work full of interest to the housewife, and when 'lifting' the fire in the morning the woman prays in an undertone that the fire may be blessed to her and to her household. The people look upon fire as a miracle of the Divine Power provided for their good," wrote Carmichael of Hebridean attitudes c. 1850, which originated in Ireland.

> *Before retiring for the night, the fire would be "smoored" with loving care. With the hearthstone normally in the middle of the floor, the embers were evenly spread in a circle, which was then divided into three equal sections, with a small boss being left*

in the middle. A sod of peat was laid between each section, with each sod touching the central boss. Then the whole circle was covered over with some ashes, and the central heap referred to as The Hearth of the Three. The woman then closed her eyes, stretched her hands, and slowly intoned "a formula." In Ireland this ran:

I cover this fire

As noble Christ did.

Mary on top of the house,

And St. Brigid in its center.

The subdivision of the fire into three around a central boss may well refer to Brigit as a trinity within the outer ring of her unity.

As a working icon her image in the hearth was also a nightly resurrection of the great fire-eye seen engraved in Neolithic tombs, such as Dowth, and was a small-scale version of the Uisnech-centered fire-eye. All three placed the believer under the protection of the ash-hidden fire goddess during darkness. F. H. A. Aalen points out that in Ireland a central hearth was once fundamental, "though now it can be found only in West Galway, having long since been moved to the gable end in other districts." (Possibly the last people to sit around a central open hearth were a Mr. and Mrs. Lawless of Menlough, Co. Galway, c. 1966.) As recently as the seventeenth century, both round and rectangular Irish dwellings were focused on a central fire, "and round it they sleep on the ground, lying all in a circle about the fire, with their feet towards it." This fire, essential to winter survival, and cooking throughout the year, was seen as a spiritual gift, blessing the entire house. The Irish word *tellach*, "hearth, fireplace," also means "household" and "family." So the central domestic light united habitation and inhabitants in a single word.

In Ulster it was considered unlucky to be the first house to show smoke on May morning. On this, the first day of the "summer half" of the year, there was a tendency for every domestic fire to fly from the house to rejoin its parental blaze in the *síd*, or in the supernaturally arising sun itself.

RIGHT *"The Churn" or
Harvest Home, Toome,
Co. Antrim, c. 1910. The
last-cut sheaf, called the
Churn or Cailleach, now
rafter-hung, presides over
the family at Harvest
Supper. A fiddler plays,
top left.*

THE POT

By speaking of the underworld *síd*, fire ran below the domestic hearth into the territory of Begoibne, Brigit's "sister," the woman of the smithy and pot-maker. Her workshop located beneath Croghan Hill offered a divine prototype to householders, who likewise buried a pot in front of their hearthstone. Examples of small "pot-oven" burials include one that was found under a kitchen floor at Mahoonaghbed, Co. Limerick, hung from two thin iron rods laid crosswise over the hole. Clare, Kerry, and Tipperary have provided all similar evidence of a "*síd*-in-miniature" underneath the cottage floor.

The buried pot represented the abyss, lower hemisphere, and fundament of Brigit. Therefore when St. Columcille was trapped in Breccán's Cauldron, the notorious whirlpool near Rathlin Island, it was to Brigit that he prayed. "He besought Brigit that a calm might come to him." She duly obliged, and he was able to reach Scotland safely.

The issue here is the elasticity of the domestic *coire* or cauldron, which reaches through the topographic scale toward infinity, a range that is reflected

THE HANGING-BOWL LIGHT

Until recent centuries, most Irish houses had no windows. Domestic life was lived largely in the dark, pierced by Brigit's fiery arrow, the shaft of sunlight coming through the south door, as Synge discovered among the Aran islanders, where the angle of the shadow still told the time of day. After sunset, illumination came almost entirely from the hearth-fire, but was sometimes supplemented by the oil light of a hanging bowl. These vessels were suspended from the roof by three cords or chains, passing through three lugs around the rim. Whether made of bronze, wood, or stones, they are generally regarded as having more than utilitarian ambitions, for they evoke the sun boat at night, transporting the wavering glimmer through oceans of darkness. With that in mind, the passage of the submarine sun was engraved in a rocking pattern around the rim of the wooden Altartate vessel that was discovered at Clones, Co. Monaghan (currently dated 500 B.C.E.–450 C.E.).

A bronze lamp from Ballinderry Crannog, on the Eiscir Riada, 2.5 miles (4 kilometers) from Croghan Hill, displays the kind of vulva symbol depicted in continental Europe since Paleolithic times. The same

in language. *Coire* means "cauldron, large pot, gulf, and whirlpool." The word *aigen* means "a large metal vessel used for washing hands," and the ninth Rule of Tallaght states that after it had been returned to the smith to be tapped all around, three times, the pot could then be employed to brew liquor, fleshment, or porridge. This tapping was a ritual appeal to the triple goddess of the waters, both clean and foul. *Aigean* also means "the ocean, the deep, and abyss." Similarly, the pot buried beneath the house floor was overflowing with meanings, connected by symbol and mythic word.

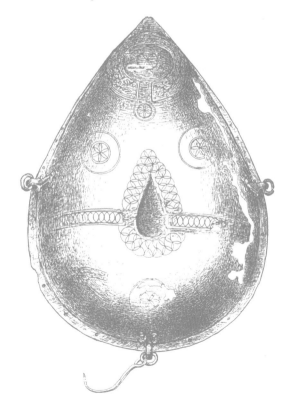

LEFT *Bronze hanging-bowl lamp from Ballinderry, Co. Westmeath, Iron Age, 9¹/₂ inches (24 centimeters) long, incised with vulva and belt symbols. It used whale oil, or sun-fish oil, appearing to come from Brigit's fiery interior.*

shape is also embossed into the base of the vessel. Seen from below (as it *would* have been seen), this magic pudendum is surrounded by the rotating pattern of incised sun circles, attached to and bordered by a belt of running solar symbols. Perhaps it evoked the east–west Eiscir Riada as the national "Belt of Brigit," complementing her straw belt, which, as we shall see, played a big part in the February 1st ritual.

The rosette at the tip of this vessel is surrounded by an applied collar, neck (or mide). Over it the wick would have floated and shone. The loops are formed by cast animals who bite the rim.

Other bowls suggest a journey to the sacred interior by showing Brigit's vulva in their overall form, as with the Kilgulbin East vessel, or by the shape of and engraving on the lugs, as at Ballynacourt.

ST. BRIGIT'S EVE

The greatest occasion in the traditional domestic year was, arguably, the festival of Brigit's birth, on February 1st, the Imbolc or Oimelg quarterday, and start of spring.

On St. Brigit's Eve it was customary to limewash the house inside. "A good big fire was put down and the animals were bedded on clean straw. The whole interior had an air of coziness and comfort ready to receive

BELOW St. Brigit. On the eve of her quarter-day, Imbolc (February 1st), she was ceremonially welcomed into the house as the infant-child of early spring.

Brigit into the house." In Co. Mayo the man of the house procured a garment to use as a mantle, or *Brat Bride* (the clothing of the infant goddess). The article chosen was the one that would be in greatest use by the member of the house whose occupation was the most dangerous, such as the muffler of a fisherman. The man took it to the yard, drew a good long sheaf of straw from the stack, and wrapped the garment around the straw to give it a rough outline of a human body. Then, carrying it as if it were a child, he set it down outside the back door and went into the house.

So placed, this straw child also evokes the birth of St. Brigit. Her *Life* states that she was born neither within the house nor without. Her pregnant mother, visiting a queen, had "put one of her two footsteps over the threshold of the house, the other foot [still] being outside . . . *Then* she brought forth her daughter, even St. Brigid."

The door is implicitly equated with the vulva of the saint-goddess's mother.

Brigit brought the wheelings of the cosmos into the cabin. By her entry she took over the house, which was accordingly born (in both senses) from the dark travail of the winter environment, toward the growing light. The occupants acted as midwives to the double event, which resacralized the entire structure in the way that a Hebridean chant suggests:

May Brigit give blessing

To the house that is here . . .

Brigit, the fair and tender,

Her hue like the cotton grass.

Rich-tressed maiden,

Of ringlets of gold;

Both crest and frame,

Both stone and beam;

Both clay and wattle;

Both summit and foundation;

Both window and timber;

Both foot and head;

Both man and woman;

Both wife and children;

Both young and old;

Both maiden and youth.

In Co. Mayo folk ritual, the straw child who was refused entry at the back door represented Brigit of the completed winter quarter. Consequently that door (which usually faced north) remained shut at the Imbolc festival, the start of spring. Instead, when the preparations for supper were complete, the man rose to say that he must fetch Brigit through the front or south door to share the feast. Going outside again, he knelt and cried to the family: "Go on your knees, open your eyes, and let Brigit in!" Inside, they responded: "She is welcome."

The formula was repeated twice more, and while the people within continued to chant "she is welcome," the man brought "Brigit" around to the front door and entered with her, whereupon all cried: "*Mush! Se beatha agus a slainte*" . . . "How wonderful! She is welcome, and seeing that, a toast." The straw baby. Brigit was then laid respectfully against a table leg, or, if need be, was placed on a sick cow's back in order to effect a cure.

At the Imbolc festival, to ensure that every member of the family came into direct contact with Brigit's power, a ten-foot (three-meter) ring of braided straw rope was made, to which three or four straw crosses were attached. It was called *Cris*, *Crois Bride*, or St. Brigit's Belt. The "belt" was carried from house to house, and all the occupants drew it over their heads and down their bodies before stepping from the golden ring. In performing this ritual they literally wore the track of the sun-goddess' annual circuit. (Irish *Cris* is cognate with Welsh *gwregis*, which takes on solar

connections in the phrase *gwregys Iau*, "the belt of Jupiter," and dives into the ocean in *gwregys'r mor*, the "sweet sea weeds, or sea belts.")

Some idea of the range of Irish *crois* comes from Keating, c. 1650, who measured the breadth of Ireland as "four and a half degrees of the solar *crois*, which is called the zodiac." The word was also applied to the "zones of heaven and earth" of earlier cosmological speculation.

As a human belt it was the equivalent of Ireland's medial road between equinoctial sunrise and sunset, the Eiscir Riada. Woven in straw, it was prophetic of a successful harvest to come, reaching from sea to sea. The Christian tradition says that St. Brigit had herself worn the belt, before giving it to a beggar girl, who in turn loaned it to the sick, for cures and general circulation. All subsequent belts were descended from the sacred prototype, worn by the saint-goddess.

To complement the *Cris*, a silk head-ribband called *Ribin*, or *Ribe Bride* was left outside the house on Bride's Eve, and was believed to lengthen during that night; afterward it was used as a cure for headaches. (In Bride, the health of mind and body were of equal importance.) Her head ribbon can perhaps also be seen wound around Uisnech, in the word *ribeann*, which O'Donovan defines as "a royal hill on which royal parleys were held." The *Ribin* is the linear form of her energy, and ultimately relates it to the monster serpent who accompanied her in the boat from Scandinavia. It surfaces again as Caoranach at Lough Derg, Co. Donegal, facing St. Brigit's well.

THE FOUR QUARTERS

Devotion to St. Brigit has survived recent transformations of house interiors. The cross of Bride, as old as the Neolithic, still hangs in many a modern Irish kitchen, at least "for luck." Made either of rush or wheat straw, these crosses combine harvest gold with Brigit's yellow flame. Whether in lozenge shape, quartered wheel, or free-legged, the dynamic of the solar year is conveyed, showing the original god-given plan for the Island and its attached Otherworlds.

Equally, the qualities of the quarters typically determined the orientation of a rectangular house. The main door should face east, or south. Only with great reluctance would a house be extended toward the west, which was the zone of misfortune. These issues were matters of spiritual (and therefore physical) life and death, because, in M. Eliade's words, every house is "the choice of a universe that one is prepared to assume by creating it."

This act of alignment with the cosmos (reiterated in the layout of the classical city) explains why in Ireland an English silver florin coin, having a quartered design on the back, was much favored as an offering to be placed under the threshold of the door. Its pattern repeated that shown on quartered gold disks made in late Neolithic Ireland. In Co. Limerick housebuilding, a florin was tossed at the outset, and work would only go ahead if the coin landed with the quartered design uppermost. This "superstition" was concerned with the correct fixing of a center and projection of horizons, in what Eliade calls the "cosmosizition" of a territory and its transformation into a replica of the exemplary universe, created and inhabited by the gods. The simplest dwelling repeats the pattern by declaring a World Center.

When considering the site for a new house in nineteenth-century Ireland, "Very few people were content with preparations of a material kind." Out of respect for them, sites of ancient occupation, or activity, such as prehistoric earthworks or megaliths, were avoided. By consulting with the oldest living inhabitants the builders also hoped to avoid accidentally blocking routes taken by local divinities, or by spirits of the mortal dead on their funeral path to the grave. Throughout Ireland a strong belief persisted that if a new house was constructed across a fairy path, then the inhabitants would suffer broken furniture, plates smashed in the night, destruction of crops, sickness among the animals, and human fatalities. To avoid these calamities, four piles of stones were left as markers at the corners of the chosen site. If the gods left the piles of stones undisturbed during

OPPOSITE *Girls and corn dollies, Kinsale, Co. Cork. On St. Brigit's Day, the entire family passed through her straw belt, called* Crois Bride, *to ensure good health.*

LEFT *A four-armed St Brigit's Cross; 12 inches (30 centimeters) broad, made of rush or straw. Such crosses still hang in many an Irish home, denoting the four quarters of the year. The fire-goddess rotates beneath her Christian veil.*

the following night, work on the house might safely start thereafter. The importance attributed to the four quarters of the Irish house reiterates Asiatic conviction, where they were held to incorporate the four winds in heaven, the four rivers of Paradise, and other zones beyond the earth.

Among Irish householders, it was the fire goddess, Brigit, queen of the sun's cardinal movements, at once so powerful, yet so measured, the bringer of fire, yet the protectress from conflagration, who carried her farflung riches back into the house, like a harvest home, and distributed them among the family.

With the help of Ulster midwives, these gifts included the "Moon of the Four Quarters," as their chant was called. It was addressed to the woman-in-labor. The midwife marked the four house corners with Brigit's crosses, and on the threshold she sang:

> Four corners to her bed.
>
> Four angels at her head.
>
> Mark, Matthew, Luke, and John;
>
> God bless the bed that she lies on.
>
> New moon, new moon, God bless me.
>
> God bless this house and family.

To this sound, the newborn child entered the world.

HOME AGAIN

Brigit's work is nearly done. Creeping secularism is making her visits unnecessary, so she stays away.

The mythless shell, a house without gods, was described by Samuel Beckett some decades ago. His *Endgame* (1957) is set in a chamber where high upon the rear wall are two small windows, like the Sandymount Martello tower, curtains closed, which "suggests that the room may represent the inside of the skull of a man who has his eyes on the external world." The scene both inside and out denotes a dying world, a Machine Age where there is "no more nature." When Clov (French *clou*, "nail") looks out of the window, he says all is "corpsed." The waves are

LEFT *Samuel Beckett, novelist and playwright. Through a largely disenchanted secular world he refined the art of spiritual homelessness.*

"lead," the sun is "zero," and the light is an even gray, "light black from pole to pole." The master of the house, Hamm (hammer) is dying, and the curtain falls as Clov teeters on the threshold of the room, neither in nor out, gazing at walls blackened by nihilistic power, and wondering if an alternative form of habitation is possible.

"No symbols where none intended," Beckett wrote at the end of his novel *Watt*, realizing that his house of nonmeaning was essentially a denial of the entire mythic tradition. Only chop down the roof tree, *Cleithe*, and the Home-on-earth, as a system of poetic interconnections, is bound to collapse. Technology will then have freedom to do what it likes with the debris. In a postsymbolic age, the tree that stands at the center of Beckett's *Waiting for Godot* is a shadow, a meaningless antisymbol, at once mocking and describing a deprived state.

Into this lassitude now breaks the sudden thunder of an ecological endgame, rumbling beyond the living-room windows like Eogabal-the-tree-god's last laugh. He is trying to say that if we do not belong in Nature we belong nowhere, and so must face final eviction and perpetual homelessness.

OPPOSITE *Brigit's sun-wheel as gold disk, c. 2000 B.C.E., from Kilmuckridge, Co. Wexford, 2¹/₂ inches (7 centimeters) diameter, over Croghan Hill, Co. Offaly, Brigit's síd, or underhill home.*

RIGHT *Malin Head, Co. Donegal. Ireland's most northerly point. Here the furious dance of gale, foam, and rock weave a crown for the island goddess Banba, mistress of Nature's hidden processes.*

The same truth may underlie a *Litany of Creation*, which was written by an Irish cleric in 1575. As he peered from his chapel window at what he was supposed to regard as a cursed, sin-laden, soulless wilderness, an apparently irresistible gust of affirmation swept over him. He suddenly loved what he saw out there. In a passionate appeal, he called up the despised glories of physical reality, so that the universal soul and the house of individual consciousness might reunite.

> *I entreat Thee by water, and the cruel air. I entreat Thee by fire. I entreat Thee by earth. I entreat Thee by land and sea unresting . . . I entreat Thee by the triad, wind, and sun, and moon. I entreat Thee by the compass of the tuneful firmament; I entreat every stately-branching order, the host of the bright stars. I entreat Thee by every living creature that ever tasted death and life. I entreat Thee by every inanimate creature because of thy fair beauteous mystery. I entreat Thee by time with its clear divisions, I entreat Thee by the darkness, I entreat Thee by the light. I entreat all the elements in heaven and earth. That the eternal sweetness may be granted to my soul . . . this, in brief, is the wise "besom of devotion".*

For us, as for him, the besom or broom belongs to Nature, and sweetness in the soul depends on inviting her back into the house of human culture, there to break into her old song once more:

Icham of Irlaunde	*I am from Ireland*
ant of the holy londe	*And from the holy land*
of irlaunde,	*Of Ireland,*
gods sire pray ich thee	*Good sir, I beg of you,*
for of saynte charite	*For Holy charity,*
come ant daunce wyt me	*Come dance with me*
in irlaunde.	*In Ireland . . .*

BIBLIOGRAPHY

ANNÁLA CONNACHT, ed. Freeman, A.M., Dublin, 1994.

ANNALS OF CLONMACNOISE, trans. Mageoghagan, C., 1627, ed. Murphy, D., Dublin, 1896.

BARING-GOULD, S., *Lives of the Saints*, Edinburgh, 1914.

BARROW, J.D., *The Anthropic Cosmological Principle*, London, 1988.

BECKETT, SAMUEL, *Endgame*, London, 1958.

—, *Waiting For Godot*, London, 1954.

BERGIN, O., "White-eared Cows," in *Ériu*, xiv, 1946.

BEST, R.I., (ed. and trans.), "The Settling of the Manor of Tara," in *Ériu*, 4, 1910.

BIELER, L., *The Irish Penitentials*, Dublin, 1963.

BOLLE, K.W., "Myth: an overview," in ER, 10, New York, 1987.

BORLASE, W.C., *The Dolmens of Ireland*, London, 1897.

BOWEN, E.G., "*The Cult of St Brigit*" in *Studia Celtica*, 8, 1973/4

Bruiden Da Choca, ed. Stokes, W., RC. xxi. 1990.

BUCK, C.D., *A Dictionary of Selected Synonyms in the Principal Indo-European Languages*, Chicago, 1949.

BUCHANAN, C., *Traffic in Towns*, London, 1963.

BUCHANAN, R.H., "Calendar Customs," in *UF*, viii, 1962, and ix, 1963.

BUTTIMER, A., *The Human Experience of Space and Place*, London, 1980.

CAMPBELL. J. and ROBINSON, H.M., *A Skeleton Key to Finnegans Wake*, London, 1947.

CARMICHAEL, A., *Carmina Gadelica*, 5 vols., Edinburgh, 1928–1941.

CASSIRER, E., *The Philosophy of Symbolic Forms*, London, 1955.

Cath Maige Tuired (The Second Battle of Mag Tuired), ed. Gray, E.A., Naas, 1982.

CHART, D.A., *Preliminary Survey of Ancient Monuments of Northem Ireland*, Belfast, 1940.

CLARKE, H.B., "Topographical Development of Early Medieval Dublin," in *JRSAI*, 107, 1977.

COFFEY, G., *New Grange and other incised tumuli in Ireland*, Dublin, 1912.

CRAWFORD, O.G.S., *The Eye Goddess*, London, 1957.

CROKER, T. CROFTON, *Researches in the South of Ireland*, London, 1824; reprinted Shannon, 1969.

—, "Antiquities of Lough Gur" in *The Gentleman's Magazine*, 103, pt. I, 1833.

CROSS, T.P., *Motif-Index of Early Irish Literature*, New York. 1969.

DAMES, M., *The Silbury Treasure*, London, New York, 1976.

—, *The Avebury Cycle*, London, New York, 1977.

DANAHER, K., *The Year in Ireland: Irish Calendar Customs*, Cork, 1972.

DANTE ALIGHIERI, *The Purgatory*, ed. and trans. Butler, A. J., London, 1892.

DAVIES, P.C.W., *Other Worlds*, London, 1980.

DAVENPORT, G., *The Geography of the Imagination*, London, 1984.

DE PAOR, L., "The Viking Towns of Ireland," in Almquist, B. (ed.), *Proceedings of the Seventh Viking Congress*, Dublin, 1976.

DE PAOR, M. and L., *Early Christian Ireland*, London, 1958.

DICTIONARY OF THE IRISH LANGUAGE, ed. Quin, E.G., et al., Dublin, 1913–1976.

DILLON, M. and CHADWICK, W., *The Celtic Realms*, New York, 1967.

Dindshenchas, Metrical (MD), ed. Gwynn, E., Dublin, 1903–35.

Dindshenchas, Rennes (RD), ed. Stokes, W., in *RC*, 15–16, 1894–5.

Dindshenchas, Bodleian (BD), ed. Stokes, W., in FL, 3, 1893.

Dindshenchas, Edinburgh (ED), ed. Stokes, W., in FL, 4, 1893.

DINNEEN, P.S., *An Irish–English Dictionary*, Dublin, 1904.

Duanaire Finn ("The Poem Book of Finn"), ed. MacNeill, E., Dublin, I, 1908; II, 1933; III (ed. Murphy, G.), 1954.

"Duanaire Ghearóid Iarla" in *Studia Hibernica*, III, 1963.

DUMÉZIL, G., *The Destiny of the Warrior*, trans. Hiltebeitel, A., New York, 1970.

—, *L' idéologie tripartie des Indo-Européens*, Paris, 1958.

DWELLY, E., *The Illustrated Gaelic–English Dictionary*, Glasgow, 1949.

Echtrae Coule ("The Adventures of Coule"); trans. Dillon, M., in *EIL*.

ELIADE. M., *Birth and Rebirth: the religious meanings of initiation in human culture*, trans. Trask, W.R., New York, 1958.

—, *Myth and Reality*, trans. Trask, W.R., New York, 1963.

—, *Symbolism, the Sacred, and the Arts*, New York, 1986.

—, *The Sacred and the Profane*, New York, 1959.

ELLIS DAVIDSON, H.R., *The Sword at the Wedding*, FL, 71, 1960.

EOGAN, G., *Knowth and the Passage Tombs of Ireland*, London, 1986.

—, *The Hoards of the Later Irish Bronze Age*, Dublin, 1983.

FITZGERALD, D., *Popular Tales of Ireland*, in *RC*, IV, 1879.

FITZGERALD, REV. P., and M'GREGOR, J.T., *The History, Topography, and Antiquities of Limerick*, Dublin, 1826–7.

FODOR, N., *The Search for the Beloved*, New York, 1949.

FOUR MASTERS, THE, Annals of the Kingdom of Ireland, ed. O'Donovan, J., Dublin, 1848–51.

FOX, C., "Chariot fittings from Lough Gur," in *Ant J*, 30, 1950.

FRASER, J. (ed.), "The First Battle of Moytura" in *Ériu*, 8, 1916.

FREUD, S., *New Introductory Lectures on Psychoanalysis*, trans. Sprott, W.J.H., London, 1933, 78–107.

GANTZ, G. (trans. and ed.), *Early Irish Myths and Sagas*, Harmondsworth, 1981.

GARVIN, J., *James Joyce's Disunited Kingdom*, Dublin, 1976.

GELLING, P. and ELLIS DAVIDSON, H.R., *Chariot of the Sun*, London, 1969.

GEOFFREY OF MONMOUTH, *Historia regum Britanniae*, in Giles, J.A., *Six Old English Chronicles*, London, 1848.

GILBERT, J.T., *A History of the City of Dublin*, Dublin, 1854–9.

GIMBUTAS, M., *Gods and Goddesses of Old Europe*, London, 1978.

—, "The Social Structure of Old Europe" in *JIES*, 17, 1989.

GIRALDUS CAMBRENSIS, *Topographia Hiberniae*, trans. Wright, T., London, 1905.

GLUCK, B.R., *Beckett and Joyce*, New York, 1979.

GOULD, P. and WHITE, R., *Mental Maps*, London, 1974.

Hail Brigit!, ed. and trans. Meyer, K., Dublin, 1912.

HALL, REV. JAMES, *A Tour Through Ireland*, London, 1813.

HALL, MR. and MRS. S.C., *Ireland, Its Scenery and Character*, London, 1841–3.

HARBISON, P., *The Archaeology of Ireland*, London, 1976.

HART, C., *Structure and Motif in Finnegans Wake*, London, 1962.

HAWKINS, P.S. (ed.), *Civitas*, London, 1986.

HEIDEGGER, M., *The question concerning technology*, trans. Lovitt, W., London, 1977.

—, *Poetry, Language, Thought*, trans. Hofstadter, A., London, 1975.

HENRY OF SALTREY. *De Purgatorio S. Patricii, in Patrologie Cureus Completus*, Scriptores Latini, II, Tom. 180, Paris, 1855.

HERITY, M. and EOGAN, G., *Ireland in Prehistory*, London, 1977.

HUGHES, K., *Early Christian Ireland: Introduction to the Sources*, London, 1972.

HULL, E., *Folklore of the British Isles*, London, 1928.

—, "Legends and Traditions of Cailleach Bheara" in FL, 38, 1927.

IFC, Schools Collection, MS 516, 1938.

IFC, MS 1799. Lough Gur and Knockainey.

JAMES, G. and JONES, T. (trans.), *The Mabinogion*, London, 1974.

JOYCE, JAMES, *Dubliners*, London, 1926.

—, *Ulysses*, London, 1937.

—, *Finnegans Wake*, London, 1939.

JOYCE, P.W., *Irish Names of Places*, 2 vols., Dublin, 1901.

KEARNEY, R., *Poetics of Imagining*, London, 1991.

—, *The Wake of Imagination*, London, 1988.

KEATING, G., *Foras Feasa Ar Eirinn* (The History of Ireland.), 4 vols., ITS, Dublin, 1901–13.

KENNEY, J.F., *The Sources for the Early History of Ireland*, Dublin, 1929.

KILBRIDE-JONES, H.E., "Excavations at Drimnagh, Co. Dublin" in *JRSAI*, 69, 1939.

KUIPER, F.B., *Cosmology and Conception,* in HR, 10, 1970.

LEASK, H.G., *Irish Churches and Monastic Buildings*, vol. I, Dublin, 1955.

LE CORBUSIER, *La Ville Radieuse. The City of Tomorrow and its Planning*, trans. Etchells, F., 8th edition, 1931.

LEDWICH, E., *The Antiquities of Ireland*, 2nd edition, Dublin, 1804.

LEHMANN, R.P.M. (trans.), *Early Irish Verse*, Austin, 1982.

LESLIE, J., "Anthropic Principle, World Ensemble and Design," in *American Philosophical Quarterly*, 19, 1982.

LESLIE, S., *Saint Patrick's Purgatory*, London, 1932.

LIETAERT PEERBOLTE, M., *Prenatal Dynamics*, Leiden, 1954.

LITHGOW, W., *The Rare Adventures and Peregrinations of . . .*, ed. Phelps, G., London, 1974.

LOOMIS, R.S., *Celtic Myth and Arthurian Romance*, New York, 1927.

LUCAS, A.T., "Furze in Custom and Belief" in *Béal*, 1960.

MACALISTER, R.A.S., *Ireland in Pre-Celtic Times*, Dublin, 1935.

—, (ed. and trans.), *Lebor Gabála Erenn*, 5 vols., ITS, 1938–41.

—, *Tara, a pagan sanctuary of ancient Ireland*, London, 1931.

—, *The Archaeology of Ireland*, London, 1928.

MACALISTER, R.A.S. and PRAEGER, R.L., "Report on the Excavations at Uisneach," *PRIA*, 38c, 1928–9.

—, "Excavations at Togherstown, Westmeath," *PRIA*, 39c, 1929–31.

MACCANA, P., *Celtic Mythology*, London, 1970.

—, "Early Irish Ideology and the Concept of Unity" in Kearney, R., *The Irish Mind*, Dublin, 1988.

MACNEILL, M., *The Festival of Lughnasa*, Oxford, 1962.

MALLORY, J.P., *In Search of the Indo-Europeans*, London, 1989.

"MANANAAN MAC LIR," "Folklore of the Months" in *JCHAS* vols. I–III, 1895–97.

MASON, T.H., "St Brigid's Crosses" in *JRSAI*, lxxv, 1945.

MAXWELL, C., *Irish History from Contemporary Sources, 1509–1610*, London, 1923.

MEYER, K. (trans.), *The Voyage of Bran*, 1903.

—, "The March Roll of the Men of Leinster" in *Ériu*, VI, 1912.

—, "Middle Irish Travellers' Prayers" in *Ériu*, VI, 1912.

MINK, O., *A Finnegans Wake Gazeteer*, New York, 1978.

MITCHELL, F., *The Irish Landscape*, London, 1976.

MULLEN, M., *The Stars and the Stones*, London, 1983.

MURPHY, G., *Early Irish Metrics*, Dublin, 1961.

—, (ed. and trans.), *Early Irish Lyrics, 8th to 12th Centuries*, Oxford, 1956.

O'BRIEN, M.A., "The Old Irish Life of St. Brigit" in *IHS*, I, 1938.

O'CURRY, E., *Lectures on the Manuscript Materials of Ancient Irish History*, Dublin, 1861.

O'DANACHAIR, C., "The Luck of the House," *UFL*, 15, 1970.

O'DWYER, M., "Three County Limerick Fairs" in Rynne, E. (ed.), *North Munster Studies*, 1967.

O'GRADY, S.O. (trans.), *Silva gadelica*, London, 1892.

Ó HUIGINN, R., "The Literature of the Laigin" in *Emania*, 7, 1990.

Ó HÓGAIN, D., "Gearóid Iarla" in *Dawn*, vol. I, 1973.

O'RAHILLY, T.O., "*Aobh, Aoibheall*," etc. in *Ériu*, XIV, 1946.

—, *EIHM*, Dublin, 1946.

O'REILLY, E., An Irish–English Dictionary, with a supplement by O'Donovan, J., Dublin, 1899.

Ó RÍORDÁIN, S.P., *Antiquities of the Irish Countryside*, London, 1965.

—, "Lough Gur Excavations, Great Stone Circle B," *PRIA*, 54c, 1951–2.

"Neolithic and Bronze Age Houses on Knockadoon," *PRIA*. 55, 1952–3.

O'SULLIVAN, S., *The Folklore of Ireland*, London, 1974.

PLUMMER, C., *Bethada Náem Érenn* (Lives of the Irish Saints), 2 vols., Oxford, 1922.

—, "Irish Litanies" in *Henry Bradshaw Society*, 62, 1924.

PUHVEL, J. (ed.), *Myth and Law Among the Indo-Europeans*, London, 1970.

RANK, O., *The Trauma of Birth*, New York, 1929; reprinted 1973.

—, *The Myth of the Birth of the Hero*, New York, 1952.

REES, A.D. and REES, B., *Celtic Heritage*, London. 1961.

RICHARDSON, J., *The Great Folly, Superstition*, and *Idolatry of Pilgrimages in Ireland*, Dublin, 1727.

ROGER OF WENDOVER, *Flores Historiarum*, trans. Giles, G.A., London. 1849.

ROLLESTON, T.W., *Myths and Legends of the Celtic Race*, London, 1985.

ROSS, A., *Pagan Celtic Britain*, London, 1967.

RYAN, REV. J., *Essays and Studies Presented to Professor Eoin MacNeill*, Dublin, 1940.

RYKWERT, J., *The Idea of a Town*, London, 1976.

"SEIGE OF HOWTH," trans. Stokes, W., in *RC*, VIII, 1887.

SIMMS, J.G., "Connacht in the 18th Century" in *IHS*, II, 1959.

SKOMAL, S.N. and POLOMÉ, E.C. (ed.), *Proto-Indo-European, The Archaeology of a Linguistic Problem*, Washington, 1987.

SMYTH, A.P., *Celtic Leinster*, Blackrock, 1982.

SMYTH, D., *A Guide to Irish Mythology*, Blackrock, 1988.

SMYTH, D., and KENNEDY, G., *Places in Irish Mythology*, Killala, 1989.

SOMMERVILLE-LARGE, P., *Dublin*, Dublin, 1979.

STEVENSON, T.G. (ed. and trans.), *The Vision of Tundale*, Edinburgh, 1843.

STOKES, W., *The Lives of the Saints from the Book of Lismore*, Oxford, 1890.

—, *The Tripartite Life of Patrick*, London, 1887.

STRICKER, B.H., *De Geboorte van Horus*, vol. I, Leiden, 1963.

STUTLEY, M. and J., A Dictionary of Hinduism, London, 1977.

Táin bó Cuailgne (The Tain . . .), trans. Kinsella, T., 1969.

TATLOCK, J.S.P. *The Legendary History of Britain*, London, 1950.

"The Burning of Finn's House," ed Gwynn, E.J., in *Ériu*, I. 1904.

"The Destruction of Da Derga's Hostel," trans. Stokes, W., in *RC*, xxii, 1901.

"The Settling of The Manor of Tara," trans. Best, R. L., in *Ériu*, IV. 1910.

Tighernach's Annals, ed. Stokes, W., in *RC*, xxiii, 1902.

Tochmare Étáin (The Wooing of Étáin), trans. Bergin, O. and Best, R.L., in *Ériu*, xii, 1938.

Tóraidheacht Dhiarmada Agus Ghráinne (The Pursuit of Diarmid and Gráinne), ed, Sheaghdha, N.N., Dublin, 1967.

TOTLAND, J., *A Critical History of the Celtic Religion and Learning*, London, 1740.

VARRO, M.T., *De lingua latina*, trans. Kent, R.G., London, 1967.

—, *De re rustica*, trans, Hooper, W.D., London, 1934.

WEBB, E., *The Plays of Samuel Beckett*, London, 1972.

WENSINK, A.J., *The Ideas of the Western Semites concerning the Navel of the Earth*, Amsterdam, 1916.

WESTROPP, T.J., "Brâzil and the Legendary Islands of the North Atlantic" in *PRIA*, 30c, 1912–14.

—, "Dun Crot and the 'Harps of Cliu,' " in *PRIA*, 35c, 1918–20.

—, "The ancient sanctuaries of Knockainey and Clogher" in *PRIA*, 34c, 1917–19.

WHITTOW, J., *Geology and Scenery in Ireland*, London, 1974.

WILDE, LADY. *Ancient Legends, Mystic Charms and Superstitions of Ireland*, London, 1888.

WILDE, SIR W.R., "Memoir of Gabriel Beranger" in *JRSAI*, 12, 1873.

WINDLE, B.C.A., "On certain megalithic remains at Lough Gur" in *PRIA*, 30c, 1912–13.

WOODMAN, P.C., "Problems in the Colonisation of Ireland" in *UJA*, 49, 1986.

—, "The Post-glacial colonisation of Ireland" in D.O. Corráin, ed., *Irish Antiquity*, 93–110, Cork, 1981.

WOOD MARTIN, W.G., *Traces of the Elder Faiths of Ireland*, London, 1902.

WOODROFFE, J., *Shakti and Shakta*, Madras, 1914–16.

YEATS, W.B., *The Collected Poems*, 2nd edition, London, 1950.

—, *Mythologies*, London, 1959.

GLOSSARY

Abcán dwarf poet of the Tuatha Dé Danann.

Adra alias Ladra: brother of Cesair, and pilot of the first boat to land in Ireland.

Aed fire god and king of Ess Ruaid, Connacht.

Aibhinn goddess and fairy queen of West Munster.

Ailech the incarcerated goddess of Grianan Ailech (Ailighe).

Aill na Mireann (The Stone of Divisions): the center stone of Ireland at Uisnech, Westmeath.

Áine sun goddess, daughter of Manannán mac Lir, the sea god; otherwise regarded as daughter of Eogabal and sister of Grian.

Áine Cli "Áine the Bright."

Aitbe Finn's wife.

Almu goddess of Cnoc Ailinne.

Amergin chief poet of the Sons of Míl.

An "The Traveller"; a sun goddess and another form of Áine.

Ana (Anu) the mother of the Irish gods, synonymous with Áine.

Anna Livia Plurabelle river goddess invented by James Joyce; synonymous with the Liffey.

Atherne (Athirne): Ulster poet, identified with furze or gorse.

Baccán suitor of St. Brigit, and the hook of her pot.

Badb a war goddess, appearing as a hooded crow; sister of Mórrigan.

Balor a one-eyed solar god of the northwest; a rival of Lugh.

Banba one of a trilogy of goddesses synonymous with Ireland, whose sisters were Ériu and Fódla.

ben síd (bean síd or banshee): literally woman of the *síd*; a fairy often supervising the transport of the dying to the Otherworld.

Bith founding god of Ireland, his name means "cosmos."

Blad (Blod): a god of the Eiscir Riada (great East–West road), who made his home at Slieve Bloom, Co. Offaly.

Bodb son of the Dagda. Bodb's *síd* was Slieve Felim.

Brâzil (Brazile): a supernatural island off the southwest coast of Ireland, named after Bres, son of the solar god Elatha, and of Ériu.

Brigit (Brigid): the great fire goddess, worshiped as poetess, lawgiver, smith, dairywoman, and deity of the house. As St. Brigit she is Ireland's foremost woman saint.

Bruiden (Bruidhean): supernatural hostel.

Cailleach (Cally Berry): old hag and winter goddess.

Cailleach Bheare (Birrn): hag goddess, believed to originate from the Bheara Peninsula.

Caoranach monster serpent of Lough Derg, Co. Donegal.

Cesair (Cessair): founding goddess of Ireland, who arrived by boat in Waterford Harbour with Bith, Fintan, and Ladra.

Columcille (Columba): mariner saint, founder of Iona.

Conaire Mór mythical king of Ireland.

Conle the Red prince of Uisnech, and voyager to the Land of Women.

Conn Otherworld deity.

Conn of the Hundred Battles second century C.E. king of the northern half of Ireland.

Crochen Croderg mother of Queen Medb.

Crom Dubh Black Stoop, the carrier of the first sheaf of harvest.

Crón brown or swarthy goddess of the Tuatha Dé Dannan.

Cúchulainn youthful warrior sun god of Ulster.

Da Derga lord who owned a Brundan of that name.

Dagda, the "Good God"; chief god of the Tuatha Dé Dannan.

Dana (Danu): mother goddess synonymous with An, and Anu, and Áine.

Delgnat wife of Partholón.

Diarmaid (Diarmuid, Dermot): one of the Fianna and lover of Gráinne.

Donn Firinne god of the underworld, at *síd* Firinne.

Eblinne (Éblenn): goddess of the Slieve Phelim (Felim, Eblinne).

Echdae skyhorse husband of Áine.

Echtga goddess of Slieve Aughty mountains.

Echtach owl sister of Echtga.

Eithne corn-maiden goddess.

Elatha sun king of the Fomorians, and lover of Ériu.

Eochaid (Eochy): a horse god.

Eochaid Airem horse plowman god of Tara, and Westmeath.

Eochaid mac Luchta blinded king of Lough Derg on Shannon.

Eochaid Ollathair "father of all," synonymous with the Dagda.

Eogabal father of Áine, and associated with the World Tree.

Ériu goddess identified with Eire, Erin, Ireland.

Erne maiden from Rathcroghan; synonymous with the Erne River.

Étáin sun goddess, wife of Midir, and of Eochaid Airem.

Étar androgynous deity of Benn Étair (Howth).

Fer Í (Fer Fí): "Man of Yew"; brother or father of Áine of Cnoc Áine.

Finn McCool (Fionn mac Cumbaill): the solar demigod of Leinster from the *síd* of Almu.

Fintan "the ancient" or "the white." Founding father, who survived the Flood at Tountinna.

Fir Bolg bag men, mythical settlers of Connacht.

Fódla (Fótla): goddess sister of Ériu, concerned with divisions.

Fomorians submarine mythic people.

Gaeth sea god of Donegal Bay.

Geároid Iarla (Fitzgerald): second Earl of Desmond; mythical son of Áine at Lough Gur.

Garaid old enemy of Fion.

Goll mac Morna demigod, one-eyed Connacht opponent of Finn.

Gráinne mistress of Diarmaid.

Grian sun goddess of Cnoc Grene, and sister of Áine.

Guaire Finn's blind poet son, alias Oísin.

Indech father of the Dagda's Fomorian mistress.

Labraid Loingsech (Moen): hero and progenitor of the Laigin tribe of Leinster.

Latiaran fire goddess of Cullen.

Lugh (Lug): a sun god, associated with a golden spear, who gave his name to Lughnasa.

Mac Cécht a sun-god plowman husband of Fódla.

Mac Cuill sun-god husband of Banba.

Mac Gréine (Gréne): sun-god husband of Ériu.

Macha horse goddess, founder of Emain Macha.

Manannán mac Lir sea god, whose home was the Isle of Man.

Manes the Good Ones, internal classical city gods.

Medb (Maev): goddess, and queen of Connacht.

Mide foster son of Ériu; also the fifth province.

Midir underworld of the god Brí.

Milesians (Sons of Mil): Iron Age gods, and rivals of the Tuatha Dé Danann.

Morrigan (Morrigu): war goddess.

Nemed leader of the mythical Nemedian invasion of Ireland.

Niet war goddess of Grianán Ailech.

Oilioll Olum king of Munster, and ravisher of Áine.

Oisín (Ossian): the blind poet son of Finn.

Partholón king of the Partholonian settlers of Ireland.

Patrick patron saint of Ireland.

Sinann goddess of the Shannon River.

Sons of Mil (Milesians): Iron Age gods and rivals of the Tuatha Dé Danann.

Tadhg serpent of Lough Gur.

Tailtiu harvest goddess of Teltown, Co. Meath.

Tea goddess of Tara.

Tír Na nÓg the Land of Youth.

Tobar lover of Delgnat at Inis Samer, the island below the falls at Ess Ruaid.

Tuan nephew of Partholón, sole survivor of the Partholonians, and fish lover of Nemann.

Tuatha Dé Danann literally, the people of the goddess Dana; a pre-Iron Age pantheon of deities; colloquially, the Fairies.

Tuathal Techmar first-century C.E. king who enlarged Mide.

Uainide green god of Cnoc Áine.

Ugaine plowman god of Leinster.

INDEX

ACKNOWLEDGMENTS

AUTHOR'S ACKNOWLEDGMENTS IN *MYTHIC IRELAND*
published by Thames & Hudson, 1992 and 1996

I am much indebted to generations of scholars for bringing so many aspects of Irish mythology to light. These workers are not responsible for my errors. I wish to thank the Irish Folklore Commission; also many helpful public and university libraries, and Mrs T. Astbury, who cheerfully typed several versions of the manuscript. Finally I recall with pleasure the heartwarming friendliness of the Irish people whom I encountered on my travels.

SOURCE OF ILLUSTRATIONS

ARCHIV FÜR KUNST UND GESCHICHTE, LONDON: 91

BORD FÁILTE/IRISH TOURIST BOARD: /Brian Lynch: 82–3, 120, 151

THE BRIDGEMAN ART LIBRARY, LONDON: 19b (British Museum), 222–3 (National Museum of Ireland, Dublin)

BRUCE COLEMAN: 148

CAMERON COLLECTION: 30

COMMISSIONERS OF PUBLIC WORKS, NATIONAL PARKS AND MONUMENTS BRANCH, IRELAND: 200, 211b

VANESSA FLETCHER: 37, 87b, 238

FORTEAN PICTURE LIBRARY: /Anthony Weir 33, 206–7

HULTON GETTY IMAGES: 121

HUNT MUSEUM, UNIVERSITY OF THOMOND, LIMERICK: 40

MIRANDA GRAY: 147

IMAGES COLOUR LIBRARY: 32, 78, 93, 99, 101, 102, 125tl, 125tr, 133, 134, 136–7, 148–9, 173, 204–5

THE IRISH PICTURE LIBRARY: 174

MICHAEL JENNER, LONDON: 7, 8–9, 11, 23, 30–1, 46–7, 118, 176, 201, 233, 240

STUART LITTLEJOHN: 181

MICHAEL MACLIAMMOR: 75

ZUL MUKHIDA: 3, 4, 10, 12–13 (National Trust, Crom Estate), 20–1, 26, 27, 36, 45t, 48, 52–3, 60, 62b, 68–9, 71t, 77, 81, 89, 94, 96–7, 100, 104, 105, 106, 110, 112–13, 115, 116, 117, 119, 123, 124, 129, 130–1, 140, 144, 146–7, 150, 153, 156–7, 158, 162, 163, 164–5, 166–7, 170, 172, 180–1, 182–3, 188–9, 190–1, 195, 197, 199, 201, 208, 209, 211t, 212–13, 214, 216–17, 218–19, 220–1, 224–5, 238–9, 241, 244–5

NATIONAL MUSEUM OF IRELAND, DUBLIN: 1, 34 (inset), 49, 52–3, 79r, 129, 171

NORTHERN IRISH TOURIST BOARD: 76

OFFICE OF PUBLIC WORKS: 192

PAISLEY MUSEUM AND ART GALLERY: 92 (Olive Carleton-Smyth: *The Faery Rout*)

REX ROBERTS A.B.I.P.P., DUBLIN: 22

THE STOCKMARKET, LONDON: 58, 86b, 87t, 135

TONY STONE ASSOCIATES, LONDON: 6, 39, 84–5, 228

WARBURG INSTITUTE, UNIVERSITY OF LONDON: 24, 25

WERNER FORMAN ARCHIVE: 56, 108, 166t, 187

ULSTER FOLK AND TRANSPORT MUSEUM: 42, 43, 44, 84t, 193, 234–5, 236–7

ULSTER MUSEUM: 143 (Jack Butler Yeats: *On Through Silent Lands*, 1951, © Miss Anne Yeats. Photograph reproduced with the kind permission of the Trustees of the National Museum and Galleries of Northern Ireland.)

REMAINING PICTURES: courtesy of the author

TEXT QUOTATIONS

The pamphlet of St. Patrick's Purgatory is quoted by courtesy of The Most Reverend Joseph Duffy, Bishop of Clogher. All material from the manuscript collections of the Department of Irish Folklore, University College, Dublin, is quoted by kind permission of the Head of the Department. Miles Dillon's translation of *Echtrae Conle* is quoted from *Early Irish Literature*, 1948, with permission of University of Chicago Press; Elizabeth Gray's translation of *Cath Maige Tuired* with the permission of the Irish Texts Society.